... a perso ... ctical day to day sense. It challenges stereotypes about Muslims to get an accurate picture of how Muslims live their lives within a liberal and democratic society. If you want to know about the pluralism within Muslim communities, this book will certainly help.'

– *Fiyaz Mughal, OBE, Director of Faith Matters*

'How do Asians in Britain feel about life and their religion? Declan Henry has fluently revealed their wide-ranging views with great competence and skill. This is an intriguing perspective seen through the eyes of an emergent and important section of our community. Definitely a work of lasting value.'

– *Paigham Mustafa, author of* The Quran: God's Message to Mankind

'*Voices of Modern Islam* offers an insight into the often little-known or misrepresented fundamentals of the faith and the diversity of contemporary UK Muslim opinion: the good, the bad and the ugly. Demonstrating that Muslims are not a single, homogeneous, uncritical mass, it debunks many stereotypes, while confirming others. Be prepared to have some of your assumptions about Islam challenged.'

– *Peter Tatchell, human rights campaigner, Director of the Peter Tatchell Foundation*

'Declan Henry has spent extensive time and effort collecting vast and accurate information about Islam and the diversity of its followers. I believe this book is a valuable resource not only for use by Muslims across the UK and further afield, but also for secondary schools, and those researching Islam and its religious and socio-cultural realities in an academic context.'

– *Dr Shaykh Ramzy, Imam, Islamic scholar and Director of Oxford Islamic Information Centre by the same author*

Trans Voices
Becoming Who You Are
Declan Henry
Foreword by Professor Stephen Whittle, OBE
Afterword by Jane Fae
ISBN 978 1 78592 240 4
eISBN 978 1 78450 520 2

of related interest

Interreligious Dialogue and the Partition of India
Hindus and Muslims in Dialogue about Violence and Forced Migration
Mario I. Aguilar
ISBN 978 1 78592 312 8
eISBN 978 1 78450 625 4
Part of the Studies in Religion and Theology *series*

Muslim Identity in a Turbulent Age
Islamic Extremism and Western Islamophobia
Edited by Mike Hardy, Fiyaz Mughal and Sarah Markiewicz
Foreword by H.E. Mr Nassir Abdulaziz Al-Nasser
ISBN 978 1 78592 152 0
eISBN 978 1 78450 419 9

**Understanding Attitudes to Personhood, Illness, and
Death in America's Multireligious Neighborhoods**
Lucinda Mosher
ISBN 978 1 78592 784 3
eISBN 978 1 78450 717 6

God, Gender, Sex and Marriage
Mandy Ford
ISBN 978 1 78592 475 0
eISBN 978 1 78450 860 9

Christian Citizenship in the Middle East
Divided Allegiance or Dual Belonging?
Edited by Mohammed Girma and Cristian Romocea
Foreword by Paul S. Williams
ISBN 978 1 78592 333 3
eISBN 978 1 78450 648 3

voices

of MODERN ISLAM

What It Means to Be Muslim Today

Declan Henry

Foreword by Dr Taj Hargey

Jessica Kingsley *Publishers*
London and Philadelphia

First published in 2018
by Jessica Kingsley Publishers
73 Collier Street
London N1 9BE, UK
and
400 Market Street, Suite 400
Philadelphia, PA 19106, USA

www.jkp.com

Library of Congress Cataloging in Publication Data
A CIP catalog record for this book is available from the Library of Congress

British Library Cataloguing in Publication Data
A CIP catalogue record for this book is available from the British Library

ISBN 978 1 78592 401 9
eISBN 978 1 78450 763 3

Printed and bound in the United States

Dedicated to my friend Diana

CONTENTS

Foreword

Dr Taj Hargey

Director, Muslim Educational Centre of Oxford
Imam, Oxford Islamic Congregation

Islam in our time is by far the most controversial and contentious of all global faiths. From its ancient origins in the remote tribal deserts of Arabia to its rapidly booming presence everywhere in the modern West and elsewhere, the religion of Muhammad is often identified with lethal intolerance, indiscriminate violence, primitive customs, belligerent homophobia, blatant sexism, amongst other execrable assertions. While most Muslims in both the Islamic heartlands as well as in the Western diaspora tend either to just ignore or to explain away these shocking and inconvenient manifestations of their creed, this self-defeating policy only confirms these disturbing allegations in the minds of many outside observers. When Muslims engage in such conscious obfuscation, they do Islam and themselves no favours as it hardens Western hostility to the (relatively) new Muslim immigrants in Europe and North America.

Instead of simply dismissing the justified criticisms levelled against Islam and its followers, it is imperative that both Muslims and non-Muslims be adequately informed about the practical dimensions of the Prophet's religion as practiced in British society today. For this reason alone, Declan Henry – who has demonstrated an admirable comprehension of Islam far in excess than most observant Muslims – has written a highly evocative and extremely pertinent volume by bravely tackling the perennial questions and pressing dilemmas facing contemporary British Muslims. By permitting a broad cross section of ordinary believers as well as professional practitioners of the faith from different sects and various denominations to articulate their own perspectives as well as their inherited sentiments about Islam, this timely book is an invaluable resource in generating an enlightening and positive public debate surrounding Islam as well as a better understanding of this hugely variegated and proliferating religion within the United Kingdom.

However, to comprehend what Islam is really about, it is vital to differentiate between what is primary and what is populist belief. The two are not the same. It is as glaring as night and day. In other words, everyone should distinguish what 'Muslims' believe and what 'Islam' believes, and not infer that that one's own personal credo is reflective of pristine Islam. Critics maintain that those who adhere to Islam's original scripture alone (Qur'an – 6:114, 68:36–37) can be termed Muslims, while those who heed the additional sources should be labelled as 'Muhammadans', as the latter focus more on Muhammad and habitually twists the Qur'an's original teachings. Indeed, there is a world of difference between what is Qur'anic Islam (derived solely from the faith's transcendent text) and what is popular Islam – stemming mainly from the much later manufactured sources like the Hadith, Sharia and fatwas (the Prophet's presumed sayings, medieval theological opinions and individual clerical rulings). This clear-cut dichotomy of what Islam promotes and what Muslims project runs throughout this highly readable book and is plainly evident in the incongruous testimonies of numerous Muslims right across Islam's theological spectrum. From the utterances of the orthodox Sunni majority to the views of the traditional Shi'a minority, from the opinions of the heterodox Ahmadi sect to the radical interpretations of Sufi mystics and Salafi zealots, the author has succeeded in weaving together a truly fascinating and compelling portrait of Muslims in Britain today.

When the multiple and often conflicting viewpoints of British Muslims are analysed and placed side-by-side, it confirms that there is no hegemonic theology within contemporary Islam in the United Kingdom. For the average non-Muslim reader, the puzzling doctrinal differences within the Muslim community are stupefying, bewildering and alarming. Most Muslim respondents in this book, contrary to what the Qur'an teaches (2:177), fixate upon a ritualistic if not robotic application of their faith that is principally predicated upon suspect non-scriptural dictates and ensuing ecclesiastical fabrications, both classical and contemporary. This largely unthinking and non-introspective belief system damages and does immense disservice to the innate intellectualism and rational foundation of Qur'anic Islam. If Muslims observe the original divine dictates of their faith, and not slavishly abide by the subsequent post-prophetic man-made dogmas that have contaminated both orthodox and heterodox Islam, then they would find themselves living in amity and concord in Western society. There is nothing in the faith's primary source (the Qur'an) that renders it incompatible with mainstream British values. But the reverse is incontrovertibly true. Should Muslims insist upon importing and implementing the Hadith, Sharia and fatwa variants of a populist Islam into the United Kingdom, they will invariably find themselves at odds with Britain's established laws and social conventions that assure intellectual liberty, religious freedom, female equity, human rights, homosexual tolerance and a whole range of other topical prerogatives. Frankly, British Muslims either need to fit in or to ship out if they want to be considered as an integral and respected segment of UK society.

What this illuminating book reveals in remarkable detail is that many Muslims in the UK – despite the fact that most have now been here for several generations – seemingly regard tokenistic, outward and superficial moves towards mainstream society as somehow sufficient by itself to be regarded as valued citizens of Britain. These Muslims incline to gloss over the absence of any worthwhile adaptation to and prudent adoption of Britain's vaunted jurisprudence and long-established customs that guarantees everyone's equality, dignity and respect. Unless British Muslims cut the entrenched umbilical cord that binds them to their ancestral homelands, whether in South Asia, the Middle East or Africa, they will unfortunately retain a non-integrationist mentality by creating a separatist and isolationist community. They will, regrettably, not become full and effective stakeholders in this successful Western nation that welcomed all their migrant forebears who arrived as workers, students and refugees. By electing to remain aloof and apart from the majority non-Muslim population in voluntary self-contained enclaves up and down the country, this apartheid-like segregation exacerbates social tensions and communal divisions. It furnishes the ideal pretext for far-right groups like the English Defence League, Britain First and others to target Muslims for their visible in-your-face culture, cuisine, clothing and creed. While right-wing racists need to be debated and defeated through convincing proof and potent counter arguments, there is no denying that Muslims are also partly liable for the growing anti-Muslim xenophobia in this country. Quite evidently, escalating Islamophobia in the UK ever since the horrific London tube bombings in 2005 is the direct consequence of repeated Muslim terrorist outrages in Britain and other European countries. Staying separately, living apart by their own volition in separatist bubbles, speaking alone in native tongues, imbibing militant theology and mixing with only their own kind have all been spectacular own goals for British Muslims. Lamentably, it has exposed every law-abiding citizen within the Muslim community to mounting right-wing vindictiveness and violence.

Given this disturbing and deteriorating situation, it behoves UK Muslims to embrace a positive two-pronged plan to neutralise insidious Islamophobia and create beneficial social interaction with the general public. First, they need to differentiate between creed and culture by not conflating religion with tradition, their customs with the creed. Once they return to a pure Qur'anic Islam that sanctions no cultural preference or any ethnic chauvinism, they can then reject those aspects of a convoluted theology that spawn anti-Islamic antipathy and anti-Muslim prejudice. Second, by acquiring genuine theological self-empowerment and a solid evidence-based mastery of their own faith, thinking Muslims will be in a much stronger position to refute both Islamic fanaticism and militancy as well as to combat stereotypical bigotry and typical misconceptions that currently exist in the public domain. Without this concerted double-edged strategy, British Muslims will not only reinforce their marginalisation from mainstream society, but will also pave the way for increasing Islamophobia. It is beyond doubt that Muslims need to put their own house in order before complaining of establishment bias and institutional discrimination. Far too often, many British Muslims reflect an expedient victimhood mentality, a 'them and us' mindset that neatly dovetails with weird foreign-inspired conspiratorial theories – diligently disseminated by a motley collection of radicalised youth, opportunist politicians, out-of-date community elders and mischievous religious leaders – instead of rigorously addressing the fundamental and root causes of their political impotence, economic disenfranchisement and social alienation. Only a thorough reappraisal and an honest re-thinking of their separatist, segregationist and supremacist stance can lead Muslims to productive integration that will facilitate the assumption of a legitimate place and role within the British mainstream. Muslims should stop blaming others. It is their paramount responsibility to fix their own problems, not to wait either for the Lord or for others to do that (Qur'an – 13:11).

What is arguably most surprising (and distressing) in this perceptive volume is that few, if any, of the disparate Muslim interviewees residing in modern Britain, irrespective of their sectarian loyalty, deal with the primacy of reason and reflection within Islam. They appear to regard this definitive Qur'anic priority of critical thinking as non-consequential or irrelevant at best. But aside from Islam's resolute championing of primeval Abrahamic monotheism (Qur'an – 2:136) and a relentless pursuit of universal justice for all regardless of their background or belief (Qur'an – 4:135), logical thinking and analytical reasoning constitute the indisputable bedrocks of Islam's sacred scripture. The text is replete with constant reaffirmation that it is a heavenly guidance for all those who think and ponder, those who contemplate and cogitate (3:190, 14:52, 15:75, 16:11–13, 38:29, 39:18, etc.). In fact, the very first Qur'anic revelations that the Prophet Muhammad received via the archangel Gabriel endorse the pre-eminence of logic and reason within the faith (96:1–5). This emphasis on intellectual inquiry and cerebral capacity was a distinctive hallmark of early Islam when the Mu'tazilites, the outstanding rationalists of their day, held sway in the expanding Islamic empire. After flourishing from the 8th to the 10th century, these original Muslim freethinkers were brutally sidelined and confined, by the repressive forces of clerical orthodoxy, to the dustbin of history. However, for today's Muslims to both survive and thrive in the West, it is axiomatic that they need to re-activate Mu'tazilite intellectualism with the Qur'anic dictum of *ijtihad* (individual analysis and critical thinking). In a progressively secular and materialistic world, mere blind belief and robotic ritualism cannot furnish effectual answers to the burning questions of the day, let alone provide convincing rebuttals to confrontational non-Muslim opponents. By resurrecting this Qur'anic truism that elevates reasoning instead of ritualism, thinking rather than tradition, British Muslims will not only become closer to the Creator and the creation, but will also be able to defend an Islam that is grounded in erudition and not emotion, on enlightenment and not extremism.

By far the greatest strength of this important collection of contemporary Muslim voices are the customary tales, myths and legends masquerading as authentic Qur'anic teachings. They encapsulate an ancestral Islam that evolved from non-Qur'anic masculine sources, which for the most part are in contravention of Islam's Holy Book. In a variety of vignettes and stories, the diverse respondents with their Sunni, Shi'a, Ahmadi, Sufi or Salafi affiliations often convey incredible insights of what many Muslims actually believe, to the utter astonishment of non-believers. Whatever the subject, their theological generalisations mostly have little or no authoritative Qur'anic substance. Throughout this absorbing monograph, some of the more eccentric interpretations of Islam embrace a distinct sectarian ideology rather than impeccable

Qur'anic canons. The interviewees have a tendency not to make actual Qur'anic references but to quote Hadith (the reputed sayings of Muhammad) without supplying full and proper citations. Although many seem to possess a rudimentary familiarity with the supposed pronouncements of Islam's founder compiled over 250 years after his death, they have far less knowledge of what is really contained in their faith's unrivalled text. Almost inevitably, many just regurgitate theological positions that have little scriptural authority. Sadly, their opinions often are the outcome of generational programming and religious conditioning not derived from Islam's supreme scripture. However, these intriguing comments by Muslims voicing their limited understanding of their own creed offers factual enlightenment about populist Islam across a plethora of topics – from the trendy fixation about women's dress, mindless ritualism, patriarchal misogyny, intolerant jihadism, ingrained homophobia, the Prophet's dynastic descendants, the apparent return of Jesus, the alleged advent of the Messiah and so forth. While not doctrinally definitive, these riveting perspectives certainly give exceptional access and intuitive entry into the modern Muslim mind.

In no way, can the author be held accountable for any of the demerits, deficiencies and defects within Muslim sectarian ideology. Whatever disputed or dubious theology is expressed by some of the denominational devotees in this exceptional volume, this is not the fault of the author who has uniquely immersed himself into the present-day vagaries and views within British Islam. He has scrupulously relayed the prevailing thoughts and the actual mindsets within the Muslim community. If these adherents of Islam have a flawed grasp of their own religion, then that is indubitably the consequence of the pernicious factionalism that is so rampant within contemporary Islam. This eye-opening book confirms that many British Muslims generally only have a partial or scant understanding of the Qur'an, which is paradoxically the product of monopoly priestly propaganda through the wretched 3M phenomenon – mullahs, mosques and madrassahs. This traditional form of unthinking religious indoctrination unfortunately remains essentially unchallenged and unchanged in Muslim society everywhere. Nevertheless, it is crucial that British-born Muslims must robustly question their own faith and return to its original uncontaminated sublimity. Living as they do in a free and democratic country, it should be their intrinsic religious duty as well as an undoubted secular necessity to familiarise themselves thoroughly with their sacred scripture by not deferring to any imposed theological misinterpretations or reactionary misconceptions circulated by an imperious Islamic clergy. Only then will British Muslims be able to disseminate an accurate Islam that is not chiefly based on ritualism and formalism, but is grounded on truth and reason, tolerance and logic – as demanded by the faith's primary text (Qur'an – 109:6).

Irrespective of the multitude of fables, myths and legends that predominate within much of present-day sectarian theology (that only serve as a brake on true social cohesion and genuine critical thinking), there is undeniably hope and scope for the future. Islam in the UK – as elsewhere in the Muslim world – requires a much-needed root and branch reform, along the lines of, but not identical to, the European Reformation, Enlightenment and Renaissance. Currently, the perverse medieval theology – that is accepted unquestioningly – originates not from Islam's divine epistle but from the toxic trio of manufactured non-scriptural sources (Hadith, Sharia and fatwas) that have long passed their sell-by date. For Islam to be relevant and germane in today's secular Britain, modern Muslims must take the bull by the horns and jettison those doctrines, beliefs and perspectives that perpetuate segregation, exclusion and isolation. Nothing less will do. Fortunately, the recent establishment of the Oxford Institute for British Islam is boldly advocating a faith that severs the hitherto injudicious fidelity to foreign cultures and anachronistic beliefs. This new academy spearheads an exclusively scriptural Islam that is progressive, pluralistic and pertinent. It seeks to advance a faith that relates to this day and age without discarding pristine Qur'anic principles. By courageously embracing a Qur'an-centric, gender equal, non-sectarian and intercultural (not disparate multiculturalism) worldview, this new think tank is set to become the intellectual engine for intrepid critical introspection, fresh thinking and novel initiatives that will inexorably foster a creed that is firmly rooted in and relevant to 21st century Britain. Rather than justifying an existing faith that epitomises ritualism, irrationalism and separatism, this new centre will be at the forefront in integrating Qur'anic Islam fully into the rich cultural mosaic that constitutes a dynamic modern Britain. In this way, the emergence of a truly British Islam will make a significant and salient contribution to authentic religious freedom and social diversity in this country.

Without doubt, Declan Henry should be saluted for producing a highly impressive, splendid and well-timed overview of Muslims in the UK today. His meticulous research and fearless investigations provide considerable food for thought, for both the non-Muslim majority as well as the Muslim minority. For the latter, this book sets into motion candid introspection and uncomfortable free-thinking, while for the former it furnishes a valid and valuable vision into contemporary Muslim life and philosophy. For anyone genuinely desirous to fully understand Islam and its votaries in the UK today, this book is required reading to gain veritable insider glimpses into the world's fastest growing religion.

Acknowledgements

I am deeply indebted to all the Muslim interviewees who generously gave me their time during my research for this book. The number of names is too lengthy to add here but I would like you to know that without your valuable input, writing this book would not have been possible. I am delighted to have created a work that reflects your opinions and hope I have accurately reflected your thoughts on the range of topics featured in the book pertaining to Islam at the current time.

I am appreciative to Paigham Mustafa who kindly allowed me to use Qur'anic interpretations from his own exposition of the Qur'an (*The Quran: God's Message to Mankind*). It was such a privilege to be given this access and consult with Paigham, who was extremely generous with his help around English translations of the Qur'an. I have used various English translations of the Qur'an in the book but upon Paigham's advice, have steered clear of using any that might be considered sectarian in tone.

I would like to extend special recognition to Dr Taj Hargey, Shaykh Asrar Rashid, Shaykh Hojja Ramzy, Shaykh M. Islam Qadri Jilani,

Imam Irfan Chishti, Imam Omar Jamaykee, Imam Mohammed Shammas, Imam Irfan Patel and Imam Kaushar Tai for all their support and guidance.

My special thanks to Imam Safeer Khan from the Ahmadiyya community in Gillingham, Kent, and to the many members of his congregation, especially Zahid Khan and Faiza Mirza who freely gave their time. I would also like to single out Ahsan Ahmedi from the Crawley Ahmadiyya mosque for all his help. To all of you, your welcome, kindness and camaraderie won't be forgotten.

Finally, I would like to say a big thank you to Andrew James, Senior Commissioning Editor, and Lily Bowden, Marketing and Publicity Executive, at Jessica Kingsley Publishers for their professionalism and expertise.

DISCLAIMER

I interviewed over a hundred Muslims for this book. In some cases, their names and some other details have been changed to protect their identities and anonymity.

Introduction

As a non-Muslim, writing this book has been one of the most profound and supremely interesting times of my life. It has also been a time of deep reflection. A time to think about God in ways I had never before considered. It has made me contemplate my own faith and assess how I perceive God. As a Catholic, it has brought me closer to my own faith, rather than pushing me away from the religion I was born into and much cherish. In the process, I have been introduced to the life of the Prophet Muhammad and have appreciated the deep respect Muslims hold for him. I too bestow this honour, and place the reverence Muslims have for him on par with the belief and respect that I and fellow Christians have in and for Jesus Christ. It was interesting to hear an imam tell me during my research about how the Prophet Muhammad once said that of all the Prophets, he felt closest to Jesus.

Muslims, Christians and Jews have so much in common and upon close examination, have far more in common which unites than divides them. But there are differences and during the course of this book, these will become apparent. However, what is also apparent is that there is a deep connection between the three faiths of Islam, Christianity and Judaism, which allows us to relate to each other, whether we personally choose to believe – or not.

Yet none of this relates to the reason why I chose to write this book. As an Irish person living in the UK, I have known many Muslims over the years and indeed consider some of them as good friends. And although I've expressed an interest in the religion, up until writing this book I have known relatively little about Islam's true essence. I therefore wanted to find out more about its depths. Writing this book has been a voyage of discovery, but my main reason has been specifically to explore the religion in light of its damaged reputation, a reputation resulting from extremism and radicalisation over the past few decades but most particularly in recent years.

This book is about Islam. It is also about Muslims living in Britain who have spoken out and given me their honest and outright opinions on a vast range of topics connected to their religion. Early on in my research, I discovered that some ordinary Muslims actually know little about Islam except for some of the basics, causing me to concentrate on approaching imams and other Islamic scholars for a deeper theological discussion. Having said that, I spoke to dozens of non-clerical Muslims and sought their views on a wide range of social issues in relation to their daily lives.

I would mislead you if I said that I have written the definitive guide to Islam. That is not my intention. The truth is, this book could be 20, 30 or 50 times the size it is and still would not be big enough to convey everything about this deep subject. Perhaps describing my book as a small stream of water might help the reader see more clearly. A stream is not an ocean and yet an ocean would not exist without the stream. Although a stream is small in size, it has the strength and capability of journeying to the ocean. Indeed, isn't every ocean in the world made up of many small streams? So with that in mind, view this book as one small stream that is alive, healthy and whose gentle flow of water leads to a vast ocean. What I present here is a taste of Islam in Britain, at one particular moment in time, and a taste of viewpoints from Muslims living in the UK about how they perceive their religion, themselves and the world around them.

Although this book is written mainly with non-Muslims in mind, I also think that Muslims could read it and learn things about Islam they didn't previously know. They may also read things that they disagree with, or wish they had the opportunity afforded to them to make a comment on some of the subject matter covered in the book. If that is the case, I would also hope they realise that every person comes with their own individual opinions which are personal and sometimes unique to them.

This book contains the viewpoints of Muslims from various groups and sects, so it is bound to spark differences of opinion. Although all groups and sects are not represented, there are sufficient to highlight some of the main key differences that exist within the religion. If anything, this book highlights the fact that Muslims are not monolithic. So perhaps, it is time for them to be prepared to respect other groups, and extend a reconciliatory handshake towards each other, bearing in mind that each believe in the Holy Qur'an and the five pillars of Islam, despite their differences.

I hope you learn much about Islam and Muslims from reading this book and that you come to realise that Islam is a beautiful religion and Muslims are good people. I hope it also enables you to gain a better understanding of the Prophet Muhammad who founded Islam. And whether you are a Muslim, Christian or Jew, or from any other religion, or have no faith of your own, I hope that Allah (God), my creator, your creator and the creator of the entire universe showers your life with many blessings. Inshallah (God willing).

CHAPTER 1

Being Muslim

There are 1.8 billion Muslims in the world, with over 55 countries whose populations are predominantly Muslim. According to the Pew Research Center, it is estimated that by the year 2030, 26 per cent of the world's population will be Muslim. Indonesia currently has the largest Muslim population with more than 200 million, but India is predicted to surpass this figure with an estimated 300 million by the year 2050. In the UK, the British Muslim population is 4 million, and although this seems a significant number, it is lower than France (5.7 million) and Germany (4.9 million). Russia's population of 14 million Muslims is the largest on the continent. However, these live in the vast geographical east of the country, east of the Urals, and are therefore considered Asian.

Statistics are useful in providing glimpses of the Muslim diaspora, but provide little insight into what Islam is or what it means to be a Muslim in today's world. The word *Islam* itself means peace and submission to God. Muslims readily point out that Islam is a very peaceful religion, knowing that the media often portrays it as the opposite. Islamic terrorists have poisoned the hearts and minds of many non-Muslims into believing that something evil and cruel lies at the heart of Islam, one of the world's great religions.

Is Islam a complex or difficult religion to understand? Muslims who I interviewed for this book said that Islam is neither complex nor hard to understand. They informed me the religion lays down clear and concise instructions as to how people should properly live their lives by serving God to the best of their ability. It is felt that confusion about, or non-adherence to, the faith is a result of Islam and culture becoming entwined, resulting in practices that are not truly based in Islam. It is worth noting that some Muslims feel that non-Muslims get caught up in incorrectly differentiating between Islam, culture and race, and that it is here where issues sometimes get mixed up.

> Islam is a simple religion. It teaches you how to treat people – how to be a good human being and how to be productive. In a metaphorical sense, it places greater importance on planting trees rather than cutting them down. To become a Muslim is simple. The first two steps you need to take are to believe there is only one God and that the Prophet Muhammad was the Last Messenger that God sent to earth. I was born in Bethlehem and I recognise Judaism and Christianity. I believe in Jesus, Moses and all of the other Prophets that lived before the Prophet Muhammad. What makes Islam unique is that we believe that Muhammad was born of human parents – resulting in his conception – whereas we don't accept the Christian teachings that Jesus was the son of God born by Immaculate Conception. **Naazir**

* * *

It's easy to describe a 'bad' Muslim or someone who doesn't adhere to the teachings of Islam: someone who doesn't pray or go to the mosque as often as they should, someone who has extra-marital affairs or drinks alcohol or misuses drugs, who has no respect for their parents, who is untruthful and doesn't give money to charity. Someone who isn't a law-abiding and integrated citizen. So one of the first questions I asked my interviewees was what it means to be a good Muslim and be recognised by other Muslims as a good adherent of their faith.

Being a good Muslim means that nobody should ever be affected by your words or your deeds. Every time we meet somebody we say 'Salam', which means 'Peace on you.' A few other worthy points to know is that half of Islam is about cleanliness. This is very important to us. We wash each time before prayers and before we touch the Qur'an. Also, it is said that if you are a Muslim, you must not sleep if one of your neighbours is in need. It's not a question of saying, 'It's their headache' and do nothing. At the very least, you should offer some help. Part of the religion is striving to help humanity at large. Of course, there are times that you can't do anything practical, but you can still pray for somebody. Even with praying for somebody, you must pray until you feel satisfied inside that you have done as much as you can. **Ehan**

A good Muslim is somebody who upholds the rights of Allah and the rights of people. He or she he is somebody who believes in The Holy Qur'an which to Muslims is the true word of God for all mankind; somebody who is good to their parents and good to their spouse. Somebody who is honest and trustworthy, who looks after their children and ensures they get a good education. Somebody who is a good role model in their community, who respects their neighbours by not making undue noise, and ensures their property is kept in a good state of repair. **Hassan**

A good Muslim surrenders his or her will to Allah and believes that the Prophet Muhammad is God's Final Messenger. To be a true Muslim, you have to affirm it in the heart and testify it on the tongue. Somebody who prays five times a day. Somebody who knows the difference between halah and haram.

This means knowing what is permissible and what is not. For example, knowing what to eat and wear. A good Muslim is also somebody who helps his Muslim brother, because when he helps his brother, he helps mankind and builds a stronger society. Sincerity is a necessary quality because a person should be unconditional in their goodness without having a motive that seeks a reward. A good Muslim always follows the path of Allah by propagating his message far and wide. Muslims firmly believe in different functions for men and women in society – men are seen as the head of the family and women are the homemakers. **Farris**

* * *

Muslims believe in one God. They believe in His Prophets and Messengers, and that the Prophet Muhammad is the final Prophet that God sent to the world to deliver his divine word, which is contained in the Holy Qur'an. Most Muslims believe in angels and like some Christians believe that each person is assigned an individual special guardian angel to watch over and protect them from harm. They also firmly believe in a Day of Judgement, when everybody will be held accountable by God for their actions. This is considered paramount because it leads a person either to the gates of paradise or towards hellfire.

Islam stresses freedom of religion for all, leaving people to follow the religion of their choice. There are two well-known quotes in the Qur'an which state this: 'There should be no compulsion in religion' (Qur'an – 2:257) and 'For you your religion, and for me my religion' (Qur'an – 109:6). The core principles of Islam are: belief in God, and the Last Day, and the angels and the scriptures and the Prophets. Islam has similarities to Christianity and Judaism in terms of scripture as outlined in the Qur'an, Bible and Torah. It has less in common with Buddhism and Hinduism – in the sense that neither of these religions believes in one God or indeed in the same version of God that binds Muslims, Christian and Jews together. There are Muslims who fully acknowledge that Christianity and Judaism are branches from the same tree and that if they are followed correctly, they teach similar morals to Islam. However, these days Christians are moving closer to secular opinion on social issues – homosexuality and abortion – along with most Christians who think it is okay to have pre-marital sex. Islam on the other hand holds firm on its teachings against these issues as well as offering a level of prescriptive and ritualistic detail about daily life beyond any other religion that believes good actions are necessary in order to be rewarded in the afterlife. Muslims believe that people should pray directly to God for help.

Praise be to God, Lord of the worlds. The Beneficent, the Merciful. Master of the Day of Judgement. You (alone) we worship; You (alone) we ask for help. Show us the right path, the path of those whom You have favoured; Not the (path) of those who earn Your anger nor of those who go astray. (Qur'an – 1:1)

* * *

Hospitality is very important to Muslims. Discourtesy and bad manners are frowned upon. Guests, including non-Muslims, are always made to feel welcome. It is customary for refreshments or a meal to be offered when you enter someone's home.

One day, Abu Dharr, who was a friend of the Prophet, was cooking a broth that was a favourite dish of the Arabs at the time. The Prophet said to him, 'While broth is being cooked for your family, add a little more water to it so that your neighbour might also share in it.' (Hadith – Muslim)

In Islam, respect is given to family, elders and religious leaders. Imams are deeply appreciated and revered for their knowledge, and are called upon when advice and guidance is needed during difficult times.

Etiquette and good manners are important in Islam, because there is a saying of the Prophet that states that people with good manners show the best character. It's the first thing you see in a person. Is there anything worse than seeing somebody with a loud mouth who is rude? Good manners lead to good morals. Muslims like both these qualities. We respect our parents, our families and relatives. We are taught from a young age not to be rude to anybody. Having shame is also something else that is high on the agenda for Muslims. Somebody who does not have the ability to feel shame will be seen to have poor morals. **Badia**

Good manners and hospitality are very important features in Islam. The Prophet placed great value on kindness to visitors. He always welcomed visitors into the mosque and made sure that they were offered some food. A warm welcome was assured to all. The needs of the visitor were paramount. If a man had two wives and the visitor had none, it was not uncommon for the man to divorce one of his wives so that the visitor could marry her to satisfy his manly desires. Women weren't forced into this against their will. In fact, they wanted to do it because for them, too, it showed kindness and respect to the visitor, which was part of their Islamic tradition. **Farris**

MISCONCEPTIONS

As in all aspects of life, ignorance and fear often lead to people hearing, seeing or assuming things that aren't true. There is a widespread misconception that Muslims all hate dogs because they seldom have them as pets. Although there is nothing in the Qur'an that criticises dogs, when you ask Muslims why they do not prefer them as pets, they will explain that this is due to hygiene. Certain parts of dogs are considered impure, particularly the nose and mouth. Allowing dogs in the house may entail moulting hair and dripping saliva, and therefore Muslims avoid having dogs as domestic pets to prevent the hassle of extra washing and purification before prayers or reading the Qur'an. But that does not mean they dislike or hate dogs. They appreciate their value as guard and guide dogs, or for herding livestock, or being trained sniffers.

Young Muslims become aware at an early age that people hold false ideas about their religion. Once during a visit to a mosque I was informed that most young Muslims growing up in the Western world are accustomed to people, either in jest or otherwise, asking if they are carrying a bomb in their bag. These young Muslims complained of bullying and teasing at school; some were asked questions such as, 'Are you related to Bin Laden?' or 'Is your father fighting for ISIS?' and 'Are you going to marry your sister?' This final question belies a common misunderstanding, because Muslims are allowed to marry their first cousins. Others have been asked, 'Why do you have to starve?' when referring to fasting during Ramadan. These conversations led me to discussing misconceptions with adult Muslims, who told me that some of the following assumptions are commonplace:

Muslims believe in a different God to Christians and Jews

Most non-Muslims think that we have our own God, but that is not God. Muslims do not worship a different God to Jews and Christians. However, they reject the idea of God having any partners or being part of a 'trinity' (Father, Son (Jesus Christ) and Holy Spirit) as believed by Christians. We usually use the word Allah, which is the Arabic for God. Muslims reject the idea though of God having any partners or being part of a 'trinity'. There are 99 names used when referring to God. They include The Maker, The All Knowing, The Gracious, The Merciful, The Master of the Day of Judgement, The Creator of Mankind, Lord of all the Worlds, The Noble, The Wise, The Protector and The Watcher, to name a few. He is the One who bestows all honour and is the wise Judge. When I think of God, I think of humbleness, kindness and forgiveness. God is perfect in every way. I pray to Him for my parents' good health and so that I can get good grades in my exams. I know people are not supposed to ask for material things but it's not really wrong either to ask, so sometimes I ask when I need something, but not all the time. **Motaz**

Muslims are all the same

The important thing to remember is that Islam is like Christianity in the way there are several different groups and sects under its name. To the untrained eye, all Muslims look the same but this is not true because there are different groups of Muslims – for example Sunni Muslims, Shi'a Muslims and Ahmadiyya Muslims. All of these have differences in customs and certain aspects of doctrine. There are also several sub-sects within these core groups each with slightly different doctrines but most of them share more similarities than differences. **Gamil**

Muslims are cruel to animals

Some believe that animal cruelty is used in the killing of animals for halal meat – particularly around the sacrificing of certain animals during Eid and other Islamic festivals. I eat meat that is not halal because I know that cattle are not killed in the country where they are sacrificed to an idol of some kind or other. So I feel free to choose meat in the supermarket or butcher shop without the need for it to be halal. Muslims get into various debates on the matter and believe that every animal for human consumption should be killed in the name of God, but the Qur'an does not request this. There is a Hadith which comments on the importance of using a sharp knife when slaughtering an animal in order not to cause it unnecessary suffering and to cause the least pain. We cut the main artery in the neck, which allows them to bleed out. They are dead in seconds. However, various disputes still occur about the need for compassion and care of animals regarding whether or not the animal should be stunned before their throats are slit. **Ahsan**

Muslims keep to themselves and discourage integration with non-Muslims

This is unfair considering that Muslims believe in being respectful to others outside their faith, and welcome non-Muslims to join with them at special times of celebration, for example meals at the mosque during Ramadan when they break their fast. Muslims also regularly share food with neighbours when there is abundance, and someone being non-Muslim is never a deterrent for doing so. Many Muslims consider the word 'integration' a word that is mis-defined. A warm smile and greeting to a neighbour or a stranger in the street is integration. Muslims work with people from many different racial, cultural and religious backgrounds and do not have any problems associating with these differences. Many Muslims have a keen interest in football and other sports and play with non-Muslims. There is no evidence that points to Muslims refraining from work or any leisure pursuit to avoid being friends with non-Muslims. **Gabriella**

Muslims have strange dress codes and cultural norms

There is a lot of sexism towards Islam with many believing that only women are forced to cover up. But there are rules for men, too, around their appearance. Ninety-nine per cent of Muslim males will have beards. Although it's not obligatory, it is recommended. It is a sign of masculinity. The Prophet had a beard and Muslims love to follow in his footsteps and emulate his habits. Males must be covered from navel to knee. They are allowed to show their chest because it is believed women are able to control themselves when seeing a bare-chested man. Men, however, are more *easily* aroused, and that is the reason why women choose to cover their bodies (except hands, feet and face). They are not forced to do this. It is their choice alone and usually through custom. The obligation lies between the person and God. **Vafi**

Female Muslims are not allowed to travel by themselves

There was a rule once in the time of the Prophet that women were not allowed to travel by themselves because it wasn't safe to do during war in early Islamic times when people used to torture Muslims. It wasn't considered safe to travel alone as they risked attack. Obviously that rule no longer applies; however, some females in Saudi Arabia keep to this rule and are usually chaperoned by a male relative when outdoors, although this has become more cultural than anything else. There is nothing in the Qur'an that commands it. **Raana**

Muslims are all Arabs, or are from Pakistan or India

Islam is a universal religion. People from every nationality, race and colour will have Muslims amongst them. Some Muslims are Arabs, but there are also Arab Christians too. A large majority of the world's 1.8 billion Muslims live in Asia. More than 300 million live in sub-Saharan Africa too. The four largest Muslim populations in the world are found in Indonesia, Pakistan, India and Bangladesh. There are also many different cultures attached to Islam, including Chinese Muslims and European Muslims. **Chaker**

Muslims don't value education

This is simply not true. A lot of Muslims are highly educated and many speak several languages. Medicine, architecture, art, mathematics and astronomy are just a few of the many areas where Muslims were at the forefront of academic achievement in the early centuries of Islam. Poverty in some predominantly

Muslim countries is the prime reason for illiteracy, as opposed to Muslims setting out deliberately to thwart people away from education. Academically, my children know that they need to do much better than English students to go forward in life. They know discrimination still exists, which will make them second choice if they only equal the exam results of their contemporaries. **Pasha**

Muslims don't believe in Jesus

The opposite is true. Jesus is highly regarded in Islam and he is referred to over 40 times in the Qur'an. He is seen as one of God's Holy Prophets who was responsible for many miracles in his lifetime. Some Muslims name their sons after Jesus, who is called 'Isa' in Arabic. Muslims have very high respect for Jesus. The Prophet once mentioned how he felt closer to Jesus than any of the other Prophets. Muslims also hold in high regard his mother, the Virgin Mary. In addition to this, Chapter 3 of the Qur'an is about the grandparents of Jesus. As an imam, I sometimes feel embarrassed when I'm in the company of Christians who appear to know very little about the family of Jesus, all of which I have learned from the Qur'an. I've stopped mentioning this to even priests and vicars when I'm in their company because experience has taught me that they won't have this level of knowledge. **Parvez**

Muslims lie about Islam being a peaceful religion and never speak out against violence

Lying is a very bad thing. The Prophet abhorred lying. He said people who lie have no faith. So if a Muslim lies about anything he is going against his religion. The majority of Muslims abhor violence and terrorist groups. Some imams speak about the evil of extremism and terrorism and organise discussions to address the subject. However, there seems to sometimes be a mistrust of Muslims in general, which would imply that some sectors of society think all of us are potentially violent. Let me tell you a funny story about a young boy at school in Dewsbury. The boy said, 'I live in a terraced house' but the teacher misheard him and thought he had said, 'I live in a terrorist house', resulting in the matter being reported to the police. **Irfan**

Muslims hate Christmas

When I was growing up we always celebrated Christmas as a holiday and had a traditional turkey dinner. Many other Muslims I know did the same. However, while many Muslims marked Christmas day with a special meal in the past, religion has now taken a firmer grip, and things have changed. If Muslims dislike Christmas these days, it's because of the way it's celebrated rather than because they dislike the fact that Christians are celebrating Christ's birthday. Muslims love Jesus because he is one of God's Prophets. Furthermore, I don't think anybody ever dislikes the festivals of others. It is every person's right to live in a country where freedom is given to its citizens to practise their faith. But if a Christian is living in Saudi Arabia or Pakistan, they are not expected to participate and celebrate Ramadan and Eid. Although most Muslims don't celebrate Christmas, they nevertheless recognise it as a special time of year for relaxing, meeting up with friends and family, and eating nice food. So, in that sense, they are sharing in the season of peace and goodwill. **Juma**

INTEGRATION AND CHANGING TIMES

Many Muslims born in the UK experience conflict with the cultural values of their parents, who came to Britain in the 60s and 70s, which are different from those of subsequent generations born and raised here. Changes in integration will continue with each new generation. In many cases, we have already arrived at the 'grandparent' stage, where the parents of young Muslims in the UK were born here when their own parents first arrived 40 or so years ago. Even so, Muslims are still more likely to live in majority Muslim areas and to speak a language other than English at home. Many have few non-Muslim friends, and in Britain only a third of Muslim females are in paid employment. There are several reasons for this. Many are economically inactive because of raising young families, or are in education or have a long-term illness or disability.

Muslims who came to live in Britain during the 1960s were economic migrants from the sub-continent, East and West Africa and Mauritius. They worked hard to give their children a good education, which they were denied. Some husbands had two or three jobs. These were parents who were very proud that their children spoke good English. But these people were materialistically orientated. They were Muslims on a Friday afternoon, but for the rest of the time their religion was put to one side. These were parents who had sent their children to the mosque to be educated in the religion because they were unable to teach them much about Islam themselves. Some imams spoke poor English and sometimes the quality of the teaching was concerning. Often the children would come home and ask the parents questions that they were unable to answer, which was very embarrassing to them. After the parents became financially stable and the children began to grow up, their perspective on life changed and they realised that there was more to life than a big house and money in the bank. So they started going to the mosque more and more, but still had very little knowledge of their faith. Overall, there was a dichotomy going on between different cultures. Some parents became westernised, while others struggled with speaking English. Things have changed these days. There is less pressure on men to work so hard as a few decades ago, and now many women work as well. Imams are better educated and most speak English. But one thing that hasn't changed is parents not being able to teach the Qur'an to their children. Divisions creep in and they are sometimes not noticed until it's too late. They can only be attributed to different perceptions of the religion between some parents and their children. Apart from not eating pork and doing Ramadan, little else is practised. The religion gets diluted because parents aren't able to teach their children, which is a barrier to them sharing a common appreciation and knowledge. They fail to grasp that Islam is a complete way of life. **Ahsan**

An insurance man used to come to our house to see my father when I was a young boy. I would sit quietly in the corner and listen to their conversation. My mother used to make tea for the man and serve it in a special mug that she kept on the windowsill for white non-Muslim people. As a result, I grew up believing that non-Muslims were different to us and were not allowed to use the same crockery as Muslims. Years later we were in a restaurant and I brought this subject up with my parents. My mother remembered the mug and laughed. My father said, 'There is no such thing in Islam', referring to this incident and how culture and religion are so easily mixed up. My mother was a child of the sixties, raised in post-partition Pakistan, and had brought prejudice with her to the UK from those times where discrimination, bitterness and distrust were commonplace between Muslims and Sikhs and Hindus, despite having previously lived peacefully beside each other for centuries. **Haanii**

I grew up surrounded by white English people in a predominantly white neighbourhood. Yes, there were times when I felt a bit of an outsider and – during my school years when I was practically the only Muslim in my school – I experienced an identity crisis. I didn't feel valued. I had poor eye contact and could barely look any of the teachers in the eye. I met one of my former teachers recently, who remarked that I was the shyest person ever at school! However, the experience of being raised in this type of isolated environment has served me well. I have many English friends and indeed a variety of friends from different cultures. I have heard of other Muslims who mainly socialised with fellow Muslims at school and in their home area and have been disadvantaged by not being able to sample other cultures outside their own. **Tabana**

I feel fully integrated into British society; I was born here, grew up here and went to university. I have a wide range of friends from different cultures and backgrounds, including British people. It's a different story for my parents. They came here as economic migrants from Bangladesh. They didn't integrate well. They didn't see the point in the investment because they planned to only stay here for a while, earn some money and then return to Bangladesh. They worked hard, sent money home to my grandparents and hoped that it wouldn't be long before they returned home. But then the war broke out in Bangladesh and they never went back there to live. Would you believe that I have never visited Bangladesh? Yet this is part of my identity and history and somewhere people associate me with. My identity is British Bangladeshi. These days you read about ethnicity and diaspora and the lives of those spread around the world away from their homelands. But you hear far less about the experiences of the second-generation diaspora and how they have almost had to cope with a double identity. **Salman**

For some Muslims Islam is unequivocally interwoven into their daily lives, with each and every action reflecting the teachings contained in the Qur'an. Muslims think of God constantly. They mention Him constantly in conversation. He is never far from their minds because the ultimate desire is to honour and obey their creator and serve the creation. Islam is sometimes lived more intensely than Christianity because it is not just part of a Muslim's life, it becomes their life, which must be lived accordingly.

Being Muslim is my identity and my way of life. I couldn't imagine belonging to any other faith. My parents raised me to be a good person, to show honourable behaviour, to have nice manners and to live life with good ethics. I was taught from a young age to be kind to my family, neighbours and friends. I was taught the importance of being charitable, of building communities; and I was encouraged to inspire others by setting a good example by my actions. The Qur'an teaches us that God created people differently. There is a great spirit of companionship in Islamic communities whereby we like to get to know one another and to value each other's company. I firmly believe that if people follow the teachings of Islam that they can live peacefully and in harmony.

I am never alone. God is always with me. I remember recently going for a job interview and before I was called into the room, I calmed myself down by having a conversation with God. I asked Him to give me a voice in the interview. My trust in Him paid off because the interview went well and I got the job. I have guidance for everyday life. I know that it is wrong to drink alcohol because being intoxicated leads to losing control of our senses.

There is a great sense of family in Islam. It feels as if you are a member of one big extended family because no matter where you go in the world, when you meet other Muslims, they welcome you into their fold. I remember travelling to Switzerland once by myself, not knowing anybody there, but a trip to a mosque put me in contact with fellow Muslims who were friendly and very helpful. There is a bond between us. I remember staying at the mosque for six hours – talking and praying with people who I had never met before but feeling a warmth and regard that I believe is unique to Islam. I have made friends from many other countries through my religion, so there is also great diversity. Islam teaches you to be a good person – how to interact with other people – to not lose your temper or get upset at little things. **Sophia**

FAITH SCHOOLS

For some Muslims there is always a seeking to get the correct balance between receiving a good education and developing an understanding of Islam from a young age. Faith schools, which are mainly mixed, have come under criticism in the media for the potential to alienate young people from British society. Young girls are ordered to wear the full-face veil from the age of 11, having no choice in the matter. The students are not allowed to sing or listen to music (because of its association with debauchery and drunkenness) and are forbidden to celebrate birthdays (viewed as a symbol of idolatry) by the orthodox traditionalists. They are also not allowed to use tampons before marriage (to prevent widening of the vagina). A major criticism of these schools is that they actively discourage integration with non-Muslims, creating a 'them and us' mentality.

This is a tricky question to answer about segregation in schools between Muslims and non-Muslims. I agree with Muslim schools to a certain extent because we want our children to have Islamic values instilled into them from an early age. We want them to be taught the Qur'an and how to pray properly. It's never a good thing to see young Muslim males in their late teens not practising their religion, and when you ask them, 'Do you believe in God?' to be told, 'I don't know.' I would like to see children raised with a sense of virtue from an early age. However, I wouldn't want young people to be disadvantaged by faith schools if it meant a watering down of the national curriculum and for young people not being able to achieve good exam results. I believe English schools are still the best in the world for getting a good education. **Gabriel**

We believe that it would be ideal if children were taught in separate schools where there is emphasis on Islamic teachings as well as the national curriculum. We don't believe that children would be disadvantaged. No, they wouldn't be segregated from everybody else, because they would be part of the society in other ways outside of their schools. It is important that their faith takes precedence because young Muslim people at school face a lot of peer pressures, which result in the lessening of their faith. Sometimes you see young females not covering themselves anymore and young men who stop attending their mosque for prayers. Naivety of youth leads to relationships, parties and sex. Unless there is strict control in the family home, secularism can easily come about bit by bit. **Omar**

RELIGIOSITY OR ITS ABSENCE

'I'm not currently practising, but I was raised in the Islamic faith, so it will always be with me', were the words of a young UK pop singer who grew up Muslim.

There will be many more people like this young man who were raised as Muslim but are now either no longer practising, or are taking a 'break' from the religion. The differences in the latter group are those who, in the main, abstain from practising for a period of time during their late teens and early twenties, those who no longer pray or attend mosques but who still do Ramadan each year. They drink alcohol, misuse drugs, go to betting shops or play the lottery and have illicit sexual relationships. They refrain, though, from eating pork because they may fear comments from non-Muslims who know Muslims do not eat pork, although they are far less aware that alcohol is forbidden in Islam.

I knew many such Muslims in London during the 1990s, some of whom were from Pakistan, Morocco, Algeria and Egypt, and others who were born in the UK. Those from Morocco and other North African countries secured residency in the UK by finding a British female to marry for a fee of £2,000. These young men enjoyed life in the UK by going to pubs and sleeping with women and men. I remember one man who caught AIDS and eventually died. However, before his death he expediently shunned all aspects of his previous lifestyle including dating men, and dutifully returned to praying five times daily.

Another young Muslim I once knew got married at short notice – I know now that this must have been an arranged marriage. I remember him saying at the time that he would never leave his wife alone in the presence of another man and that his wife must always be 'covered' when she left the house. He, too, had returned to practising his faith and attended the mosque every day. He also began making disapproving comments about the lifestyle choices of other people – both Muslims and non-Muslims – as he deemed these incompatible with the teachings of Islam. Only a few months earlier, he had frequented nightclubs, drank alcohol and had random sex. It occurred to me at the time that those who take breaks from Islam and who later return were capable of great hypocrisy.

I wondered if these experiences from a generation or so ago remain true today, and began to ask practising Muslims to reflect on the cultural and/or religious differences between young Muslims in the past two decades. The conclusions from my research show there are still young Muslims who take leave of absence from their religion, mainly those who leave home and/or go to university. They sample freedom and aspects of life that they were unable to experience when they lived under the watchful eye of their families.

Sexual expression forms a big part of this new-found freedom. When I asked some young Muslims who no longer practise, a recurring answer to my question was that initially they felt Islam had too many rules which they found too difficult to keep, but when narrowed down this mainly involved relationships and alcohol. However, in certain areas of the UK, particularly in large cities, I was told that more female Muslims are wearing the hijab and are more moderately dressed than in previous decades. In some parts of Britain, girls as young as five are wearing hijabs and even niqab when they start primary school, although traditionally, girls are only expected to start wearing them when they reach puberty.

Despite mosques having failed to attract young Muslims who attend regularly, they have found knowledge on the internet or via other technology that has helped them embrace Islam. Many Muslim youths follow different imams or channels where information is given out in an easier way. Some find it easier to YouTube or Google an explanation of something than to read a book. There are phone apps, for example, which remind them when it's prayer time.

However, the decline in the number of young Muslims attending mosques has resulted in fewer being able to recite the Qur'an in Arabic, and learn more about the life of the Prophet. It was also felt that young Muslims who don't stray from their faith are those who sustain regular links with their mosques and communities.

Halal food is now a billion-pound industry with more and more young people insisting on eating it in a wide range of settings, including universities and hospitals. A growing number of restaurants have introduced it to their menus, and because of increased awareness in the food industry, the eating of non-halal food is no longer considered acceptable as an alternative choice in the absence of halal meats.

Human resource departments in businesses have also broadened their diversity and inclusion policies within their work environments, resulting in managers being more sensitive to the religious needs of their employees. Some employers run cultural awareness events – for example, some do 'Ramadan-athon' during the month of Ramadan, which requires fasting one day during the first week of Ramadan, two days in the second week, three days in the third week and finishing with four days in the fourth week.

Retail industries have progressed too and it is not uncommon now to see Eid cards and gifts available for sale in some shops. There are also many Muslim fashion influences now, especially with the rise of social media. Through their success on YouTube and Instagram and gaining many followers, mainstream fashion brands have collaborated with them to cater for the Muslim female market. Many Muslim women have launched their own fashion brands and seen success.

Sport and younger Muslims have also played a part in shifting perceptions as well. There are definitely more role models for young Muslims now such as Mo Farah, Amir Khan, Yaya Touré and Ibtihaj Muhammad (female Olympian for the USA). These Muslim sportsmen and women have an identity that Muslims can relate to, like wearing a headscarf or praying before a game. This could encourage younger Muslims to become involved in sports.

Muslims tend to get married earlier these days, some as young as 23, 24 and 25 in comparison to 28, 29 and 30 in past decades.

The main reason for settling down earlier in life is because many young people can't afford a mortgage, and so instead they decide not to delay marriage if they have to rent a home anyway. In the past it was more of a priority to find a job and buy a house before marriage was even contemplated, but life is no longer necessarily played out in this sequence.

Many Muslim women are now more empowered than ever before in the UK, but this is not reported in the media mainly because it has not fully come to mainstream prominence. Young Muslims these days are Westernised and are un-accepting of what their parents and grandparents endured. Women are better educated and have careers. They are often not reliant on their husbands, and this has resulted in a huge reduction in misogynist behaviour and even domestic violence because the younger generations do not tolerate this kind of abuse. Cooking and cleaning is no longer exclusively a woman's role and this in turn has resulted in Muslims, in the main, being able to differentiate more clearly between culture and Islam than ever before.

Some other younger Muslims appear less fearful of asking questions about homosexuality because they know more LGBT people and see same-sex marriages taking place in other communities. However, homosexuality in Islam remains seen by many as sinful and taboo. This will be covered in detail in a later chapter.

Muslims, in my research, also commented that prisons still seem to be full of people wanting to be good Muslims, which is a trend that has not changed much with time, except that there are far more Muslims now in prison than in previous decades. While incarcerated, it is thought that these prisoners practise their faith more than they did previously because they like to be seen as good and virtuous to help with early release. How true this might be is difficult to determine, but this does not stop some from having suspicions.

Most of my friends at college are non-Muslims and non-religious. They ask me questions like 'Why can't I eat pork?', 'Why do women wear the burqa?', 'Why can't I have sex before marriage?' or if I have ever been tempted to have sex. I don't mind them asking me because it increases their understanding. With regards to the question about having sex, I tell them I am not tempted because that is the way I have been taught and have accepted.

Islam is sometimes about adapting to your surroundings. We don't live in an Islamic country and therefore it's only reasonable that people will ask me questions like this. My parents are from Pakistan. I have visited there twice. The call for prayer, which is called Azaan, is so loud but is so beautiful to hear. In fact, it can be heard a couple of miles away.

Islam is sometimes stricter in Pakistan. It's an Islamic state so therefore people have to be more mindful about levels of respect, which includes more attention towards their clothing. When I am there I don't usually wear Western clothing. Most males wear a shalwar kameez, which is a pair of baggy trousers covered by a tunic that comes down to your knees.

I'm not as religious as my father. He has grown a beard and only wears Islamic clothing. I pray only two or three times a day. He balances work, family commitments and prayers, and he is also on the board of trustees at the mosque. He is always busy, but he never complains. I guess when I get married my priorities, too, will change. I imagine that I will begin then to have a greater appreciation of my religion and become more committed to my prayers and going to the mosque. **Abbas**

Muslims between the ages of 18 and 25 have mixed-up values. They say, 'We don't drink, but it's okay to smoke weed' and 'We will have sex with non-Muslims but must marry a Muslim.' I would estimate that 70 per cent of young Muslims find it hard to follow rules and therefore pick and choose. Some go to Friday prayers and never eat pork, but in the same breath they drink, smoke and have sex before marriage. Some are Muslim because they have to be. It is rare for a Muslim to convert to another religion, but I know at least three people who stopped practising completely and who now have a strong conviction against Islam, to the degree that one of them calls himself an atheist. For me, being a Muslim makes you a better person because you have been given a moral code. It teaches you to be caring and not to lie. Through believing in God, a person tries to do the right thing. I wouldn't say I am a perfect Muslim. I'm slack sometimes at praying, reading the Qur'an and helping out in my community. But I would score myself seven out of ten for mainly being good. I pride myself on having had a good upbringing. My parents are well integrated in British life and therefore I am too. I know other young Muslims, who I estimate make up about 30 per cent of us in the UK, who are extremely good at practising their religion and keep to every rule but for some reason or other, mainly owing to upbringing and culture, there is a social awkwardness about them rendering them unable to socialise and integrate properly with their peer group including non-Muslims. I really believe that people need to have a balance in life whereby they don't lose themselves in religion to the degree that it dominates their entire life. They need to live a little too and this doesn't mean being untrue to yourself or being deceitful to your parents or others. **Muji**

Young people going to college or university often escape from their parents' rules, restrictions and cultural expectations. The more religious a family is the more its members will be critical of each other. Leaving home brings new-found feelings of 'freedom'. Although this can start at secondary school, parental influences still loom in the background, but living away from home brings independence and freewill. Sometimes this new-found freedom brings about poor behaviour. I witnessed this myself during my time at university. I was shocked at the behaviour of other Muslims – males and females – who spent their student loans on partying and drinking. Being impressionable and having maybe previously lived sheltered lives, they availed of these opportunities without reservations. This saddened me greatly, but I got used to it and this experience taught me never to be fooled by a single woman wearing a hijab, because they may not be all virgins underneath. **Saif**

I'm like a bee that sticks to a flower. Anything I put my mind to, I embrace it fully. I returned to live life as a better Muslim ten years ago after a few years in the wilderness. I no longer needed football, going to the pub with friends and dating women. I've since discovered you can be a Muslim and live a fulfilling life. You don't have to destroy yourself with alcohol and sex in the hope of happiness. To embrace Islam in earnest, I grew a beard and started wearing a full-length tobe (male traditional dress), which helps maintain modesty, especially when praying as it covers my body down to my ankles, because God likes people to be covered. I wear a white tobe for the Friday service because the Prophet wore a white one on the special day of prayers. I no longer see old friends or acquaintances because they all go to the pub, something that I do not want as part of my life. Muslims don't drink alcohol because although it is recognised as something that might be fine in moderation, the evil of misusing it outweighs the goodness, so therefore as a general rule, it is completely banned in Islam. I still have to suppress my desires when I see a beautiful woman. I also blank out provocative music. But these are small sacrifices when you know that relinquishing them is for the greater cause of Islam, which is to live one's life for God alone. These days, I keep my life simple. I enjoy a cup of coffee and occasionally watch *Countryfile* on television. **Binyamin**

I have become more adaptable to the environment around me. Most of my current networks are people I met in the mosque. My new motto is: If I meet somebody it should be for the sake of God. I have great discussions with other Muslims and elders in the mosque about what is above the sky and what is below the earth. We love to debate about science and the universe. There is so much valuable knowledge in the Qur'an about these issues. But the most important thing about being a Muslim is the constant drive to be a better Muslim. Mosques are like a hospital in that respect. People are in recovery because we are all there to improve and to live better lives. A person does not have to claim to be religious to be religious. You can be of any ethnicity or creed, but if your heart believes in one God and you do good deeds, then you are religious in a very special way. You help contribute to a good society where there can be justice and freedom from oppression. People need guidance to bring them to the purpose. We need to develop better ways of bringing people back to Islam and teach them the Qur'an as well as the teachings of the Prophet. **Farris**

* * *

Muslims are frequently asked about why they don't drink alcohol, especially since wine features frequently in the Bible. Jesus enjoyed drinking wine – most people are familiar with the biblical story of the wedding feast of Cana, when the guests' wine supply diminished so Jesus performed the miracle of turning water into wine. But for most Muslims, alcohol is strictly taboo and must be avoided. Ironically, some Muslim countries allow alcohol to be produced; for example, Pakistan is renowned for some of their malt whisky, and Tunisia and Turkey are well-known producers of red and white wine, which they export around the world.

> Consumption of alcohol not only destroys the individual, it destroys their family, their economy, their physical and mental health and in the long term, it damages the community at large. As a direct outcome of alcohol consumption, it has been proved beyond any doubt that morality and a sense of responsibility cease to exert any influence on those afflicted. People who heavily drink often turn towards crime and commit offences such as thefts, burglaries, violence, domestic violence, child abuse, rapes, suicides and death by dangerous driving, to name but a few. The teachings of Islam in this regard have given the perfect answer, the perfect antidote and the perfect reasoning. The Qur'an states: 'They ask thee concerning wine and the game of hazard. Say: "In both there is great sin and also some advantages for people; but their sin is greater than their advantage"' (Qur'an – 2:219). **Musa**

Muslims also get asked why they don't eat pork. People know that the consumption of pork is also forbidden by Jews. The pig is simply not seen as a clean animal, and so its meat is to be avoided. Other prohibited food by some Muslims includes certain fish and creatures from the ocean including prawns, shellfish, jellyfish, turtles and frogs.

The pig eats filth and is utterly shameless. The reason for the prohibition of its flesh is obvious, as by the laws of nature its flesh would have a foul effect on the body and the soul of one who eats it. As food affects a person's soul, there can be no doubt that the flesh of such a foul animal would also be foul. Islamic philosophy proposes that eating food has two effects. The first affect is on the body, and the second affect is on the soul. Therefore, if you eat a foul animal there will be foul effects on the body and the soul. Effects on the body from eating pork include the passage of viruses, such as swine influenza virus, which may cause a flu-like illness, (as well as) the passage of parasites, such as the adult tapeworm, which can lodge in the gastrointestinal tract and cause malnutrition and blood loss. Pork also has an extremely high fat content – we know that the high intake of fat predisposes to high blood pressure, and the gradual blocking of arteries with fatty material leads to heart attacks and strokes. Effects of pork on the soul, according to Islamic philosophy, would affect moral qualities such as chastity, modesty, humility, honesty and integrity. As Islam is a complete religion – no absolute ban has been declared. Therefore anybody experiencing extreme hunger that may lead to their death is allowed to eat pork as stated in the Qur'an 5:3. **Ezaz**

DEATH AND THE AFTERLIFE

A dead body should be treated like a live person. Muslims respect the dignity of the dead person. The Prophet instructed this and said the coffin should not be shaken because it's not good for the dead body; rather you should be as gentle as possible to the dead person. Muslims believe that the dead feel pain so therefore it is important to not mishandle the body or change it in any way. Beards must not be trimmed and hair must not be cut, and neither should a person's finger- or toenails be cut. The body is washed and scented and wrapped in a shroud. It is believed the dead body still has a connection with the soul. Post-mortems are allowed if it becomes a legal requirement but should be avoided if possible because cutting up a dead body is not respectful to the dead person's dignity. However, Islam allows organ donation because this is seen as giving life to another person. Muslim funerals are usually held within 24 hours of the person's death and use burial. This is a cultural tradition, especially in hot climate countries. Many Muslims prefer burial to cremation. Although coffins are mainly used in the UK, there are some local authorities that allow shrouds. A groove is made in the grave, which the shroud is slid into. On the Day of Judgement, the body is put back together again. This begins with the coccyx bone (tailbone) which seldom rots but whose DNA remains untouched even if it does. Muslims believe everybody resurrected will be aged 33 except prepubescent children who will return at the same age as they were when they died.

> Children who die before their fifteenth birthday automatically go to paradise. That is the age when somebody becomes an adult in the eyes of Islam. Likewise for people with mental health problems and those with learning difficulties; they too go automatically to paradise. On the Day of Judgement, God will resurrect all of the people from these three groups as Muslims. On the other hand, he will punish 'Muslims' who are like cattle or sheep with outward markings, but who inside are devoid of the principles required to be a good Muslim. If they do not believe their faith with a full heart and act according to their convictions of faith, they will be resurrected on the Day of Judgement as non-Muslims. **Nazzar**

Descriptions of heaven in the Qur'an are always represented by love, peacefulness and beauty. We are told that people entering paradise will get dressed in beautiful robes and will drink from gold goblets, waited on by servants while being surrounded by virgins. It will be beautiful beyond human description. It will be like finding true love. People strive in life to meet their true love but encounter barriers in doing so. But heaven, we are told, is like meeting that perfect person who is your true love, because it is here you encounter God, your creator. You won't meet God face-to-face but you will feel his essence, his presence, his love, and it will really be divine beyond anything ever experienced. **Baber**

Descriptions of hell in the Qur'an are always represented by images burning in fire. The horrendousness of it is relayed to instruct people that unless they repent their sins and live their lives according to the word of God they will be burnt in hell as punishment. To warn people against this disaster, they are told that the punishment will consist of their skin burning, and not just their existing layer. After the first layer burns, they will be given another layer and this too will burn, repeating the pain and agony. The person's cries will not be heard, because essentially hell is about being cut off from God, being cut off from goodness. Of course, only God decides who goes to hell because it is he who sees inside the person's soul. **Yassir**

KAFIR

The word 'kafir' is invariably used by Muslims as a derogatory term for non-Muslims – people who reject Islam and the Prophet Muhammad (otherwise referred to in English as either an unbeliever or disbeliever). The plural of the word is 'kuffar'. The term 'infidel' is always used within this context.

'Kafir' was used in the time of the Prophet to mainly distinguish between Muslims and non-Muslims who were primarily polytheism worshippers (those who believe in more than one God). In more modern times it is generally used to mean anybody who is non-Muslim, irrespective of whether they believe in God. Islamic scholars say that 'kafir' implies that the legal rulings of Islam do not apply to a particular person who is considered spiritually inferior. It can also be used more harshly by inferring that anybody who is non-Muslim will not get to paradise, although more scholarly Muslims say this is not technically correct and believe that certain people who are non-Muslims will be saved in the afterlife. A verse in the Qur'an implies that this is the case:

> Those who believe (Muslims), and those who are Jews and the Christians, and the Sabians (or those of some other faith) – whoever truly believes in God and the Last Day and does good, righteous deeds, surely their reward is with their Lord, and they will have no fear, nor will they grieve. (Qur'an – 2:62)

Although this verse indicates paradise is the reward for all good and righteous people, whether they are Muslim or not, there is still a tendency for most orthodox Muslims to bypass this verse and believe that paradise is mainly for Muslims only, with only a small window of opportunity open for all others.

It is a question of whether the message of Islam reaches people or not. Somebody living in the wilderness of the Amazon jungle will be exempt from hell, for example, as will an elderly person who can't comprehend Islam. But there is a chain of others who may not automatically be exempt, ranging from Catholic priests to Jewish rabbis, and atheists to Israeli soldiers fighting in Israel. The difficulty with this latter group is deciding whether the message of Islam reached them but they did not understand it, or they understood but rejected it. This too leads to another layer of debate. Did the person reject Islam and verbalise this outwardly? Or did they appear to reject it but accepted it in their hearts, but for some social or political reason or other, were unable to convert to Islam?

The core essence of all of this is that salvation is between the person and God. Take you for example, Declan. I don't know whether you will go to paradise or hell. When you die, it might be seen that outwardly you are a Catholic and therefore you will have a Catholic funeral, but who can say that some time during your life, or before your death, that you will not have supplicated to God and fervently asked Him to save you. How do I know whether or not you hid your true beliefs by not declaring them openly? Salvation between a person and God will never be a black or white issue. There is no such thing as a general judgement. Islam is not that dogmatic because there is such great depth to it. It is based on individuality. You may look at somebody and judge them but you will never be able to see the unseen. Therefore nobody should ever consider themselves better than others. **Purdil**

CHAPTER 2

The Prophet and Islam – A Brief History

The Prophet Muhammad was born in Mecca in the year 570. Arabia was a harsh and desolate environment, full of mountains, desert and arid regions where access to clean drinking water was scarce. It was also a country without a government and cut off from others by vast oceans of sand. This was an age of ignorance, when idolaters were an intrinsic part of the Arabian fabric.

Abdullah, Muhammad's father, died before he was born. It was the custom at the time for single mothers to send their children to live in the desert, resulting in his mother, Amina, sending Muhammad to live with a foster mother called Halimah eight days after he was born.

During his early childhood in the desert, Muhammad learnt Arabic in its purest form. Despite its many drawbacks, Arabia possessed a highly developed language – which was spoken by the ancient nomadic Bedouin people whose oral traditions (including poetry recitation) were renowned. This training helped Muhammad develop a strong and pleasant speaking voice.

Muhammad stayed in the desert until he was five years old before returning to live with his mother. Sadly, she died a year later.

He then went to live with his grandfather for two years until he too died. Muhammad then went to live with his uncle, Abu Talib, and remained with him until adulthood.

Muhammad grew into an extremely handsome man and his companions would comment on his good looks. He was of medium height, average weight and had broad shoulders. He had a clear complexion, dark eyes, good teeth and a well-framed jaw and chin. His beard was thick and black, as was his hair. He took great care of both and always applied oil before combing. He also walked with a fine gait. The Prophet was a clean man and always wore clean clothes. It was said his perspiration smelt more beautiful than any musk or perfume ever created. Between his shoulders there was what was believed to be the seal of prophethood – a raised area of skin the size of a pigeon's egg. Muhammad's genealogy can be traced back to the Prophet Ismail – the first son of the Prophet Abraham.

Muhammad became a merchant dealing in the sale of horses, camels and donkeys, and also sold spices at markets. He gained sales experience with his uncle before starting to work for a wealthy widow, Khadijah, who he eventually married at the age of 25. He had a few opportunities to travel beyond the borders of his own country, and sometimes undertook business trips with the Arab trade caravans to Persia, Byzantium and Egypt. These journeys often took months, as the traders carried their wares to and from these regions.

Khadijah was 40 when she proposed marriage to Muhammad. She was a pious lady who took an active interest in everything he did and she trusted Muhammad so much that she handed over her entire wealth to him. This included her slaves, who Muhammad instantly set free. Khadijah is commonly regarded by Muslims as the Mother of Believers. She and Muhammad had four daughters and two sons (who died early). He adored his daughters and felt blessed by them, highly valuing them in an era that placed little worth on the birth of females. Men wanted their wives to have sons, fearful that without male heirs the family lineage would be compromised; these were cruel times that often saw baby girls being buried alive because they were perceived as being burdens. Muhammad admonished this idea, and by example planted the seed that would stop these barbaric practices. He had an excellent relationship with his daughters and felt blessed by God for their creation. He would often take them on donkey rides and buy presents for them. Later in life he used to take his grandsons to the local courts so they could listen and learn about justice and the difference between right and wrong, as he felt this was a good way of helping them learn how to make decisions.

The Prophet remained faithful to Khadijah for the 25 years they were married until her death. He was 49 when she died, and from that time until his death – aged 63 – he married a further ten times and had another son who also died in infancy by Mariyah, one of his wives. These subsequent marriages must be viewed in context of the traditional patriarchy, and the enduring wars and attacks against Islam. The Prophet was part of a society in Mecca that helped orphans, widows and other people in need during the aftermath of war. Widows and divorced women were likely to fall on hard times rendering them helpless. His kind heart and desire to care for and protect these women – particularly widows and other vulnerable females – from living in extreme poverty could be one of the reasons why he married so many times. Before Islam, Arabs could have unlimited wives, but this was reduced to four by the Qur'an. As a special privilege to the Prophet, in acknowledgement of his status, he was allowed to marry more than four times. The Prophet married the youngest of his wives, Aisha, when she was aged six and he was 53, although it is also claimed that the marriage was not consummated until she was nine. Child marriages and considerable differences of age were no impediment within the cultural context of seventh-century Arabian society. A lot of men married young girls but did not consummate the marriages until the females reached maturity. Sex was not allowed until menstruation had commenced. At the time there was greater stigma in Arabian culture attached to a man marrying an older woman than a young girl.

During the lifetime of the Prophet many enemies thought, because of his revelations, he was a mad fortune teller who dealt in black magic. However, Muslims point out that there is no evidence to support this and they do not accuse him of sexual wrongdoing because these practices were commonplace during this era. There are so many fabrications these days, such as the far-right lobby and propaganda videos, which claim that if the Prophet were alive today, he would be jailed for many crimes, including sexual inappropriateness and paedophilia. There were preposterous claims that the Prophet liked the practice of 'thighing' (placing the penis between the thighs and massaging until ejaculation) and had developed this practice during the three years he was married to Aisha before lawful consummation took place. These absurd allegations are meritless. The truth is the Prophet was kind and gentle to all his wives and would never do anything to hurt them. But just as during his lifetime, there will always be people who try to besmirch his reputation. **Madani**

In addition to Aisha, there is also a small controversy about another of the Prophet's marriages. This relates to the ex-wife of his adopted son Zayd, who was previously a slave of the Prophet's wife, Khadijah. He asked if he could be allowed to stay because he liked having the Prophet – who he considered to be very kind – as his Master. The Prophet grew fond of Zayd, and treated him more like a son than a servant. Sometime after Zayd had divorced his wife Zaynab, the Prophet proposed to her, and they got married.

Except for Aisha, all of the Prophet's wives had been married before. It is worth noting that in those times virginity held significant status. This, therefore, is a sign that the Prophet wasn't lustful and his reasons for having so many wives in later life were purely honourable and caring.

MUHAMMAD: MAN AND PROPHET

Like Jesus and the other Prophets, the Prophet Muhammad came to earth and lived as an ordinary man. His heart did not possess a morsel of vanity, like his predecessors. He too was destined to live amongst a nation, and in doing so lived out the most extraordinary existence without realising his true greatness; such was the extent of his humility. Muslims will revere him until the end of time and whenever the name of the Prophet is mentioned, it is usually followed with the words *'peace be upon Him'*, although there is no scriptural injunction to do so.

I want to tell people how merciful the Prophet was to everybody. He loved animals and stipulated that they should be treated well, fed properly and allowed to rest. He was ahead of his time because in those days there were no animal rights in Arabia, but the Prophet often taught people that if they were riding on a camel or horse and stopped to speak to somebody, they should get off the animal and let it rest.

The Prophet was also a believer in human rights. He believed that slaves should have rights. Remember, slavery was so common in the world back then. His call for rights and better treatment were indeed the first steps that anybody had taken and this eventually led to their eradication centuries later.

Wives of the Prophet commented that despite his status as Prophet to the outside world, when he was at home he did not seek any special treatment. He used to play hide-and-seek with his children or crawl about on the floor to amuse them. They were also allowed to sit on his knee or climb on his back. His love for them was tender and enduring. When it came to practical tasks, the Prophet would sew his own shoes to repair them, but could have easily asked someone else instead.

Companions of the Prophet also commented that during journeys away from home when it came time to eat, the party would arrange tasks amongst itself. Some would hunt, others would skin the animal and others would cook it. The Prophet, who could easily have been excused of any task, would insist on gathering firewood to start the fire. This showed he was a down-to-earth man. Time and time again, companions of the Prophets used to comment that he was a warm, friendly and good-humoured man who never walked around without a smile on his face. So it's easy to imagine him having dinner around the fire and enjoying the camaraderie. **Raamis**

The Prophet was very gentle with children. He could speak to them on their level without lecturing if they had done anything wrong. He could brighten the mood of any sad child. Once, when a small boy's pigeon had died, the Prophet was at hand to offer him some tenderness to ease his loss. The Prophet perfected everything. There was never anybody like him before and never will be again. His conduct was always perfect. He was the first amongst equals. I have met lapsed Muslims who have stopped practising Islam, and their faces always light up when I tell them stories about the Prophet. I firmly believe that he is the final barrier that stops them leaving Islam. Once a member of Aisha's (his wife's) family spread slander about her supposedly having an affair with another man. The Prophet knew it was a lie but did not seek retaliation against the person who started the false rumours. To me, he was the ideal role model who taught that even when you are treated badly in life, you must not retaliate. He taught us to forgive and let it go. **Dabir**

The Prophets were chosen from eternity at the divine will of God rather than acquisition on earth by character or deeds, and therefore all the Prophets had divine souls. Muslims believe the Holy Prophets came to connect humankind to its creator, since our intellect is limited, and the Prophets have always informed us about the differences between good and bad, virtues and sins, benefits and harm, and rights and duties. Islam teaches that God loves his creation 70 times more than we love our own mothers and he gave us the best of Prophets who were all blessed with certain qualities to fulfil their mission:

Noah was given persistence.
Abraham was given courage.
Moses was given leadership.
Jesus was given patience.
And Muhammad was given wisdom.

> *But Muslims believe that their Prophet was also given the qualities*
> *of the other Prophets as well and have bestowed many titles upon*
> *him including The Leader of the Prophets, Imam of the Prophets*
> *and Master of the Prophets. (Qur'an – 33:40)*

Muhammad never sought personal benefits such as wealth, high status or power. He only sought approval from God because he knew his destiny and role for mankind as stated in the Qur'an.

From an early age, the Prophet became known for being truthful. As he grew up, he was respected and admired by his community, and at quite an early age was nicknamed 'The Honest' or 'The Trustworthy'. People liked being around him because of his kindness and wisdom. He led by example, and his companions were led by the examples he set. He was an intelligent man who was also known as 'The Seeker' because of his quest for knowledge. He became one of the hanifs who were a group of proto-monotheists around Mecca. They believed that Abraham had walked their land and dedicated Arabia to the one God, the God of the Jews and the Christians. They called God 'Allah'. Muhammad knew of the Old Testament and part of the Gospels. Like many Prophets before him since Abraham's time, he too began calling for people to believe in one God.

> The origins of Islam started simply, with a few followers, consisting
> of the Prophet's cousin, Ali, and a friend of his named Abu Bakr.
> Interestingly, the Prophet's uncle, Abu Talib (Ali's father) was the
> head leader of a tribe called Quraysh – who believed in statues
> and other idolatries – but not God.
>
> The Prophet's message, calling for everyone to believe in
> one God, was met with ridicule and rejection by Quraysh, who
> viewed it as a direct threat to their way of life. Firstly, they began
> spreading rumours that the Prophet was insane. When this failed
> to have effect, they came to harass him and plastered excrement
> on the doors of his house and the houses of his followers. They
> also threw stones at them in protest.
>
> Later on, the Quraysh plotted to kill the Prophet – after

holding a meeting amongst fellow tribes and agreeing for each tribe to nominate a strong man who was a good swordsman. They planned to go to the Prophet's house when he was asleep and for all the men to plunge swords into him in one swoop. However, an angel appeared to the Prophet earlier that day and told him not to sleep at home. His cousin, Ali, slept in his bed instead.

That night, when the tribesmen broke into the Prophet's house, they were about to stab the body in the bed believing it to be that of the Prophet, but saw at the last minute that it was Ali, and they withdrew and fled. By the time of this aborted assassination, Islam was growing more widely, but because of the constant threats against them, the Prophet and his followers decided to leave Mecca and broke into different groups.

Some of the Prophet's followers found refuge in Ethiopia as they fled their pagan persecutors. Here they met the Negash, a Christian king who welcomed them because he recognised they shared a common belief in one God. The Prophet himself relocated to Medina where hundreds turned out to hear his message. During his time in Medina, Islam really flourished, prompting the Prophet to build the first mosque. The only problem was that he couldn't decide on the most suitable place to build it so as not to offend anybody. He decided to let his camel roam around, knowing that camels are known to choose comfortable spots to lie. The mosque was built on the spot where the camel eventually lay and was called The House of Muhammad. **Kaied**

THE HOLY QUR'AN

Muslims believe that, before the Qur'an, God's scriptures were delivered through various Prophets – the Scrolls of Abraham, the Psalms through David, the Torah through Moses, and the Gospels through Jesus. But somewhere through history God's Word became corrupted. Time after time, the holy scripts had become diluted, tampered with or in some way altered. That is, until God chose the

Prophet Muhammad to be his Messenger, on whom he would bestow his Word and then leave the task of delivering its message to his people.

This was no ordinary command. God wished for the Qur'an to become the source that would never become diluted or corrupted. It would remain pure to the end of time – untouched and unblemished. Muslims believe that God chose the Prophet because he was illiterate; knowing that nobody would accuse him of writing down falsehoods but instead would realise that the revelations came straight from the Almighty. Liberal Muslims, however, dispute that the Prophet was illiterate by questioning how an intelligent man who was a successful trader could not know how to read and write. Before Islam, Muslims believe that earlier Holy Books have been changed and corrupted and that parts are missing. One omission being that of Mary, mother of Jesus, who is spoken of in the Qur'an with special fondness: 'In a miracle unreported in the Bible, the infant Jesus supposedly spoke up from the crib to defend his mother's honour when ill-wishers accused her of fornication' (Abbot 2013). Muslims believe that only the Qur'an is the pure word of God and that Muhammad has revealed the accurate correct revelation of God, which had been lost or corrupted before him. This will reside in the words of the Qur'an for all time. It is with this understanding and conviction that Muslims hold the Qur'an, believing in it above any of the previous Holy Scriptures written prior to Islam.

The first lines of the Qur'an contains the essence of the teachings contained within the whole of the Qur'an:

> *In the name of God, the Gracious, the Merciful*
> *All praise belongs to God, Lord of all the worlds,*
> *The Gracious, the Merciful,*
> *Master of the Day of Judgement.*
> *You alone do we worship and You alone do we implore for help.*
> *Guide us in the right path –*
> *The path of those on whom You hast bestowed Your blessings,*
> *those who have not incurred displeasure, and those who have*
> *not gone astray. (Qur'an – 1:1–7)*

The Prophet was a spiritual man who liked to spend lengthy times by himself in prayer and contemplation. Eventually he began to withdraw to a cave on Mount Hira for quiet meditation. It was here one night in the year 610, at the age of 40, that the archangel Gabriel appeared to him and the process of the Qur'an revelations began. This signalled the start of Muhammad's prophethood and the beginning of Islam. The revelations continued for 23 years, up until the time of the Prophet's death in 632.

It was reported that the angel Gabriel appeared to him and said 'read'. The Prophet told Gabriel that he couldn't read. Gabriel embraced the Prophet before instructing him a second time to 'read'. The Prophet once again told Gabriel that he was unable to read. Once again Gabriel embraced the Prophet before instructing him a third time to 'read'. The Prophet pleaded, 'I can't read.' Once again Gabriel embraced the Prophet before telling him for a fourth time to 'read'.

The Prophet was overwhelmed by the appearance of Gabriel and the first revelations resulting in his wife taking him to see a monk, who listened carefully to what was revealed to him, before declaring, 'You are a Prophet', then adding, 'He came to Moses, He came to Jesus and now he has come to you.'

The monk warned him that he would have a struggle on his hands and that people would reject him to the point that they would throw him out of the town. From that moment onwards, the Prophet understood his role and his destiny. He pressed ahead knowing that it was God's will. Sometimes the revelations bestowed upon him were so powerful, he felt weighed down with the emotional pressure. The Prophet rode a camel and it was noticed that during these times the camel would have to sit down because of the weight the Prophet generated. **Jaan**

The Qur'an consists of 114 chapters and is divided into 30 parts. The shortest chapter is three verses and the longest 286 verses.

There are five core themes to the Qur'an:

Almighty God
Revelations to the Prophet Muhammad
Previous Prophets
Life of the hereafter
Commands for living day-to-day life

During the lifetime of the Prophet, the entire text of the Qur'an was written down and committed to memory by thousands of Muslims, a practice followed to the current day. This is one of the key reasons that the text has been preserved in its original form. The Prophet dictated the revelations given to him to his appointed scribes over a 23-year period. According to Islam, the Qur'an contains every concept, principle and law necessary for mankind's ethical, moral, intellectual and spiritual development.

The Prophet's followers wrote the revelations on palm leaves, stones and bones. After the Prophet died, the first caliph (successor), Abu Bakr, gathered all the revelations together but they were not put into book form until Uthman ibn Affan, the third caliph, took charge, some 15 years later.

The Qur'an was written in classical Arabic and was first translated into English in 1649. The text is considered by Muslims to be the pure word of God. The Qur'an is always held with respect by Muslims, who generally feel the book should never be touched without first carrying out an ablution. Copies of the Qur'an should be placed in a high place, like a bookcase, and never left on the floor or taken into the toilet. Muslims believe the Qur'an is to be used until the Day of Judgement, and that in the meantime it will assist them in living their day-to-day lives.

The Qur'an is recited in Arabic in the form of a mild chanting. There is a beautiful, touching sound to it, like a great melody. It is lyrical, poetic and elegantly rhythmic in a way that is unequalled by any other religious text.

The Qur'an is the source of God's wisdom for Muslims throughout the world. Thus many who heard the words in the original Arabic won't understand them without a translation. Muslims are encouraged to read the Qur'an to fully appreciate the importance of focusing one's life to the will of God.

The true believers are those only who believe in God and His messenger and afterward doubt not, but strive with their wealth and their lives for the cause of God. Such are the sincere. (Qur'an – 49:15)

Many children learn to recite the Qur'an from cover to cover. I once knew a nine-year-old boy in London who learned to recite the entire Qur'an in a little over a two-year period. It was amazing to watch somebody pick a chapter for the boy who would then recite it without hesitation. Most children are usually only able to accomplish this between the ages of 13 to 17.

Children and elderly Muslims are the two best categories of Muslims who are dutiful at reading and reciting the Qur'an. Adults in-between are neglectful and often ignore this responsibility. It is no good just reading the Qur'an, you have to understand it. To do this you have to read commentaries. Sometimes you have to do your research to understand things. There are so many wonderful creations and discoveries in the Qur'an worth pondering, from how mountains are created to the origins of how honey is made. **Taaib**

The Qur'an is protected by there being only one version in Arabic of the Qur'an for all Muslims, ensuring that even the slightest dot in it will never be changed. There are many translations of the Qur'an in English and other languages, although it is noted that the true interpretation of the original is sometimes lost in translation from Arabic into other languages. Muslims insist these divine revelations must be protected to remain pure and uncorrupted. Yet, like the Bible, there are certain texts and verses in the Qur'an that are perhaps more suitable to the time in which they were written than now. The Prophet Muhammad died in the sixth century and although the Qur'an does not contain dates or name specific places, it appears to be indicative of life during the times of the Prophet. And just like the

Bible, discussion continues in society, mainly in non-Muslim circles may I add, as to whether the Qur'an is relevant for our current times.

The Qur'an sometimes gets interpreted differently by individual Muslims and communities, and indeed in different countries and continents. For example, Muslims in parts of Africa and Asia may understand aspects of the Qur'an differently to Muslims in the UK, with one key to these differences being that around the world people speak and read many languages and experience a wide variety of cultural influences. But the Qur'an is designed to facilitate good lives for all Muslims wherever they live and to make, by its message, life easier and more straightforward. Muslims also believe that the Qur'an contains a universal message for eternity, that it is the blueprint which directs people as to how to live their lives to get to paradise. They also consider it to be 100 per cent in accordance with science, without any part of it contradicting scientifically based knowledge.

> The Qur'an is very helpful. Many things in science have shown what Allah said in the Qur'an over 1400 years ago. Examples of this are when he said that 'everything living thing is made from water'. Modern science has proven that every organism consists of a high proportion of the water and if it lost as much as 25 per cent of its water, it would die. Another example is, 'We built the heaven with might and it is we who are expanding it.' Cosmologists have stated that galaxies are flying apart from each other, but there must have been a time when galaxies were closer together; and a time earlier when all the galaxies and material in the universe were crunched up together into an incredibly small space. **Dadvar**

THE HADITH

In addition to the Qur'an, most Muslims have another religious text that they follow and refer to frequently. This is the Hadith, which comprises the practises and sayings of the Prophet that were compiled several hundred years after the Prophets death (I use the word Hadith throughout this book for both the singular and plural forms). It is through the Hadith that Muslims learn the general habits and actions of the Prophet. The whole body of traditions about the life and wisdom of Muhammad is known as the 'Sunnah'. As Clarke (2013) points out, the Sunnah is the second and subordinate religious text after the Qur'an upon which Muslims refer to for their faith and life. The body of traditions circulated orally for decades, even centuries after the Prophet's death, with the word Hadith basically meaning report or statement or the telling of something 'new'. The records of the practice, words and confirmation of other people's words and deeds in relation to the Prophet, therefore, were called Hadith. But the name for the practice is Sunnah (custom or usage) whose plural is Sunan.

The Hadith, written in Arabic, consists of a collection of books containing several million of the Prophet's sayings, actions and things that he approved of during his lifetime that gives rise to its credibility or questions it. There is no other comparative collection to compare it to, and it far outweighs anything that has ever been recorded about the life of Jesus.

The Hadith are reference books that were compiled by followers of Islam starting around a century after the Prophet's death and concluding 300 years afterwards. They comprise a chain of narrations, which were heard and passed on through the generations and were accepted provided they came from people of good character. Muslims, in general, believe that the Hadith lead them to the correct way of living life based on how the Prophet lived – based on what he did and said including his daily routines, what time he got up and went to bed, how he did his ablutions, how he prayed and the food he liked (milk, dates, bread, cheese and shoulder of lamb).

The Hadith were passed on by scholars and their students, who in turn passed them on to their students. The Hadith are mainly studied by Islamic scholars – with imams imparting information to ordinary Muslims because the books of the Hadith are difficult to read, often contradictory and best avoided unless they are to be studied carefully and interpreted correctly. Some of the contents can be seen to be conflicting unless they are explained within the context of the times of the Prophet. Although the Hadith runs into several volumes and consists of numerous collators who put together the Hadith, which were transmitted orally for generations, the two most widely read collections are by *Bukhari* and *Muslim*.

Here are two examples of the Prophet's wisdom as outlined in the Hadith:

> *Religion is very easy and whoever overburdens himself in his religion will not be able to continue in the way. So you should not be extremists, but try to be near to perfection and receive the good tidings that you will be rewarded, and gain strength by offering the Salah (prayers) in the morning, afternoons and during the last hours of the nights. (Hadith – Bukhari)*

> *Whoever believes in Allah and the last day, let him not annoy his neighbour; whoever believes in Allah and the last day, let him honour his guest; whoever believes in Allah and the last day, let him speak good or else remain silent. (Hadith – Muslim)*

Examples of his famous sayings, which run into their thousands, include:

- Like for others what you like for yourself. (Hadith – Muslim)
- Man cannot be a true believer if his neighbour is not safe from his behaviour. (Hadith – Bukhari)
- You say salam to everybody whether you know him or you know him not. (Hadith – Tirmidhi)
- When a respectful person of a people comes to visit you, pay him due respect. (Hadith –Muslim)

Islamic scholars consider it important to read books with background commentary books for the Hadith texts so as to ensure a proper understanding of why the Prophet said and did certain things –

and the meanings behind his actions. Some Muslims believe that everything that the Prophet did or said was a revelation. Islamic scholars say the Hadith serve as an explanation to the Qur'an because without the Hadith the Qur'an is difficult to understand.

I sometimes think Muslim clerics have not done enough to get the correct message out to people and that is one of the reasons why Islam and the reputation of the Prophet get attacked. Ninety per cent of Muslims have never read the Qur'an in a language they understand. They know how to recite it in Arabic but do not understand it. Muslims seem to just read simple books on virtues in Islam (i.e. the benefits of doing this and that if you practise certain elements). Likewise, Muslims in general will have diluted and ill-informed knowledge of the Hadith, and hence their knowledge about the life of the Prophet is also thinned and superficial.

When studying the Hadith, it must be taken into account that the Prophet used Mosaic Law in the majority of cases, unless a revelation contradicted it. Revelations from God to the Prophet were piecemeal, and sometimes they may have come after the Prophet had administered a punishment that was previously recorded in the Hadith, without acknowledging that the punishment preceded a revelation, and which might have determined a different outcome. It is important for Islamic scholars to check the authenticity of the narrators by looking at a chain of them to see if they knew each other and were connected. They may have lived in the same country or city, and therefore it was possible they could have met or have known each other.

> Hadith has different categories; many are of an authenticity to the level of Qur'an, some are lower, and there are fabrications. Only Muslim scholars of Hadith can recognise the authenticity of Hadith, through the chain of narratives which determines the validity or weakness of a Hadith. **Kabeer**

Some scholars have stated that about 10 per cent of Hadith are total falsehoods while others feel the percentage is much higher.

There is a verse in the Qur'an which refers to the night that the Prophet was taken on a 'journey' which could be reasonably interpreted that he had a vision, a spiritual experience, which took him in a trance where he felt the presence of God close to him:

Glory be to the One who inspired His servant to endeavour during the night from the Sanctioned Submissions to the fringes of submission that We blessed in order to show him Our signs. Indeed He hears all things and sees all things. (Qur'an – 17:1)

In a Hadith, which refers to this verse, it states that on the night in question God took Allah up to heaven and during his journey back, he saw a glimpse of hell, which was three-quarters full of women. The Hadith said that these women were put in hell because they were ungrateful to their husbands as well as being guilty of swearing and gossiping.

For me the Hadith must pass a double litmus test: 1) They must not defy or contradict the Qur'an and 2) They must not defy logic or reason. I firmly believe that anything in Islam that is bizarre, strange or inhumane comes from the Hadith, which in my opinion are mainly manufactured sources. These are secondary sources and not the Qur'an, which is pure and untouched. Another example of manufactured Hadith is the one about female genital mutilation, which originated in Egypt thousands of years before Islam. There is no mention of this procedure whatsoever in the Qur'an so why would the Prophet have ordered women to be 'cut lightly' as some Muslims believe? Besides, if this was so important to him, why didn't he request it to be done to his daughters? On seeing a Hadith, I can tell whether the Prophet could or could not have said it because after extensive study and practice I have developed academic insights and can intuitively sense the veracity or otherwise of the Prophet. **Dr Hargey**

There are various interpretations of the Hadith where the Prophet speaks about there being 73 groups, all of which except one would go the hell. Some scholars question if he meant that within Islam, his nation would be split into 73 sects and that he was condemning the formation of these groups of Muslims that would come about after his lifetime. Others question if he was referring to 73 different types of religious groups around at his time and that from these, only Muslims would be saved. I consider this a weak Hadith that was incorrectly told. I believe all Muslims will enter paradise provided they do not reject the article of faith that binds the religion together. **Asrar**

THE LAST SERMON AND FINAL DAYS

The Prophet worked hard all his life. He was a humble man who never feared manual tasks like digging ditches or helping in the building of mosques. It was not until shortly before his death that he became ill for the first time with a high fever. The fever was so high that 13 buckets of water were thrown over him to bring down his temperature. Although he eventually became free of the fever, the illness left him in a weakened state and he never fully recovered. His farewell sermon to his community took place two months before he died. Like most of the Prophet's speeches, it wasn't particularly long but what set it apart was not just the poignancy of the occasion being the last time he would ever publicly address his people but the message that his speech conveyed. Here he outlined the perils of racism by saying:

> 'A white man is not superior to a black man and a black man is not superior to a white man.' He went on by saying, 'Asians are not superior to Arabs and Arabs are not superior to Asians.' Then the Prophet added, 'A Christian is not superior to a Muslim and a Muslim is not superior to a Christian.' (Hadith – Ahmed)

The Prophet spoke about women and reminded his people to always treat them well. He also spoke about civil war and discouraged infighting amongst Muslims after his death; instead, he instructed people to concentrate their time and energy in spreading the message of Islam to the world.

Shortly before the Prophet died, he knew he was seriously ill. He called all of his wives together and sought their permission that he go to the house of his youngest wife – Aisha – for her to take care of him. Aisha was known to be very instinctively attuned to his needs and all his other wives readily agreed to this plan without any ill feeling amongst them.

Despite Aisha's great care of the Prophet, his health did not improve. His love for praying remained with him until the end. A few days before he died he was very weak, but was still determined to go the mosque and pray. He barely had the strength to walk and had to rest his weight on the shoulders of two of his followers who accompanied him to the mosque. A few days later the Prophet died. Before he died though he told his followers that it was God's will for him to be buried wherever he died. His followers made a literal interpretation of this and buried the Prophet in Aisha's chamber. At the Prophet's funeral in Medina, thousands came to his funeral and each took turns to visit his body in the chamber to pay their last respects.

* * *

The Qur'an outlines the reasons for which the Prophet was granted permission to engage in warfare:

> *Those who have been driven out of their homes unjustly only because they said, 'Our Lord is God' – And if God did not repel some men by means of others, there would surely have been pulled down cloisters and churches and synagogues and mosques, where the name of God is oft commemorated. And God will surely help one who helps him. God is indeed Powerful, Mighty. (Qur'an – 22:41)*

The vast majority of Muslims believe that Islam is a peaceful religion and that its teachings do not allow instigating war. Muslims are allowed to use self-defence if under attack. Throughout history the Prophet has faced accusations that he was a violent man. There is no evidence that this is true; as the author Ruth Cranston pointed out in her book *World Faith* (1949), 'Muhammad never instigated fighting and bloodshed. Every battle he fought was in self-defence. He simply fought defensively in order to survive. And he fought with the weapons and in the fashion of his time.' Would it be reasonable to assume Muslims who believe the Prophet's character to be without blemish are correct, considering that there are 1.8 billion people in the world who follow Islam? Would that number of people who believe and trust in the Prophet so fiercely believe in Islam if its founder was a violent man?

And God did help Muslims who bravely fought to protect themselves from death. The first great battle of the Prophet's time was the battle of Badr in 624, and it became the defining moment in Islamic history. Prior to the battle, the Prophet and his army had fought several smaller skirmishes against the pagan Meccans in late 623 and early 624. Badr, however, was the first large-scale engagement between the two forces. Despite having only 313 men, 70 camels and two horses against 1000 soldiers, 700 camels and 300 men on horseback, the Prophet and his soldiers claimed victory. Had the Prophet and his men lost against this much stronger army, Islam would have been eradicated forever. The Prophet said later there are some things in life that can't be explained and that it could only be God's will and divine intervention that brought about a result favourable for Islam and its future survival.

A friend of the Prophet once returned from battle and went to the Prophet and told him with great pride how he had defeated an enemy that day. The enemy was very strong and put up great resistance before being outmanoeuvred. Before the Prophet's friend was about to plunge a sword into the enemy's chest, the man made a declaration of faith to Islam. However, the Prophet's friend didn't believe his sincerity and thought he had only said it so that his life could be spared. The Prophet's friend wasn't prepared for the response he received and said afterwards that in all of his life being Muslim, he had never seen the Prophet get so angry. With his face bright red, the Prophet asked his friend what he would do on the Day of Judgement when his own declaration of faith would be read out. How would he be able to justify making the decision to kill the enemy on his own accord? The Prophet concluded by saying that even if he ripped the man's heart out, that he still wouldn't have been able to tell whether he was telling the truth or not – so he should have taken the enemy at his word and believed him. The Prophet's friend later remarked how he had wished he hadn't been Muslim before that day because of his terrible error of judgement, which had left him feeling guilt-ridden. **Safeer**

* * *

Some historians are of the view that warfare was used to spread Islam in the centuries following the Prophet's death. However, it cannot be conclusively proven that what was written recorded the precise truth of what occurred all those centuries ago, and therefore some matters previously accepted as facts may lack authenticity. At the Prophet's death he left the religion in a good place, but he had predicted divisions, fractions and human greed for power. Muslims had taken over full control of the Arabian tribes, with Islam holding sway and peace being reached amongst its people. Some historians and scholars argue that Muhammad may not have intended to go any further militarily but that his successors grew greedy and after his death sought more power, which the only way they could achieve was by invasion and warfare. They spread their wings and gained lands in the Persian Empire and the Byzantine Roman Empire. They went into Syria, North Africa and Central Asia.

Young, handsome Arabs were portrayed as dynamic, virile and full of enthusiasm under a new religion that they wanted to spread across the world. The devout believed in an eternal reward. They imagined a heaven filled with delicious food and dark-eyed virgins waiting to satisfy their sexual desires. The quest to take Islam into new areas of the globe had mixed motives by those spreading the word.

Many of the Islamic soldiers sought gold and glory for their spoils, which were divided amongst commanders and warriors. Within a century of the Prophet's death the influence of Islam had spread over the known world. It had become a world faith and a political force to be reckoned with. And so the quest for further growth and the spread of Islam continued.

Within a 20-year period the Byzantine and Persian empires were taken over by Islamic forces. These two dynasties were locked in continuous battle with each other, but overlooked the Arab warriors waiting in the wings to strike. The two empires were exhausted from their long-waged wars and the Arab warriors outmanoeuvred them in terms of strength and vigour, eventually capturing the Byzantine Empire, which included Jerusalem, Alexandria, Asia Minor, Syria, Palestine, Turkey, the Balkans, North Africa and Italy. The Persian Empire also fell into their command, a territory that included Iran, parts of the Middle East and India. This was followed by the formation of several Islamic empires, including the Umayyad Empire, which captured Damascus, and the Abbasid Empire that built Baghdad.

The Christian Crusades started in the late tenth century and continued until the late twelfth century and saw almost 200 years of fighting between Muslims and Christians. Muslims saw the Crusaders as violent people who wore crosses and preached destruction. The Crusaders were ultimately defeated on a massive scale, which left Christianity as a minority religion in most of the Middle East. As time passed, more of the populations under new governorship converted to Islam. The primary aim of the conquerors was not to impress Islam by force, though lower rates of taxation levied on those who adopted Islam as their religion may well have been instrumental in many conversions. There is no evidence that conquered populations were compelled to convert. Christians and Jews, considered as 'People of the Book', were allowed to practise their respective religions with the proviso that they refrained from criticising the Prophet Muhammad and the Qur'an.

There were other smaller empires including the Safavid Empire, in the sixteenth century, which conquered Iran. This was a Shi'a Muslim empire whose leader Shah Isma'il believed he was a direct descendant of the Prophet. It collapsed in battle at the hands of Afghan rebel Sunni Muslims. Then there was the Mughal Empire in India established also in the sixteenth century by Zahīr ud-Dīn Muhammad Barbur who claimed he was a descendent of Genghis Khan and of the great Turkish conqueror, Timur. This was a fraught empire with constant infighting that eventually led to its extinction.

The Ottoman Empire was established in the early 1300s. It expanded rapidly through Turkey, before the Ottomans started invading neighbouring countries, one after the other. Their vision was to create a world that had Islam as its sole religion. This resilient empire endured until 1922, when it collapsed after a long period of decline. From Geneva, the League of Nations carved up the remains of the Ottoman Empire, resulting in Britain taking over responsibility for Iraq, Palestine, Jordan, Egypt and Sudan. France was placed in charge of Morocco, Algeria, Tunisia and Lebanon. Italy took authority over Libya. The end of the Ottoman Empire and the transfer of care of the countries it held under its power lasted until after the Second World War, before the respective member countries gradually gained their independence.

Osama Bin Laden believed the collapse of the Ottoman Empire in 1924 to be a humiliation to Islam, the sultan being removed as caliph and forced to go into exile in Switzerland. Bin Laden alluded to this at the time of 9/11 by stating that it was now the West's turn to taste humiliation that Islam had endured for the 80 years since the caliphate was forced to disband. Indeed, this century saw the return of militant groups across the Middle East – Al-Qaeda and ISIS, both of which went on to become merciless in their quest to spread Islam by force. Extremism will be explored in detail later in the book.

THE FIVE PERSONALITIES OF ISLAM

The Prophet often told his people he had conveyed the message of God to them but did not want any gifts in return. Instead, he requested they honoured and respected his household, which he valued dearly:

> *And settle in your home; and do not display yourselves, as in the former days of ignorance. And perform the prayer, and give regular charity, and obey God and His Messenger. God desires to remove all impurity from you, O People of the Household, and to purify you thoroughly. (Qur'an – 33:33)*

But it is believed that what the Prophet referred to as 'Household' in this verse began long before His time on earth. It went back to the beginning of creation and to Adam, its first person. Made of clay with no earthly parents, God blew the soul into his body. When Adam opened his eyes he saw five lights, which God explained were the five lights of creation. Afterwards, God caused Adam to fall into a deep sleep and then extracted one of his ribs to create Eve. To this day, some Muslims believe that is why some humans are born with a rib less than others to signify what God had done.

Who exactly these five lights were, which God had shown to Adam, has raised mixed opinion amongst Islamic scholars. When the Prophet talked about his Household, some thought he meant his entire Household including all of his wives, while others construed it as being his closest family members. It is said the Prophet understood the prophecy that was bestowed upon him precisely, and pinpointed exactly who these five lights were. These were the Prophet himself, his daughter Fatima, her husband Ali and their two sons, Hasan and Husayn.

I have provided you with a glimpse of the Prophet's great character in this chapter. Here is a snapshot of the others involved in this story.

Fatima was the most beloved youngest daughter of the Prophet. He loved her dearly next to God. Even when Angel Gabriel appeared to him, he never stood up but every time Fatima entered a room, the Prophet would rise to his feet and kiss her hand. Fatima was born without the need to menstruate and gave birth to her children, without losing any blood. She is regarded as the Queen of all Saints in paradise. When the Prophet was dying he told Fatima not to be sad because they would be reunited together shortly afterwards in paradise. Fatima died six months after the Prophet.

Ali's mother was walking in Mecca around the Kaba when she went into labour. She looked to the sky and asked for His mercy. The walls of the Kaba were split allowing her to enter inside and give birth to Ali, a great honour never given to anybody before or since. This in itself symbolises the importance of his birth and the role he would play on earth as well as in paradise. Ali was the first cousin of the Prophet. They grew up together after the Prophet went to live with Ali's father when his grandfather died, and so they were very close. Ali is regarded as the King of all Saints in paradise who supervises the saints, and who Islam believes is responsible for controlling and stabilising the universe at the behest of God.

When Fatima gave birth to Hasan and his brother, she did so without pain and blood loss, resulting in a supernatural birth. Hasan was said to have resembled the Prophet from his navel up to the crown of his head. He was incredibly clever as a child and grew up full of wisdom that surpassed his biological years. He appeared to always have a great insight into the future. History, too, has been kind to him and credits him with stopping warfare in the years after the Prophet's death, saving the lives of many thousands of Muslims as a result. But the Prophet had foretold this history and told him before his death to save his people from great destruction.

Husayn was like a carbon copy of the Prophet from the navel down to his toenails. The Prophet loved him dearly. One day, Husayn was sitting on one knee of the Prophet and on the other sat Ibrahim, the Prophet's son, when Angel Gabriel appeared with a message from God. Angel Gabriel asked the Prophet if he loved the two children, to which he replied he did before being told that God required one of them. The Prophet replied that both were the property of God, but if he had a choice he would sacrifice his son, Ibrahim, because that way he would be able to bear the pain. He could not imagine the pain his daughter would endure if she lost her son. A short while afterwards Ibrahim died of natural causes.

Ahmed ibn Hanbal, an eighth-century imam, had a premonition that on the Day of Judgement, the Prophet and Fatima will be at the *sirat* – a narrow bridge that every person must pass over to enter paradise – to help them cross safely. Once they have crossed they will be greeted by Ali (who will be joined by other leading Islamic figures) and given a drink from the Kauthar, a special river on the banks of paradise where the water is whiter than milk and sweeter than honey. However, not everybody who successfully crosses the bridge will be allowed this drink. Hypocrites who have tried to fool God in their lifetime will be dragged away to hell, but those who are allowed its drink will never thirst again and will be guaranteed paradise. Afterwards, once they have entered paradise they will be greeted by Hasan and Husayn, who are regarded as the two Princes of Jannah (paradise).

Controversial, admired and loved

The Prophet will always be a controversial figure because of his greatness. Anybody as powerful as the Prophet causes division, rivalry and jealousy. Sadly, that's human nature. And it's not just non-Muslim enemies from when he was alive or current-day non-Muslim critics – history is littered with many people who have said uncomplimentary things about him, including some Islamic scholars. These included the thirteenth century Turkish theologian Taqī ad-Dīn Ahmad ibn Taymiyyah. As Rapoport (2010) points out Taymiyyah opposed Muslims visiting the grave of the Prophet or doing intercessions to him. He said the Prophet was an ordinary man whose body had rotten in his grave. He worried that people were following him too closely and in doing so risked putting him on par to God. Some say that part of the beliefs of Taymiyyah were wrong and dangerous and helped form the ideology that has led to extremism in later centuries.

Various sects within Islam either agree or disagree with Taymiyyah's ideology.

Barelvi Muslims

> We believe the Prophet is present in many places at the same time – that he is still witnessing all that goes on in the world and that he has knowledge of that which is unknown, including the future. **Laqeet**

Other orthodox Muslims only believe that God is omnipresent.

Deobandi Muslims

> We believe the Prophet is alive in his grave, but that is all. When we pray to God, we use the word 'yaa', which signifies somebody is near to you, but when we refer to the Prophet in prayer we use the word 'ala', which signifies somebody who is far away. **Samik**

The Prophet's predictions

The Prophet was renowned for his predictions and seeing into the future, so great were his gifts from God. He predicted that 72 events would occur in the period close to the Day of Judgement. Here is a selection of the prophecies he foretold that would occur in the world before the Last Day as outlined in Jalal-ul-Din (2006):

> People will begin to miss their prayers and pay no attention to them.
> People will begin to consider lying to be lawful. Telling lies will become an art.
> Divorce will become common practice.
> Sins will be on the increase.
> Wine will be drunk freely.
> Men will imitate women and women will imitate men.

A man will not hesitate in causing harm to his friends.

Wrongdoing and tyranny will be looked upon as acts of pride.

The meanest man shall become the leader of the community by their consent or votes.

Justice will be sold (with bribery) in the courts of justice.

'The Burdha'

'The Burdha', otherwise known in English as simply 'The Cloak', is an ode written in praise of the Prophet by Imam Sharaf al-Din al-Busiri in Alexandria in the eleventh century. He was a scholar of Arabic and poetry who had previously written poems about kings but decided he would write a poem to honour the Prophet.

'The Burdha' is one of the most famous pieces of literature in Islamic poetry and is known all over the world where it is memorised, recited and sometimes sung by many admirers of the Prophet. It was written by the poet after he was afflicted with paralysis following a stroke. Imam al-Busiri recounted that, after he had written the poem, in his dream he saw the Prophet Muhammad, who covered him in his cloak. He said the Prophet wiped his face with his blessed hands and covered him in his cloak. After Busiri woke up he found that he was able to walk and therefore was cured of his stroke.

The ode consists of 160 verses and is a story about Busiri's love and admiration for the Prophet. It is a piece of literature that easily appeals to many people including scholars and non-scholars, religious and not-so-religious, adult and child, by its simplicity and sincerity. It is said anybody who belongs to Muhammad will always be invited to celebrate in his great life – whether they have grave sins on their back or they speak with Muhammad upon their tongue.

Here is a selection of verses from 'The Burdha' describing the attributes of the Prophet:

... Our Prophet, who is commander and forbidder – there is No one more true in his saying no or yes than he is. (3:35)

... He is the sun of esteem to which they are as if moons: Reflecting its lights in darkness to humanity. (3:53)

... How grand the form of a Prophet brightened by character, Enveloped by handsomeness, distinguished by jollity! (3:54)

The gentlest of souls until the enemy forced the fight, abusing him and all his companions so brutally. (8:117a)

The many years of their torture, murder, and tyranny He chose to bear and endure – and those with him – patiently. (8:117b)

O my beloved, I beg of you in life and in death, To wrap your burdah of special care and love over me. (10:151a)

Most noble of All creation, What refuge do I have But you at the coming of the global emergency? (10:152)

Disrespecting the Prophet

A Hindu youth in a remote village of Bangladesh wrote something on Facebook insulting the Prophet Muhammad resulting in drastic consequences. A crowd of 20,000 Muslims travelled from neighbouring villages and burnt down 30 homes in the Hindu village, practically decimating it in the process. They did it in the belief that they were protecting the honour of the Prophet but none of them questioned if the Prophet needed defending. I wonder how many of them had ever read the Qur'an because if they had, they would have discovered nowhere that says that these are the actions man must take if one of God's Prophets is insulted (Revesz, 2017).

In recent years several magazines in Europe have presented a caricature of the Prophet as a violent, troubled and ancient nomad. This naturally upsets many Muslims who dislike seeing the Prophet being mocked and insulted in such poor taste. Despite Islam being a peaceful religion when practised correctly, the reactions of a minority of Muslims to these caricatures have brought Islam into disrepute.

The situation in Paris regarding negative images of the Prophet published in the *Charlie Hebdo* magazine saw extremists attack its offices and shoot dead its editor and several other members of staff.

What happened in Paris was totally wrong and against the teachings of Islam. Instead of exercising patience and being democratic in the response to the publication, what the extremists did was bring shame and dishonour to Islam. Naturally, Muslims were upset by the publication, but no ordinary Muslim would ever dream of carrying out a barbaric attack like what happened. The appropriate response for all parties was to have challenged the magazine and ask them why they had deemed it fit to insult the Prophet. The Prophet has never been to France. He never did anything wrong against the country. But the magazine knew that similar material had been published in Norway and had upset Muslims. They decided to test the reaction of the French people. However, its publication ended in tragedy. **Nassem**

* * *

Every Muslim finds it easy to recount their favourite story about the Prophet – stories that they heard in childhood or some other point in their lives – stories that are personal to them and have touched their hearts. Some are from the Hadith while others are folklore. Here is a selection of stories Muslims shared with me which provide many interesting glimpses into the Prophet's character and humanity.

The Prophet used to walk past a certain street every day and encountered each time a woman who disliked him and his religion. She used to stand at her window and throw rubbish at him every time he passed. The Prophet never responded or reacted to the woman. Others might have sworn or shouted at the woman, but the Prophet did neither. Each time he calmly walked past and ignored the woman's abuse. Then one day he noticed the woman was no longer at the window. The next day there was also no sign of her, so he decided to knock on her door and enquire if she was alright. He discovered that she was ill and went in and sat with her. They eventually became good friends. (Hadith – Bukhari) **Zara**

There was once a companion of the Prophet who had served him for many years. He knew the Prophet's habits very well. When the Prophet observed a fast, he usually broke it with milk and dates in the small hours of the night. One day, the Prophet's companion knew that the Prophet was fasting so he kept milk and dates for his meal; however, the Prophet did not appear at the appointed hour. The companion thought that the Prophet might have accepted an invitation and broken his fast elsewhere, and so he ate the food himself. When the Prophet entered the house later with another companion, the first companion discovered that the Prophet had been dealing with some urgent work, hence his delay, but had not eaten. The Prophet's companion felt so ashamed because he had no food left in the house he could offer the Prophet. He felt so mortified that he had eaten the food and would have to tell the Prophet what had happened, but the Prophet sensed his companion's hesitancy and retired to bed without asking for food. (Source unknown) **Kaied**

My favourite thing about the Prophet is that he believed in us, he believed in 'me'– yet there are over 1400 years between us. The Prophet Muhammad said (paraphrased): my real believers will be those who come after you all, and without seeing me they will believe in the religion. This makes my heart shake. On the Day of Judgement, as we are tested for our good and bad deeds, the Prophet Muhammad will cry 'Ummati Ummati' (save my people). That is love like no other – and this is what makes me a firm believer in being a good human, a loving human to all society. (Hadith – Bukhari) **Ayesha**

There was once a Jewish man who lived with his young daughter. He hated the Prophet and would often shout and curse at him. Then the Jewish man lost his eyesight. His daughter was very upset and ran away in the hope of finding a cure for her father's blindness. She was sitting crying when a companion of the Prophet found her. The companion asked the girl why she was crying and she told him about her father. The companion advised the girl to go and seek the help of the Prophet. And so she went to the Prophet's house, but when she got there she discovered that he was asleep and did not want to disturb him. Having once heard that anything attached to the Prophet was blessed, the girl picked up the Prophet's sandals and scrapped the dust from the soles onto the lap of her apron before running back to her father in excitement. She rubbed particles of the dust into the corner of her father's eyes and to everybody's amazement his eyesight was restored. The man then asked his daughter what the cure was that she had found. But instead of gratitude, he reacted with severe anger after she told him that it was the dust from the Prophet's sandals. Such was the extent of his rage that the man started to stab his eyes, but even this did not stop him seeing. Then he heard a voice telling him that for as long as the dust from the Prophet's sandals was in his eyes, his eyesight would never be taken away again. (Source unknown) **Aamir**

Several people sought to harm the Prophet during his lifetime. When the Prophet fled Mecca to find refuge in Medina, a reward of 100 red camels was advertised for anybody who could murder him. A man named Suraka – who was known to the Prophet – followed him on horseback. He caught up with the Prophet while he was walking with his companion, Abu Bakr, en route to Medina. But each time Suraka was about to attack the Prophet with his sword, his horse fell down on its knees and sunk deeply into the sand. This happened three times and rendered Suraka to understand that neither he nor anybody else could ever touch the Prophet. It also made him accept the Prophet before he returned to Mecca and misled his enemies as to which direction he chose to leave the city. Suraka became a Muslim and years later met up again with the Prophet who smiled and asked God to shower him with blessings. (Hadith – Bukhari) **Dabir**

A man once went to the Prophet's home and told him that he had lost his young son and that it was now three days since he was last seen. The man was very upset and requested that the Prophet prayed for his safe turn, while mentioning how the Prophet's prayers were always answered. The Prophet raised his hands and supplicated to God for help in finding the missing boy.

Within minutes, another man walked into the Prophet's house and asked the man if he had lost a child, adding that he had seen him playing along with some other young children in a nearby area. A beautiful, happy feeling came over the father of the missing child and instantly he wanted to rush to the area to find his son. But just as he was ready to leave, the Prophet asked the man to do one thing for him. 'Oh Prophet, what is that?' asked the man. The Prophet told the man that when he went to the area to find his son, that he must call him by his name, rather than to call out to him 'son'. The man enquired the reason for this. The Prophet replied, 'Look, you have not seen him for three days and look at how much you have missed him. In that area, there will be many orphans. If they hear you speak the word, "son", what will they think or feel? It will break their hearts realising their fathers are dead.' (Source unknown) **Youssef**

People sometimes talk about imaginary dinner parties to which they would invite famous or well-known people as their guests. These guests might be historical or contemporary, but are always people who have great significance for them. I have even read where people have suggested having Jesus as their ideal guest. Undoubtedly, if this was possible I imagine he would be captivating company. But why not invite the Prophet Muhammad also? Wouldn't he, too, be a superb guest to have at the dinner table, with his handsome features and friendly graciousness? Wouldn't it be fascinating to listen to his wisdom, his philosophy of life, his religious conviction and belief in God? A fellow Irishman, George Bernard Shaw, once said that he greatly admired the Prophet:

I have always held the religion of Muhammad in high estimation because of its wonderful vitality. It is the only religion which appears to me to possess that assimilating capacity to the changing phase of existence which can make itself appeal to every age. I have studied him – the wonderful man and in my opinion far from being an anti-Christ, he must be called the Saviour of Humanity. (UKIM, 2015)

Personally, I believe that if I had known the Prophet I would have got on well with him – that he would have been a friend. So I would definitely have invited him as a dinner guest and know that I would be touched by the holy, gentle and humble spirit of this great man.

There was once a man called Abd-Allah ibn Ubayy, a chief in an Arab tribe who was in constant dispute with the Prophet and did everything he could to belittle him and to mock Islam. The Prophet's companions grew weary of Abd-Allah and sought permission from the Prophet to kill him, but their request was refused. Sometime afterwards, Abd-Allah's son became a Muslim and he too grew tired of his father persistent abuse of the Prophet. He also went to the Prophet and asked permission to kill his father, but again the Prophet refused. Later when Abd-Allah died, everybody was surprised the Prophet donated one of his shirts for him to be buried in and even offered to say his funeral prayers. The companions were taken aback by the Prophet's kindness, but asked him, had he not taken notice of a teaching in the Qur'an (9:80) which states that even if you pray 70 times for somebody who has wronged Allah, that he will not be forgiven? The Prophet thought for a moment before replying that he would pray then for more than 70 times. (Hadith – Bukhari) **Faiza**

One day the Prophet was praying in front of the Kaba when members of the Quraysh spotted him. They went and killed a nearby camel and cut out its guts before going over to the Prophet and throwing it all over him. The camel's intestines and blood were smeared all over his head, face and body. The Prophet did not say a word or even move but kept on praying. He did not allow the situation to distract him from his prayers. Later one of his daughters came and helped to clean him. (Hadith – Bukhari) **Abdul**

Once there was a big dispute amongst the Meccans, with each chief wanting to be the leader who placed the black stone on the Kaba. They couldn't decide amongst themselves which one most deserved the honour. Finally, they agreed to wait until the next morning, when the first man who appeared would be tasked with deciding which chief would erect the black stone.

The next morning the chiefs were waiting and the first man to appear was Muhammad. The chiefs were very pleased about this because Muhammad had a good reputation as a trustworthy and honest man. The chiefs, though, were surprised by what he asked of them.

Muhammad put a cloth sheet on the ground and took the black stone and placed it on the cloth. He asked the chiefs to hold the corners of the cloth sheet and to lift it onto the Kaba. This meant that everybody got an opportunity to lift the black stone, which resulted in everybody being happy to be participating in the task.

Once the chiefs had raised the black stone onto the Kaba, Muhammad fixed it firmly into place without the chiefs realising what he had done. Muhammad later commented that this was what God had wanted in order to stop the conflict amongst the chiefs. (Hadith – Muslim) **Shahid**

Once the Prophet travelled by himself to Ta'if – a town about 40 miles from Mecca – to call people to Islam and tell them about the oneness of God. He preached to the people and invited the residents to come and join him in Islam. They instantly rejected him and his message, and then viciously threw rocks and stones at him. They made it clear that they did not want Islam. Angel Gabriel appeared to the Prophet, who was bleeding, and told him that he was accompanied by the Mountain Angel. Gabriel asked the Prophet if he wanted the Mountain Angel to kill the people who had mocked and attacked him, adding that the angel would crush the two mountains which surrounded the city. But the Prophet told Gabriel that he didn't want this to happen. Instead he complained of his own weakness for not being able to properly convey the message of God to the people of Ta'if, adding that the people needed to be spared because one day their children would be Muslim. (Hadith – Bukhari) **Enna**

There was once a man who had sex with his wife during Ramadan, in a period when he should have been fasting. He went to the Prophet and announced that he had destroyed himself. The Prophet told the man that he should fast for 60 days to atone his sin, but the man pleaded with the Prophet and said that he would not be able to fast for such a lengthy period. The Prophet then told the man to go and free one of his slaves. The man told the Prophet this would not be possible because he did not have any slaves to free. The Prophet then told the man to go and feed 60 poor people. The man told the Prophet that there was no poorer man in the region than himself, and that he did not have enough food for himself, not least 60 people. The Prophet, being the kind and gracious man that he was, gave the man an ample amount of dates and asked him to go and feed 60 poor people, before adding that he could use whatever was left over to feed his own family. (Hadith – Dawood) **Yasmeen**

One day the Prophet was out walking when he came across a woman carrying some heavy bags. He instantly went to help her and offered to carry the bags home for her. The woman did not know who the Prophet was as she had never seen him before, but she accepted his help. In those days it was an unusually kind gesture for a man to help a woman in such a manner.

During the journey the woman started to talk about a man that was referred to as the Prophet, reciting bad stories she had heard about him and saying she disliked his beliefs. She believed he played tricks on people in order for them to convert to Islam. She added that she didn't want to fall victim to his magic and trickery. The Prophet listened but remained silent. When they got to the woman's house, somebody close by recognised the Prophet and asked the woman, 'Why is the Prophet carrying your bags?'

The woman turned to the Prophet and said, 'Why didn't you tell me that you were the Prophet?' to which He replied, 'If I had told you, you wouldn't have allowed me to carry your bags.' However, sometimes miracles happened. The woman was so overcome by the excellent moral kindness of the Prophet that she felt guided by God to say to him, 'I accept you', and thereby became a Muslim. (Source unknown) **Miji**

CHAPTER 3

The Essence of Islam

THE FIVE PILLARS OF ISLAM

The declaration (Shahadah)

This declaration is seen as the password into Islam. It is essential to repeat this with sincerity to become a Muslim and to convert to Islam.

This is a simple line that Muslims repeat over and over again: 'I bear witness that there is no deity but God and that Muhammad is His messenger.'

There is nobody worthy of worship but God. From the moment a Muslim opens his or her eyes, they must remain focused on their faith every moment of the day. That is why there is a prayer to say after waking and a prayer before sleeping. A Muslim must live their life by this first pillar. Everything they do throughout the day must be around this sentence of faith. It has to be a lived experience everyday through actions more than words. You have to take your love of God to the extreme by knowing that you love Him over anybody or anything else. He is all you will ever need to feel complete and whole. Muslims constantly talk about the Prophet Muhammad and try to live by the examples he set in his lifetime. It is not unusual to hear parents remonstrate with their children if they have made a mistake or done something wrong: 'The Prophet wouldn't have done that' – so great is his influence. **Zain**

This is the cornerstone of the religion. The Prophet emphasised so much about worshipping one God. This is mentioned too in the Qur'an. If this part of the faith is contaminated, then the person's entire faith will become contaminated. It's like a manager running a company and then somebody else comes along and says to the employees 'I am the manager', leaving everybody confused and dissatisfied. So the importance of there only ever being one God is paramount to the Islamic faith, because if there was ever more than one God, there would be destruction on earth. As well as believing that Muhammad is God's Messenger and his final Prophet, Muslims also believe in all the Prophets who preceded him. **Rayaan**

Prayer five times a day (Salat)

The Prophet advised Muslims that they should pray five times a day and outlined to them the specific times between sunrise and sunset that worship must take place:

- Before sunrise (Fajr)
- Sun at the highest point (Dhuhr)
- Before sunset (Asr)
- Sunset (Maghrib)
- Late evening (Isha)

Muslims are allowed to perform their prayers anywhere, whether they are at work or at home. However, the mosque is the preferred place for prayers because it allows for fellowship. Muslims always pray and prostrate to God towards the direction of the Kaba in the south-east. Prayers are always said in Arabic with the opening words Allahu Akbar (God is Great). Muslims must be clean before they pray and carry out an ablution (Wudu), which combines respect for God with purification before the start of worship, and consists of the following cleansing:

- both hands are washed up to the wrist
- the mouth is rinsed out three times
- nostrils and the tip of the nose are washed three times
- face is washed three times
- arms are washed three times
- water is passed over the head down to the back of neck
- ears are cleaned
- nape of the neck is cleaned
- feet are washed up to the ankles.

Women have the same prayer obligations as men, although they are excused from attending the mosque if they choose to. A lot prefer to stay at home to pray instead, but many women attend Friday prayers. The Hadith states that it not obligatory for women to go to the mosque daily (due to practical issues such as minding young children, etc.). Men prefer to pray in the mosque where they join in congregational prayers. There is companionship to be found in the mosque for them – looking out for one another, people with problems are helped. Children are encouraged to attend the mosque for lessons in the Qur'an. There are female teachers for this, too, who carry out Islamic teaching – etiquette on how to eat and dress, respect for parents and elders. Islam has had fine women scholars – starting with the Prophet's first wife. **Vafi**

Saying prayers five times a day makes you conscious of God all the time. You are continuously touching base. Prayer is like a key to your home. Without a key, you are not able to get inside. The Hadith says that saying your prayers five times daily is the key to paradise. A person is only excused from praying if they are travelling or they are sick. Of course, there will be others who do not stick to the rule of praying five times a day, mainly through laziness and lack of commitment, especially when it is winter time and they have to get up very early. To me, praying is about making that commitment to your Maker because he is the one who provides me with all of my needs. Muslims pray for themselves, their families, their community and for Muslims who have died. We also pray for non-Muslims and can seek forgiveness for those in difficulty. We are not allowed to pray for non-Muslims who have died because they failed to revert to Islam before their death. **Afia**

Alms giving (Zakat)

This is the practice of charitable giving. It consists of spending a portion of one's accumulated wealth for the benefit of the poor or needy. Muslims usually give 2.5 per cent of their income to charity. This is obligatory – not voluntary. Islamic voluntary institutions are then responsible for the just distribution of this money. Needy non-Muslims may be included as beneficiaries – for example, in a country where there has been a disaster such as an earthquake.

As soon as somebody starts working full-time, they must start paying the Zakat. Older students must also contribute some of their allowance. The Zakat is paid to orphans, the injured and the poor. A large percentage of this goes abroad, but you are allowed to give Zakat to anyone in need anywhere in the world, including Britain. Many people choose to pay their Zakat to Muslim charities. There are several in the UK, including Muslim Aid and Islamic Relief. **Parsa**

The Zakat is obligatory for every male and female Muslim. Every person is assigned a Zakat date from the first time they pay it, and this becomes the date each year thereafter that they pay it for the remainder of their lives. You have to look after the poor. Islam is fair to everybody. Giving Zakat is not a high amount of your wealth.

We make mistakes in life even in wealth, so paying Zakat is like a spiritual purifier of our wealth. Every Muslim contributes to the poor in one way or another.

Zakat starts when somebody starts earning money where they have a surplus left over after having paid their monthly bills and debts. When this is complete, they must then check the daily market rate of silver and gold for that date, as directed by the Prophet, and if the price does not surpass what money they have left over, then they must pay 2.5 per cent of their remaining money. If the price of the silver and gold exceeds their surplus cash, then they are not incumbent on that occasion. However, because the price of silver and gold fluctuates on the markets, they would be expected to repeat this exercise to ensure they remain ethical and honourable in the giving of Zakat.

If they fall beyond the threshold of not being able to afford to pay the Zakat, then they must do what is called Sadaqah, which entails doing charitable deeds instead, like buying food or helping somebody in need through practical assistance of some kind. More often than not, charity begins here at home. There is the National Zakat Foundation in the UK, which gives out cash donations to poor people or those struck by sudden tragedy, like the victims of the Grenfell Tower fire in London, which left hundreds of people homeless. **Ridhwan**

Ramadan (Sawm)

Ramadan is the month when the Qur'an was first revealed to the Prophet. It lasts between 28 to 30 days and is considered by Muslims to be a month of goodness, blessing and prayer. Ramadan is the ninth month in the Islamic calendar, which is based on the lunar cycle. The Islamic year is shorter than the solar year, and therefore Ramadan moves backwards 11 days each solar year, so that over a lifetime it will take 33 years to complete a cycle.

Muslims are not allowed to consume any food or drink during Ramadan from the first light of daybreak, almost two hours before full sunrise, until breaking their fast after sunset. This is done with an 'iftar' meal (first meal eaten to break the fast). This means that when Ramadan falls in the summer there are long periods of fasting with only about a six-hour gap between breaking the fast and starting it again, resulting in Muslims experiencing around 18 hours without food or water.

Fasting is meant to allow Muslims to seek nearness with and forgiveness from God, to express their gratitude to and dependence on him, to atone for their past sins, and to remind them of the needy. During Ramadan, Muslims are also expected to put more effort into following the teachings of Islam by refraining from arguments, anger, envy, greed, lust, profane language and gossip, and to try to get along with their fellow Muslims better. Those under the age of 12, the elderly, pregnant or breastfeeding women, and those who are ill or have a serious medical condition (for example cancer, diabetes or are HIV positive) are excluded from fasting during Ramadan.

It is sometimes hard when you are living life in a country where Islam is in a minority because it is difficult to practise completely, especially if you work full-time and you have to go and pray in a room at work. Sometimes non-Muslims don't understand this. I also find that I don't read the Qur'an as much as I ought to. Although Ramadan is not easy, I really welcome it each year because it means I spend more time in the mosque. Here the environment is geared towards people getting closer to God through prayer, listening to sermons from visiting imams and reciting the Qur'an. Everybody is on the same page during the month of Ramadan. They say that the devil is locked up for the month of Ramadan so this means that you are less likely to be drawn astray during this special month. **Aneel**

Ramadan is the holiest month in the Islamic calendar. For 30 days Muslims fast and pay particular attention to their prayers. The start and finish of Ramadan is determined by the sighting of the moon. The month of Ramadan entails practising patience and tolerance in the absence of food or drink. Ramadan is designed to make people more connected to Islam and increases their time in the mosque. The key rules are that you can only eat a light meal from sunrise and do not eat or drink anything else again until after sunset. Every day during Ramadan, a chapter and a quarter of the Qur'an is read aloud after evening prayers so that by the time Ramadan comes to an end, the entire Qur'an will have been recited. This is why the Qur'an is divided into 30 parts. **Owais**

There is also what is called a 'Night of Power' in Ramadan.

It is mentioned in the Hadith that the Prophet was upset when realising the short life span of his people in comparison to the lengthy ages enjoyed by other Holy Men from previous nations – like Noah and Moses, who both lived for several hundred years. Because of this, Allah gave the Prophet a Night of Power during Ramadan in order to bring about special blessings to each person who makes extended worship that night.

Each year the Night of Power falls on one of the last five odd-number nights in the latter half of Ramadan. By virtue of praying and worshipping longer than is required on that night, this becomes the equivalent of worshipping for a thousand months. Muslims are encouraged to make a special effort to make extended worship and to avoid disobedience on all of these odd nights because it is not always clear which night is the special one, although the Prophet stated that there are some signs to watch out for, including there being no wind on the night resulting in clear skies and calm oceans before the next morning being sunny, clear and light. (Qur'an – 97:1–5) **Irfan**

Some men sleep in the mosque for the final ten days of Ramadan in order to make sure they receive the blessing of God and to follow in the practice of the Prophet.

I usually go to sleep in the mosque after I have finished the first prayer of the morning just before sunrise and sleep until 10.30am.

During the day, I spend as much time as possible praying and reading the Qur'an. I try to only leave the main mosque to go to wash or to the toilet but usually try to be as fast as I can before returning. **Hassan**

Festival of Eid al-Fitr

This festival takes place the day after Ramadan ends. The fasting period is over. The Prophet said that nobody should fast immediately after Ramadan because Eid is a day of celebration. The month of struggle is over and it is time for a family celebration with good food to eat, the exchange of gifts, and the thanking of God for all his blessings and goodness. After the purification of their 30-day fast everybody who has completed Ramadan 'starts again' as a new person, appreciative of the effort they made during the Holy Month. On the day of Eid, there is an extra prayer Muslims, both men and women, say in thanksgiving, in addition to their other five prayers. This is called the Eid Prayer.

The pilgrimage to Mecca (hajj)

All Muslims are expected to complete a pilgrimage to Mecca at least once in their lifetime – if they are in good health and can afford it. Both men and women are expected to make the pilgrimage; Muslims dress in white during this time. There are several rituals to be made during the pilgrimage. One such example is walking around the Kaba, the small shrine located near the centre of the Great Mosque in Mecca, considered by Muslims everywhere to be the most sacred spot on Earth. Here, they touch the black stone of the Kaba, which was erected by the Prophet. Pilgrims also visit Mount Arafah, a hill outside Mecca where, according to Islamic tradition, the Prophet delivered his last sermon. In addition, they travel seven times between Mount Safa and Mount Marwah to symbolically stone the devil. Islamic teachers say that the hajj should be an expression of devotion to God, not a means to gain social standing. A male who completes the pilgrimage is known as a hajj and a woman who completes it is known as a hajja.

When I arrived at Jeddah airport my legs were shaking and I started to cry. It felt humbling to be there as a sinner who God had chosen to come. Every year the Saudi government only allows up to four million visas for the pilgrimage, or otherwise the crowding becomes too great. On my way by taxi into Mecca to visit the Kaba, I calmed down and started praying, asking Allah to forgive me for my sins and thanking him for accepting me on the hajj.

It was joyous seeing so many Muslims gathered together in one place to honour Allah – men, women and children. Young and old all gathered together with one purpose of honouring Allah almighty.

All of the pilgrimage is special throughout, with moments of joy and peace, but the part I found particularly touching was travelling to Medina and visiting the Prophet's grave. Doing the hajj is like starting life all over again – you feel like a newborn baby because all of your sins are forgiven. Since returning I feel I have become a better man and am more truthful. I hope to return again next year with my older sister. My mother did the hajj during her lifetime, but sadly my father was unable to make it. My next hajj will be in his honour.

The Prophet said that the first time you do the hajj, you must do it for yourself, but another subsequent trip can be dedicated to another person. The cost of the 15-day trip from the UK cost me £4000, although people can spend much more than this if they want to stay in a luxurious hotel, but the blessings from Allah are the same whether you sleep in a tent or a five-star hotel. **Ali**

Festival of Eid al-Adha

There is a second Eid festival that Muslims celebrate at the end of the hajj pilgrimage. This takes place exactly two months and ten days after the first Eid and is sometimes referred to colloquially as the 'Big Eid' because it lasts for three days. In addition to celebrating the end of the hajj, Muslims use the occasion to commemorate the Prophet Abraham's willingness to sacrifice his son, a well-known story in the Qur'an and the Old Testament of the Bible. In Muslim countries, animals are slaughtered in Abraham's honour.

> The second Eid is when an animal – cow or a lamb – is slaughtered. Here in the UK, we are not allowed to slaughter animals, so instead we give money to a halal butcher on our behalf or we send money to our home countries. My family send money to Pakistan for an animal to be slaughtered on our behalf.
> The slaughtering of an animal is seen as a symbolic gesture of Muslims giving something back to God to thank him for his blessings. The Eid Prayer, the same used as the first Eid, is said again every day for the three days. **Salma**

TYPES OF ISLAM

There are different types of Muslims, like there are different branches of Christianity, and within each type there are different sects, though their differences are sometimes slight. The three main types of Muslims are Sunni, Shi'a and Ahmadiyya. Overall, amongst these types, there are more similarities than differences, but nevertheless divisions exist – often causing dislike, distrust and discrimination. This may be surprising to those outside the religion who think Muslims belong to just one group or those who think all Muslims look the same and therefore are presumed to be the same. This introduction to the main types and to some of the better-known sects of Islam will hopefully shed light on the at-times complex nature of Islam, while also illustrating its richness.

Sunni Muslims
Over 85 per cent of Muslims worldwide are Sunni. Adherents believe this is the purest form of Islam. They believe they are the authoritative voice of original Islam. Nevertheless, Sunnis are divided into several sects, although there are sometimes only minor

differences between these sects. Sunni Muslims do not have a chief leader; rather they are divided into separate communities with their own mosques and imams. For the Sunnis, the term imam is used for any prayer/worship leader in a local mosque. This may be any Muslim, and not necessarily a trained clerical leader.

Sunni Muslims are the overwhelming majority of Muslims, and already existed before the sectarianism of the first and second centuries of Muslim history. There is a narration from the Prophet that states:

> *Allah all mighty will never allow my nation to unite upon misguidance and incorrect beliefs. Allah's mercy, blessings and protection are with the largest group of Muslims. (Hadith – Tirmidhi)*

The majority of Sunni Muslims in the UK are either orthodox Deobandi or orthodox Barelvi. It's estimated that over 70 per cent of Muslims in the UK are Deobandi Muslims. Deobandism came into existence in the nineteenth century where a school was established in a town in India called Deobandi. They are a sect who are traditional in their practices but lean towards sectarianism. Barelvi Muslims are another similar sect but have leanings towards spiritualism. Like Deobandism, the origins of Barelvism originated in its namesake town (Bareilly) in India. Barelvis are accused of overly worshipping the Prophet and for absorbing foreign customs in their practices (e.g. reciting the Qur'an on the third, sixth and fortieth day after somebody dies in honour of the dead person).

Most Sunni Muslims adhere firmly to the Qur'an and Hadith. They say they have a direct unbroken chain of teachers that go back all the way to the Prophet Muhammad. This they claim is unique, the chains in various other sects being broken. Furthermore, all other sects have failed to produce a chain of teachers that doesn't include a Sunni scholar.

Sunni Muslims often refer to the four caliphs who took charge of Islam in the years following the Prophet's death, a period which saw the growth and expansion of the religion and the completion of the Qur'an in book format. Each of the caliphs held the title 'Amir', meaning leader.

1. The first caliph was Abu Bakr (573–631). He was among the first people to accept Islam after the Prophet and was deemed the most suitable to take over from the Prophet after his death. Abu Bakr was the Prophet's father-in-law, the Prophet having married his daughter Aisha. He was also considered to be the Prophet's closest friend and confidant. The Prophet once said, 'I owe everything to Abu Bakr' and on another occasion, 'I have repaid every person's favour except Abu Bakr.' After the Prophet's death Abu Bakr helped gather together all of the writings of the Qur'an. He was caliph for two years before dying of natural causes, aged 61.

2. The second caliph was Umar ibn al-Khattar (579–644). He was a faithful companion of the Prophet, and also his father-in-law after allowing one of his daughters to marry the Prophet. He was a very intuitive man who predicted many of the revelations given to the Prophet. During his time as caliph he was regarded as a moderniser in politics and public services, and was especially helpful to those in need. He also encouraged women to cover themselves and banned alcohol. Umar was caliph for ten years before being murdered by a slave, aged 65.

3. The third caliph was Uthman ibn Affan (579–656). Uthman was a quiet and unassuming man, regarded by those closest to him as being modest. His reputed achievement was his compilation into book format of the Holy Qur'an, which remains the same today as it did when he completed his work. Uthman was known by the Prophet as the 'Holder of Two Lights', having married the Prophet's daughter, and after her death, marrying a second daughter. He worked hard at bringing peace and unity to Islam and did all he could to ward off those who sought power in Islam for the wrong reasons. Uthman was caliph for 11 years before being martyred in battle, aged 76.

4. The fourth caliph was Ali ibn Abi Talib (559–661). He was married to Fatima, the Prophet's youngest daughter. Ali was a very brave man and was greatly trusted and admired by the Prophet. He was the first 'boy' to become a Muslim and remained loyal to the Prophet his whole life. He was trusted to guard the Prophet's property and valuables after the Prophet fled for his safety to Medina from Mecca. After the Prophet's death he waited patiently until his time came to be caliph (being passed over thrice), and remained in this position for 5 years before being assassinated by an enemy, aged 62.

After the death of Ali, the caliphate gradually went into decline. Some Muslims were very unhappy following the Prophet's death, when his son-in-law Ali wasn't chosen as his immediate successor. (I will look at this later when discussing Shi'a Muslims.) At one point after the death of Ali there were two caliphs in power at the same time. Hasan, Ali's eldest son, became leader of the Muslims of Kufa. Muawiyah bin Abi-Sufyan, a former companion of the Prophet (and who later established the Umayyad Dynasty) ruled over Muslims in Syro-Palestine. Hasan grew tired of conflict amongst various groups of Muslims and handed over his leadership to Muawiyah to curtail further bloodshed and bring unity to all Muslims. Sadly, his intentions failed because infighting continued, and years later Hasan was poisoned by his opponents.

* * *

All Sunni Muslims believe that God will send one of his people, who will be named Imam Mahdi, as the chosen one to restore order to Islam and to bring with it a new sense of revival and growth. This man will be from the ancestral family of the Prophet Muhammad. His arrival will be part of the second coming before the Day of Judgement. Sunni Muslims believe that just before Imam Mahdi returns there will be two signs to indicate his arrival. The first sign will occur in the River Euphrates in the Middle East – the river will reveal a mountain of gold. People will fight to possess this gold, but 99 out of every 100 will die. The second sign will occur when an army tries to cross over from Syria and march towards Medina, when during their journey they will be swallowed up by the earth.

> Some scholars will tell you there is no such thing as Imam Mahdi, that he is a mythical image, but for others he is destined to be the prophesied redeemer of Islam. Ordinary Muslims may never have heard of him, and there will be some who are vaguely aware of his purpose but who don't bother getting too engrossed in the finer details as they do not see him as relevant to Islam at this time. **Maysam**

> Imam Mahdi will be born an ordinary man but will never be a Prophet. How and when he will arrive is unclear because God hasn't revealed this information, but some scholars predict that it will be near the end of time. Imam Mahdi will be a leader who will eliminate injustice in the world and bring about equality between Muslims and non-Muslims, including Jews and Christians. He will have many fine qualities as a man including a flair for justice and fairness. He will help the oppressed and the poor, and his goodness will spread across the earth from corner to corner. According to the Hadith, he won't have an easy time nor will he readily take to his responsibilities – although he will know who he is and his role in Islam; he will be frightened and will run away from his responsibilities, but he will be chased and reminded that he is the chosen leader until he relents. **Atif**

Sunni Muslims believe that Jesus, too, will have involvement in the Second Coming, and they hold many fascinating views about him that differ to those within Christianity. A passage from the Qur'an says:

> *And they're saying, 'We have killed the messiah, Jesus, son of Mary, and the messenger of God.' They have neither killed nor crucified him; but it was made to appear so unto them...rather God raised him unto Him. God is mighty and wise. (Qur'an – 4:157–8)*

Sunni Muslims do not believe that Jesus died on the cross. They believe that when he was about to be crucified, God decided to be kind to him and worked a miracle. Jesus was placed in a room by himself before the crucifixion, but God sent angels to the room and took him up alive to heaven and then replaced Jesus with a lookalike, somebody who had similar facial features. Some Sunni Muslims believe that Jesus went straight to heaven and converted to Islam, although later in this chapter you will see a different view of this offered by one of my interviewees. Regardless of differences of opinion, all Sunni Muslims believe that Jesus will return to earth.

> The Prophet once had a dream about Jesus. He saw two individuals near the Kaba in Mecca. One of the men had a reddish complexion and broad shoulders. He recognised him as the anti-Christ. The second individual was dark skinned and looked like his hair and body were wet after a shower of rain. He recognised him as Jesus. **Sultan**

Some Sunni Muslims believe that Jesus will descend from heaven aged 33 and will carry on with his life as when he was last on earth. He will arrive in Damascus and there will be a big bird at each side of him as he comes down from the sky. From Damascus he will travel on to Jerusalem. They believe that Jesus will stay for 40 years and during this time will get married and have children. He will ask the people to follow Islam and to believe in one God. Jesus and Imam Mahdi will become allies and together they will lead Muslims in preparation for the Day of Judgement.

> There is an entire chapter in the Hadith that gives an account of Jesus descending from heaven. He will not return as a Prophet, rather he will be an ordinary man because the prophethood is now complete since Muhammad. Jesus will return to take on Dajal – the anti-Christ – who will be the greatest corruption the world has ever seen. Jesus is the only person who will be able to defeat him. Muslims believe that God has already written this fate.
>
> Many lies have been told about Jesus. The real truth is that

when Jesus was last on earth, he was a Prophet of Islam. He was born Muslim and when he returns next time he will correct and rectify all of the misconceptions that Christians have spread about him. He will tell people to stop believing that he is the 'son' of God, because this was a complete fabrication. **Zena**

Sunni Schools of Thought

There were several existing and emerging schools of thoughts in early Islam, but it was not until the twelfth century of Islam that a leading Sunni scholar named Imam Al-Ghazali restricted the religion to just four schools of thought. He chose four of Islam's most intellectual scholars and from this came what is known as the Four Schools of Thought.

Hanafi

Imam Hanafi was from Kufa in Iraq – a city known at the time for its diverse community. He was a very intelligent man with great depths of knowledge who was extremely clever in debating. He is seen by some as the only imam from the great Islamic scholars to have met companions of the Prophet. His aim was to discover as many solutions as possible for issues, problems and possibilities. He once said that you can devise 100 lessons on one Hadith alone. Imam Hanafi developed principles for extracting information from the Qur'an into Hadith about certain issues –for example rules around ablution before praying. He concluded that as long as Muslims perform four rituals before praying that they had fulfilled their obligation (washing of face, arms up to the elbows, wiping of head and washing feet up to the ankles) although Muslims are free to wash other bodily parts during ablution. Imam Hanafi discussed the different body positions when praying and debated what was more acceptable – the crossing of hands or placing hands by your side. In the end, both were deemed acceptable.

The Hanafi School of Thought is predominantly found in the UK, Turkey, the Balkans, Syria, Lebanon, Jordan, Palestine, Iraq, the Caucasus, Russia, Turkmenistan, Kazakhstan, Kyrgyzstan, Tajikistan, Uzbekistan, Afghanistan, Pakistan, India, China and Bangladesh.

Maliki

Imam Malik lived in Medina where the Prophet died and, in the main, respected the practices of the people of the city because of the Prophet's influences there. He was a brilliant scholar and knew the teachings of great world philosophers like Plato. Physically, he was a big man and good-looking with blond hair, a beard and blue eyes. He never met any of the Prophet's companions, only some of the followers of the companions. Imam Malik met Imam Hanafi on many occasions and engaged in lively debates. Imam Malik disliked the hypothetical questions which Imam Hanafi frequently addressed in public debates – for example, somebody might ask him, 'What would happen if a husband went travelling and after a period of time his wife thought he had died and remarried, only for her first husband to return alive and well?' On one occasion Imam Hanafi rebuked Imam Malik, who thought these types of questions unnecessary, but Imam Hanafi reminded him that the Prophet often used hypothetical questions and answers in his sermons when addressing solutions to human dilemmas.

The Maliki School of Thought is predominantly found in North Africa (excluding northern and eastern Egypt), West Africa, Chad, Sudan, Kuwait, Bahrain, the Emirate of Dubai (UAE) and in north-eastern parts of Saudi Arabia.

Shafi`i

Imam Shafi`i grew up in Palestine before moving to Mecca. He, too, was an extremely intelligent man who was able to recite the Qur'an in full from a young age, such was his excellent memory. In fact he was known to be able to memorise a page immediately upon reading it. Imam Shafi`i was a student of Imam Malik, and studied the Islamic law of Medina. Imam Shafi`i became an expert at comparing and contrasting Islamic laws in various parts of the world and identifying similarities. He was able to identify what the Islamic scholars of Kufa said that was the same or only slightly different to the scholars of Medina. Overall, there was approximately a 25 per cent difference. Imam Shafi`i went to Kufa to study the Hanafi School of Thought. Later he moved to Egypt for the remainder of his life and it was there that he started to write principles of Islamic law and decide how best to develop and apply rules from the Qur'an and Hadith. Imam Shafi`i also recommended that Muslims should strike a balance between being spiritual and celebrating their faith, as opposed to being scholars of the religion.

The Shafi`i School of Thought is predominantly found in Somalia, Eritrea, Ethiopia, Djibouti, eastern Egypt, the Swahili coast, South Africa, Kurdish regions of the Middle East, Dagestan, Chechen and Ingush regions of the Caucasus, Palestine, Lebanon, Indonesia, Malaysia, Maldives, Sri Lanka, India, Singapore, Myanmar, Thailand, Brunei and the Philippines.

Hanbali

Imam Hanbal was a student of Imam Shafi`i. Like the other great Islamic scholars, he too was a remarkably intelligent man with a brilliant memory. He had a full memory of the Hadith's 100,000 narratives, including the chain of previous transmissions right from their original source. Hanbal saw people theorising more about the Qur'an with their main question being if the Qur'an was created. However, this did not acknowledge that God is uncreated, and because he is uncreated his speech is uncreated. After endless debates on this subject Imam Hanbal concluded the argument by stating that the spoken words of the Qur'an are uncreated, like God himself. Then people switched to asking about anthropoids and wondered if God had had a body like his Prophets, and again Imam Hanbal addressed them on this topic and satisfied their queries, saying that God was never a human being – didn't operate as a human being, and therefore never had the need for a human body.

The Hanbali School of Thought is predominantly in Saudi Arabia and Qatar, Bahrain, Oman and Yemen and amongst Iraqi and Jordanian Bedouins, and is considered the most rigid and puritanical of the four schools.

Muslims are free to choose a preference when deciding which School to follow. There is only an estimated 10 per cent difference between the respective Schools and these differences are usually around customs, etiquette and restrictions. It is found that sometimes two or three Schools may be in agreement over a topic or all four could be in disagreement, or only one in disagreement.

The following is an example of how all four Schools differ on how a Muslim should pray:

- Hanafi School – When standing in prayer, a person should place their hands below the navel.
- Maliki School – When standing in prayer, a person should loosely place their hands by their sides.
- Shafi`i School – When standing in prayer, a person should place both hands between chest and navel.
- Hanbali School – When standing in prayer, a person should place their hands on their chest.

Other differences include:

The Hanafi School says a woman can get married without her guardian's permission provided the marriage has two witnesses. All the other three schools say that a woman has to have permission.

The Maliki School states that in certain circumstances people are allowed to combine their prayers (for example if they are at work and not able to pray), whereas the Hanafi School states that combining prayers is not allowed unless you are on the hajj pilgrimage. Both the other two Schools, Shafi`i and Hanbali, remain neutral on the matter.

The Shafi`i School states that if a man touches a woman after he completes his ablution, this breaks the ablution and he needs to wash again. The Hanafi School says the ablution still holds. The two other Schools, Maliki and Hanbali, remain neutral.

The Hanbali School states that men must grow beards whereas the other three schools say shaving is disliked, but a beard is not mandatory.

It is generally found that ordinary Muslims know little about the Schools of Thoughts and mainly rely on local imams for guidance and instruction on various matters. Other Muslims, like Salafis, disagree regarding imams restricting guidance to just one particular School of Thought and feel that matters should never be constrained to the views of only one School.

> One thing we do in Salafism is we extend encouragement for education and reading. We like the person to gain a better understanding of Islam and therefore they should read books by approved scholars in order to gain a better knowledge. We always encourage others not to believe everything an imam says because sometimes to do so would mean to be blindfolded. We believe in not being restricted by staying in the one box. That's why we believe in comparative studies, looking at many various and brilliant scholars, some of whom are relatively unknown and outside of the traditional four Schools of Thought.
> **Imam Jamaykee**

* * *

Most Sunni Muslims believe that the Day of Judgement will come after Imam Mahdi and Jesus have completed their work of reviving and uniting Islam across the entire world. There will be signs, though, before the actual day begins, indicating its arrival as a last chance for Muslims to seek atonement for their sins. These signs include a sighting of the 'Dabbah', which will be an ugly beast that will appear in the Middle East. Nobody will ever have seen the likes of this animal before and its origins will be a mystery. Then there will be the 'Dukhan', a combination of something between a smoke and a fog that will cover the whole world. Another sign will be that the sun will rise and set in the west as opposed to the east.

Shi'a Muslims

Shi'a Muslims make up the second-largest group of Muslims in the world and constitute over 10 per cent of the world's Muslim population. There are over 300,000 Shi'a Muslims living in the UK, less than 10 per cent of the Muslim community. They mainly reside in Iran, Iraq, Afghanistan, Bahrain, Lebanon, Yemen, Saudi

Arabia, India and Syria. Shi'a and Sunni Muslims have been rivals for 1400 years. Shi'a comes from the phrase 'shi'at', meaning 'the party of Ali'. This was the group who supported Ali ibn Abi Talib as the fourth caliph, and believed that it should be his descendants alone that succeeded as caliphs after his death. Ali was married to the Prophet's eldest daughter, Fatima. They believe that Ali was the natural successor of the Prophet and discount the first three caliphs as illegitimate. Throughout history the Shi'as have cursed and disrespected the first three caliphs, believing that they acquired their positions through deceit.

> The last sermon of the Prophet clearly stated what the Prophet wanted when he said: 'When I pass away, I want Ali to be leader – he is leading you after me.' Ali was the commander of the battle. He was trusted. He was the Prophet's son-in-law. Those around the Prophet did not like this and when the Prophet died they plotted against Ali and gathered secretly in a mountain, even before the Prophet was buried. They did not accept Ali as their leader, but accepted Abu Bakr instead. Ali pleaded that he should be the caliph, but he did not have enough money or soldiers to mount a challenge. **Yusuf**

Ali, who was the fourth caliph (and first imam by Shi'a belief), was assassinated by the Khawarij – a fundamentalist group that arose some decades after the Prophet died. They were initially members of 'the party of Ali' but later rejected his leadership. The Khawarij wanted power, and they plotted to kill Ali and two of the Prophet's companions in the belief that if they succeeded their ascendancy was guaranteed because there was nobody else left capable of being the caliph. An opportunity arose and Ali, who was 62 and had been caliph for five years, was struck in the head by a poison-coated sword while praying in a mosque during Ramadan, in Kufa in Iraq.

> Nobody questioned what God would have wanted. The disagreement over the caliphs was never sorted. People tended to

choose 'old' over the young. Age was seen as wisdom. Ali was a young man and although he was clever, the context of the time would mean that he would never have been an automatic choice to become the first caliph. Tension had festered over the years. Before the Prophet died, he left his farm (some fields) to his daughter Fatima and to Ali. However, a lingering argument ensued amongst the companions and their supporters who believed that the Prophet's estate should have been left to the people of Islam and not Fatima and Ali. Fatima and Ali did not want to give back the farm that the Prophet had given them. This resulted in her getting attacked in her room by Sunni Muslims – she had her hips broken and died. Ali was a clever man. There is a huge book entitled *Nahj al-Balagha*, which outlines his sermons, letters and sayings. It is a masterpiece that conveys the wonderful life of Ali. Most Shi'a Muslims value this book dearly and it is a firm favourite of theirs after the Qur'an. We can never forgive the Sunnis for what they did to Ali. I don't know if God will forgive them either. **Moshin**

Upon the death of Muawiyah bin Abi-Sufyan, his son Yazid took over as caliph and ruled from Syria. Unlike his father, he was considered an impious Muslim because he drank alcohol, didn't pray and was promiscuous. Yazid angered Shi'a Muslims who were appalled by his poor behaviour. They wanted Husayn, the Prophet's grandson, to be the caliph and started making petitions for him to come and be their ruler.

Husayn received over 1000 requests from Muslims living in Kufa asking him to be their leader. When Yazid heard of this, he too sent word to Husayn requesting his allegiance, believing if he received this that those dissatisfied with his leadership would accept him. Husayn refused allegiance, which greatly angered Yazid and resulted in him ordering Husayn's assassination. Husayn was at first reluctant to travel to Kufa, but he eventually decided to travel; this ended in tragic consequences. Husayn was travelling with 72 people in his group but was ambushed on the way by 1000 of Yazid's troops. Husayn died in battle before his killers delivered his head on a tray to Yazid. This resulted in what is described by Shi'a Muslims as the 'worst day for our religion'. **Subhan**

The Battle of Karbala is one of the most significant events in Shi'a history and each year they commemorate the anniversary of the death of Husayn, who they believe was martyred in battle by Umayyad forces in 680. His tomb in Karbala in Iraq remains one of the holiest sites for Shi'a Muslims other than Mecca and Medina. Millions of pilgrims visit his tomb and some participate in symbolic acts of self-flagellation, cutting themselves to shed blood in his memory. This rarely happens outside of Middle Eastern countries, but in the UK it is suggested that Shi'a Muslims donate blood on Husayn's feast day in recognition for the love that Shi'as have for him.

Temporary marriages
Although it has no Qur'anic basis, Shi'a Muslims still participate in temporary marriages, to the disapproval of Sunni Muslims, who believe that this practice was only allowed during the lifetime of the Prophet. They said it was only used then during times of war and feel that its use in today's world is inappropriate. Shi'a Muslims disagree with this viewpoint.

This is good for widows and for women with children who can't marry. It was legitimised by the Prophet. I know Sunni Muslims disagree with this and view it as something that is not very decent and feel it is adultery made legal. They believe that the Prophet had abrogated it from Islam before he died, but Ali confirmed that the Prophet had not done so. It's a balancing act between being practical and being a puritan. I believe it is a good thing. Instead of it being seen as wrong, I believe it helps many people be more moral, especially young men and women in their early twenties who have sexual desires that need to be met. This keeps them faithful to each other. A contract has to be made by the couple and a dowry called a 'mahr' (as little as £100 or as large as £1 million

– whatever amount the 'groom' can afford) is given to the 'bride' with the agreement that the union is for a set period and once the date expires, each person will go their separate way. Of course, if they grow particularly fond of one other during their time together, they can get married after a small period has elapsed once their contract has expired. **Danesh**

Shi'a Muslims generally accept the traditional Five Pillars of Islam, but have added further cultural appendages of their own. They are:

- making offerings for the benefit of the community
- commanding good
- forbidding evil
- loving the family of the Prophet
- turning away from those who do not love the Household of the Prophet.

Besides the additional appendages there are occasional differences in how Shi'a follow some of the traditional Five Pillars when compared to Sunni Muslims.

During Ramadan Sunni Muslims break their fast at sunset, Shi'a Muslims 30 minutes later. With prayers too there are time differences. Although both Sunni and Shi'a Muslims do morning prayers and afternoon prayers, Shi'a Muslims often combine both afternoon and evening prayers together as opposed to keeping them separate. Shi'a Muslims state that the Qur'an is first and foremost God's word and that the Prophet and Hadith are secondary to this, rather than the other way around, which is preferred by Sunni Muslims. We don't say in the first instance, what did the Prophet say, or what did Abu Bakr or Uthman say; rather we ask what does the Qur'an say? **Qasid**

With regards to Imam Mahdi and the Second Coming, there is a key difference in what Shi'a Muslims believe in contrast to Sunni

Muslims, with Shi'as believing that Imam Mahdi is the twelfth descendant of the Prophet. Despite the violent times they lived in, a son from each generation of the Prophet's descendants managed to survive, although each of these imams were either killed in battle or in a mosque or were poisoned – or in Ali's case while he was praying. The twelfth imam is currently in 'hiding' (in a metaphysical sense) having been last seen when he was aged 74 in 878. He hid because there were fears that enemies would kill him. Shi'a Muslims believe that God has taken him to a place of safety where he has remained ever since. He will one day reappear when God feels the moment is right and his role will be that of completing the message of the Prophet.

They believe he will be the last leader of the people in the world. He will return with 360 good people who God wants to help him. Present-day Shi'a leaders, often called ayatollahs, are seen as caretakers awaiting the return of the twelfth imam, who will triumph over evil and rule over the world at the end of time. Shi'a Muslims believe that just before the Day of Judgement the world will enter into a new state of existence. It will be completely destroyed in its current form and shaped anew.

> The second coming will take place at a time in the world when it is in a real poor state – when Muslims are not offering enough prayers, when there is famine, despair and crime. He will come and rule for 60 years by the grace of Allah. We will know the time has arrived because there will be a conquest in Turkey and a severe famine will follow afterwards. Imam Mahdi will return with features of the Prophet Muhammad. He will perform many miracles and he will bring the world back into order. **Farhad**

When this process is complete, the Day of Judgement will come. Shi'a also believe that all Shi'a Muslims will go to paradise because the twelfth imam and his 11 predecessors will defend Shi'a Muslims on the Day of Judgement. There will be those who are punished for their bad deeds – a week in hell – but they will be taken back after that to paradise.

Jokes that mock the beliefs of Sunni and Shi'a Muslims against each other still prevail, and it is not uncommon to find people on both sides accusing the other of not being a 'true' believer, so engrained is their distrust and dislike of each other. Of course this is not indicative of all people from both groups but it is nevertheless a common feature.

There was once a meeting between Imam Hanafi and a Shi'a Muslim. Imam Hanafi arrived at a designated meeting place with some books. He entered the mosque but instead of leaving his shoes on a rack outside he took them off and placed them under his arms before entering the mosque. The Shi'a noticed his shoes under his arms and asked him why he didn't leave them outside like everyone else. Imam Hanafi replied that in the time of the Prophet, Shi'a Muslims were known to steal shoes. The Shi'a Muslim laughed and told him that there were no Shi'a Muslims at the time of the Prophet – to which Imam Hanafi replied, 'Exactly, so where did you come from then?' **Harris**

There has been a rise in the violence between Sunni and Shi'a in the last few years. Scores are being killed every week in a vicious tit-for-tat cycle between extremists on both sides in Iraq, Syria, Pakistan, Lebanon and other places. I have now heard that tensions between the Shi'a and Sunni communities in Britain are also increasing. When Muslims are required in the Qur'an (55:61) to co-exist peacefully with people of other faiths and no faith then why cannot Sunni and Shi'a co-exist peacefully? Leaders from both sides should be giving clear authoritative guidance from the Qur'an and Hadith about how Sunni and Shi'a should live side by side peacefully. However, they showed hatred amongst each other and focus more on what is common to both of our communities, so that people can get on with their lives with peace and security. The bottom line is that any differences that exist, political or theological, should never (make anyone) resort to violence and killing. **Kaushar**

Shi'a Muslims are split into three main types, although there are small sects, including one called Dawoodi Bohras, which is featured in a later chapter.

The first of the main groups is the 'Twelvers', who believe in the 12 imams and make up 85 per cent of Shi'as. They believe the twelfth imam will remain in hiding until God appoints a moment for him to reappear towards the end of time. For Twelvers, their trust and hope for revival lies with the twelfth imam, who to them is the true Imam Mahdi.

The second largest group is the 'Fivers', who only accept the legitimacy of the first five imams from the descendants of Ali. The fifth imam was Zayd, the grandson of Husayn, who got killed in battle when he challenged the corrupt Umayyad Empire.

The third largest group – 'Isma'il Seveners' – are called this because they believe that Isma'il ibn Jafar, son of Ja'far al-Sadiq (the sixth imam, whose teachings Shi'a Muslims follow as their school of thought) and grandson of Zayd, was the seventh and last imam – the natural hereditary line of Ali ending with him. They also believe, however, that his son, Muhammad ibn Isma'il, will return as the Imam Mahdi and bring about an age of justice.

Shi'a School of Thought

Shi'a Muslims do not follow the traditional Four Schools of Thought, which they view as Sunni ideology. Having said that, their School of Thought, which is called the Jafar Sadiqu School, incorporates most of the principles contained in the Hanafi, Maliki, Shafi`i and Hanbali Schools. Imam Sadiqu was the sixth imam and a direct descendent of the Prophet. He was highly respected and regarded as an intelligent person with great knowledge. Shi'as believe that Sadiqu's knowledge and guidance was inspired by God, and that he understood life, the future, how best to live a good life, and the choice mankind must take between good and evil. Shi'a Muslims state that Imam Hanafi was Sadiqu's student, explaining the similarities between the two Schools concerning customs, etiquette and restrictions.

Ahmadiyya Muslims (also known as Ahmadis)

With an estimated number of between 10 and 20 million worldwide, and over 30,000 of these living in the UK, the Ahmadiyya branch of Islam was founded in India by Mirza Ghulam Ahmad Qadiyani (1835–1908) who is believed to be the promised Messiah as foretold by the Prophet. Both Sunni and Shi'a Muslims believe the Messiah is yet to come. The Ahmadiyya founder believed he was the promised Messiah, or Imam Mahdi, for the Muslim community. He is referred to as their 'Messiah', who saw himself as the man chosen by Allah to revitalise Islam. Although Ahmadis share many similarities with Sunni and Shi'a Muslims, the one major belief that sets them apart is that the Prophet Muhammad is not the last Prophet. This breaks from fundamental Islamic orthodoxy, and sits uncomfortably with other Muslims. While Ahmadis believe the Qur'an is the final word of God and that there will never be a Prophet after Muhammad that will bring new revelations, they do not believe that he sealed God's prophethood. They say that the Prophet himself once said:

> *Islam would reach a time when Muslims would be Muslim in name only, the Qur'an would not be read or understood, and mosques would be filled with people who would receive little guidance. He also said leadership would be poor – when imams and mullahs would cause disorder and be the perpetrators of problems. (Hadith – Mishkat al-Masabih)*

Ahmadis believe their founder is a subordinate Prophet to the Prophet Muhammad. Ahmadis, who were originally Sunnis, have gone from strength to strength over the last century – and currently have 15,000 mosques in 209 countries.

Mirza Ghulam Ahmad Qadiyani is considered to be the Messiah of Islam and also for every other religion that believes a Messiah will come. The Messiah's return was prophesied in a Hadith and predicted to occur 13 centuries after the death of the Prophet Muhammad. The exactness of the time referred to a period where a 'donkey fuelled by fire would carry passengers inside its belly and would announce its departure'. We now know that to be a ship or an aeroplane. In addition to being seen as the Imam Mahdi, who came to revive Islam, he is also seen as the spirit of Jesus because of his similar qualities – strength of character and the humility he showed when facing those who refused to believe he was God's chosen one. **Shezad**

There has been widespread persecution of Ahmadis in some countries, particularly Pakistan and Saudi Arabia, who classify them as non-Muslims. This has also led to Ahmadis being arrested for religious practice in Pakistan. Several hundred have been murdered and 50 of their mosques have been destroyed. Nevertheless, Ahmadiyya Muslims are very proud and never try to hide their beliefs; instead they acknowledge the differences between themselves and Sunni and Shi'a Muslims.

Therefore it is the responsibility of God Almighty to send a leader to the people – to become an imam of the people of Islam. This is not intended to discredit the Prophet Muhammad because any leader after the Prophet is classified as a subordinate. Their job is to revive Islam. The founder of the Ahmadiyya community was appointed by God to revive the religion. He did not bring anything new to what was already there. Everything remained the same. Our interpretation of the Qur'an tells us that he is not the last Prophet. Ahmadiyya Muslims have endured much violence and death in Pakistan. They have been particularly targeted and persecuted – both historically and presently. In 1953 there was much agitation against the community, resulting in many houses being burned and people killed. The year 1974 saw a huge rise in opposition, and subsequently another wave of killings with thousands martyred, homes burned down and dead bodies scattering the streets.

The National Assembly of Pakistan invited the Supreme Head of the Ahmadiyya community to answer some questions. But despite full co-operation, the community was declared outside of the Bill of Law and constitution, and all Ahmadis were classified as 'non-Muslims'. Although the persecution continued, this did not stop Ahmadis from declaring their faith or from practising.

Then in 1984 a further amendment was passed by the National Assembly of Pakistan, known as Ordnance 20, which said that if any Ahmadi declared by word of mouth, action or gesture, or implied in any other way that they believe in Islam, they would be sentenced to three years in prison because they are not allowed to declare, say or do anything in the name of Islam. As a result of this, Pakistani Ahmadis are excluded from doing the hajj because they are not allowed to get a passport – and they refuse to denounce their religion to obtain one. Therefore, Ahmadis are refused permission to make the hajj, because the Pakistan government has reported to Saudi officials that Ahmadiyya Muslims are not true Muslims. **Imam Rashed**

The motto of Ahmadis is '*Love for All – Hatred for None*'. These were the words of the group's third caliph, and they have continued to be at the heart of the community ever since. They are written on the outside of all Ahmadiyya mosques worldwide. There is a welcoming vibe and friendly atmosphere to be found in Ahmadiyya mosques. Here, ordinary Muslims tend to have a greater understanding of Islam than their Sunni and Shi'a contemporaries, where, for me at least, it seemed the norm when asking non-academic Muslims questions about their faith to be asked to speak to the imam. I formed the opinion that their reticence was due to a fear of giving a wrong answer. I found the opposite when talking with Ahmadiyya Muslims, who take pride in knowing all aspects of the Islamic faith with a particularly good understanding of the Qur'an and Hadith. The reason for this, I was informed, was because there is a great emphasis on parents within the Ahmadiyya community. Children are taught about their faith from an early age. This means children get a good understanding of their faith and this is, in turn, passed onto the next generation.

My passion is helping people in life. I remember as a young boy, seeing the horror of 9/11 on television, and thinking this couldn't be part of what I believed in. It was not based on the real teachings of Islam that I was brought up to believe in, because I believe people can live in peace with each other, irrespective of religion, race or background. What saddens me most is that in terms of materialistic matters, technology and inventions, the world continues to make massive advancements, but when it comes to morality, we have gone backwards. This needs to change now and I believe the answer can be found in my community. **Safeer**

Ahmadis also hold a different perspective about the life and death of Jesus to Sunni and Shi'a Muslims. They say that to pacify the Jews and the Imperial Government in Rome, official records showed Jesus had died. But this is untrue. They base this argument on the reality of what the crucifixion entailed.

Because of blood loss from wounded hands and feet, physical exhaustion, pain, hunger and thirst, criminals generally took several days to die on the cross. The minimum time of death by crucifixion ranged from 24 to 28 hours, but the execution often lasted much longer. In such cases it was customary to break the bones (legs and arms) of the criminal so death would be hastened by internal bleeding. The Qur'an (3:56 and 4:158) declares that Christ did not die on the cross and that God saved him from crucifixion. The real story, according to the Qur'an, is that Jesus hid from the Jews of Judea (his persecutors) with the help of Joseph of Arimathea.

Pontius Pilate was thoroughly convinced of the innocence of Jesus and devised a scheme to save him. He chose Friday afternoon as the time for the crucifixion so he could not remain on the cross after sunset because of the Sabbath. The bones of the two thieves crucified on either side of Jesus were broken to ensure their deaths, but as Jesus appeared to be already dead, his bones were not broken. Joseph of Arimathea received permission from Pontius Pilate to have Jesus' body taken from the cross, and he placed it in a rock-hewn chamber of his family's sepulchre, where a pharisee named Nicodemus treated Jesus with spices and ointment until he was restored to consciousness.

Jesus had previously said his mission on earth wasn't complete and that he had to convey his message to the lost sheep of the House of Israel. Indeed, it was his mission to preach to all the 12 tribes of Israel – only two of which were in Palestine. So, after recovering from his wounds, he travelled to the east through Syria and then to Turkey, Iraq, Iran and Afghanistan, visiting all the lost tribes before completing his travels in India. He was known as Yuz Aasif – The Prince – Prophet. The latter part of his life was spent in Kashmir in India, where he lived to the ripe old age of 120 before being buried in the city.

There are other interpretations of Jesus that set Ahmadiyya Muslims apart other Muslims including this Hadith:

> And I swear by the Lord who holds my life in His hands that the son of Mary shall surely appear among you as just arbiter and shall break the cross, annihilate the swine... (Hadith – Bukhari)

Most Sunni Muslims take this Hadith literally believing it says Jesus will return to earth and eradicate Christianity as well as exterminate all the pigs in the world. Ahmadis believe this Hadith has metaphorical meaning and implies that breaking the cross is understood as demystifying the doctrine of trinity. With regards to annihilating the swine, they believe this means removing ills and vice from the society with preaching and spirituality.

Mirza Ghulam Ahmad Qadiyani believed that the jihad of the sword should be annulled and replaced by the jihad of the pen to win the hearts of the people. The concept of violent jihad (holy war) is viewed as unnecessary in modern times – with the right response to hate being love and kindness. Instead the Ahmadis view jihad in the Qur'anic context as the struggle a person has against their own basic desires. This core philosophy has continued within the community ever since the death of their Messiah, when a caliphate was devised. The Ahmadiyya caliphate does not view itself as a separate entity to the original caliphate, which was founded after the death of the Prophet Muhammad, but rather a continuation. Their response is that although various dynasties existed after the death of Ali and his sons, these were mainly in bloodshed and conflict. They did not align with the true teachings of Islam and were materialistically motivated hence their caliphate was reignited to regenerate the teachings of Islam. Ahmadis firmly believe that the words contained in the Qur'an are the final words of God and nothing else will ever be added.

The following is a short summary of the work of each Ahmadiyya caliph.

1. Hazrat Maulana Hakeem Nooruddin (1841–1914). Nooruddin was a well-educated man and a physician by profession. His main task was to keep the Ahmadiyya community together after the Messiah's death and to carry on its teachings throughout the sub-continent. He is particularly remembered for making known the falsehoods about Jesus' death and the coming of the Messiah – ideas which were rejected by other Muslims. He also concentrated on humanitarianism, including building hospitals and offering aid to the poor and destitute. He was caliph for six years.

2. Hazrat Mirza Bashiruddin Mahmud Ahmad (1889–1965). Son of the Messiah, Ahmad was only 25 when elected. He was strong, clever and energetic. Some were unhappy that a relative of the Messiah had taken over as caliph, resulting in a tiny split. Political divisions regarding the partition between India and Pakistan brought challenges, bloodshed and threats against the community. This did not stop him expanding missionary works in Africa, as well as building Ahmadiyya mosques to spread the faith far and wide. He was caliph for 52 years.

3. Hazrat Mirza Nasir Ahmad (1909–1982). He was the son of the second caliph and grandson of the Messiah. He was educated at Oxford and studied philosophy. His intellect and talents were used widely, and he expanded on his father's work. He set up many missionary projects in developing countries, including

the building of hospitals and schools. It was he who formed the motto 'Love for All – Hatred for None' for the community. He was caliph for 17 years.

4. Hazrat Mirza Tahir Ahmad (1928–2003). He was the younger brother of the third caliph, educated in London and a qualified homeopath. He practised homeopathy widely before his term in office, and he wrote a book on the subject. He continued his brother's work and set up missionary training colleges, and the building of new hospitals, schools and mosques. He also oversaw the move of the Ahmadiyya headquarters from Pakistan to London because of continued persecution, and set up a television channel for the community to spread the faith to every part of the world. He was caliph for 21 years.

5. Hazrat Mirza Masroor Ahmad (born 1950). He has been the caliph since 2003. He is the great grandson of the Messiah. An agriculturist by profession, much of his younger life was spent working on various projects in Ghana. He is responsible for the current moral reformation of Ahmadiyya Islam, preaching the need for man to turn back to God. He has spoken in parliaments throughout the world. He has spent the past ten years talking about world peace and teaches widely about the true teachings of Islam. He too, like his grandfather, is passionate about homeopathy and advocates its usage.

I encountered some Ahmadis in their mid- to late twenties, who told me they had all types of Muslim friends while at university, and that being united with them wasn't a problem. Some had shared student accommodation with Sunnis and Shi'a and they had got on well together. This might well be true, but based on the Sunni and Shi'a Muslims I interviewed, I formed the opinion that integration amongst them and Ahmadis is rare, with rejection and non-communication being the norm.

Three Muslims – an Ahmadiyya, a Sunni and a Shi'a were waiting on the railway platform for a train to take them to Victoria station. As the train was pulling into the station, the sign above the driver's cabin was clearly marked Victoria, denoting its destination. The Ahmadiyya Muslim boarded the train and travelled safely to Victoria station without any difficulty. The Sunni and Shi'a did not board the train and decided to wait for another train instead because they did not trust that the first train would take them to Victoria. So they waited for the next train and when it came the same situation occurred. The train was clearly marked Victoria but neither man believed it would take them there. And with that, this unappealing and nonsensical situation continued and both men were unable to complete their journey because of their mistrust. **Akram**

The Lahore Ahmadiyya Movement

There is a splinter group to the Ahmadiyya community called 'The Lahore Ahmadiyya Movement'. The founder of this group, Maulana Muhammad Ali, had connections to Lahore where he died. Lahore Ahmadis hold a distinctive theological difference to the main Ahmadiyya community – they believe the founder was not a subordinate Prophet to the Prophet Muhammad, rather that Muhammad sealed the finality of the prophethood and no further Prophets or subordinate Prophets will ever come after him (which is also the mainstream Sunni–Shi'a belief). They believe that Mirza Ghulam Ahmad referred to himself as a subordinate Prophet in metaphorical terms but that other Ahmadis mistakenly took this literally. However, they share the belief that he was the Messiah (Imam Mahdi) who came as the reformer of Islam for future generations of Muslims. Unlike the main group, they have gained greater acceptance from other Muslims by believing that Mohammed was the last Prophet. However, Lahore Ahmadis are liberal in the sense that segregation between men and women is not as strict, and most women do not wear the hijab. Another point of difference is that they do not give their allegiance to the Ahmadiyya caliphate, and are, instead, governed by a president (a former president has been a woman). Women are also allowed to lead prayers and give Friday sermons, although this does not frequently occur. Lahore Ahmadis are far lower in number than mainstream Ahmadis with an estimated number of 30,000 worldwide, mainly in India and Pakistan, and only around 150 members in the UK.

Salafism

Salafism, similar to Wahhabism, is viewed as being an ultra-conservative, austere, fundamentalist and puritan form (sect) of Islam. Wahhabism, founded by Mohammad ibn Abd-al-Wahhab in Saudi Arabia in the eighteen century, is an austere form of Islam that insists on a literal interpretation of the Qur'an. Followers of Wahhabism claim that they are trying to purify Islam. Wahhabism is considered a puritanical form of Sunni Islam and is largely connected to current-day extremism and terrorism. Many people believe that Salafi Muslims follow a similar pathway to Wahhabism. Salafism is divided into three categories: those who are politically engaged, those who are not political, and a minority who strongly believe in jihad (holy war) and therefore are sometimes linked to terrorist groups. Some Salafi Muslims question and reject traditional Muslims who follow the teachings of the four caliphs – saying that you should only follow the Prophet. This leaves them open to accusations of leaving the law pertaining to Islam from the Qur'an and the Hadith without any scholarly interpretation, which their critics claim results in opinions that are ill-informed or without strong foundation.

Salafism strives to go back to the original teachings of Islam. It does not accept any change or any form of addition. An example of the latter is the zealous love that some Muslims have for the Prophet, resulting in celebrating his birthday, the anniversary of his death and including additional prayers during the month of Ramadan. None of these are in the original teachings. Salafism aims to restore Islam to its true and proper form, to the original ways of how it was worshipped in the time of the Prophet. We want Islam to be like how the Prophet left it, and how his companions understood and applied it. Salafism is not a School of Thought. It is a method of approach – a way to gain proper interpretation and proper clarity, of looking at how the Prophet and his companions practised Islam.

We are not restricted to what is considered by other Muslims to be the main four Schools of Thought. We advise Muslims from restricting themselves to just these four Schools. It's not a question of not agreeing with them but of looking beyond these four Schools of Thought to other renowned scholars who have valuable things to say about Islam.

It's wrong to think Salafism is about a Muslim going directly to the Qur'an and Hadith and forming their own interpretations. In fact, we strictly advise against such practices. We are only interested in how the Prophet's companions interpreted it, or that of students of the companions, or students of the students. Salafism has become more popular in the past 50 years, although it has been around for centuries. We believe in the same type of jihad as other Muslims, in that self-defence against attack is permissible, but we fully condemn senseless killings that occur to non-combatants in warfare in both Muslim and non-Muslim countries, resulting in the deaths of both Muslims and non-Muslims. This is totally wrong. Salafism does not encourage terrorism. Some people mix us up because we have the zest to apply Islam and its Sharia in its purist form and while this may look similar to outsiders who do not know much about Islam, I can assure you Salafism and extremism are on entirely different pages. Their method is, 'If you are not with us, you are against us', and this includes Muslims as much as it includes non-Muslims. This is categorically the wrong way to portray Islam because Sharia strictly forbids the killing of innocent people. **Imam Jamaykee**

Many Muslims I spoke to felt that Salafism is a Saudi-funded brand of Islam that has become too dominant in the West, its followers harbouring a dislike for any who are not part of their ideology. Some Muslims view them as aggressive clerics who portray Islam as a religion of power through violence, seeing them as often-frustrated individuals locked in hate and anger for other religions and non-Muslims. All Muslims I met who were Salafi denied advocating jihad and spoke against violence and terrorism in the strongest manner. Notwithstanding this, jihadism is generally seen as having its roots in Salafism, with many claiming that all Sunni jihadists are Salafis, although not all Salafis are jihadists. This would be indicative of my personal experience of visiting Salafi mosques and talking to imams and members of their community who all condemned violence. But for those who are not of peaceful means, their minds are firmly on jihad, and the only way they will stop hating non-believers is when they embrace Islam, because they want non-Muslims to be brought to their version of true freedom in this life and salvation in the hereafter.

We are against innovation in the sense of some Muslims becoming over-pious and going beyond what is expected – for example we disapprove of Muslim faith-healers and don't encourage people who are sick to see them. Help should only be sought from God. Then there are those who go to Medina where the Prophet is buried and pray to Him. Muslims should only pray directly to God. It is God you pray to and nobody else. We don't use prayer beads. We feel if a person wants to count their prayers, they can use their fingers. We also don't believe in it being mandatory in mosques that group supplication is required to offer praise and thanks to God. We feel it is most appropriate to follow the example of the Prophet and offer your own individual supplication of thanks rather than feeling obliged to do it as part of a congregational format. **Owais**

The dress code of some Muslims in the UK requires attention. You see women wearing headscarves but failing to adhere to other degrees of modesty. Wearing tight jeans or showing legs is not acceptable. The same is true for men who wear ripped or tight jeans or shorts instead of traditional Islamic clothing. Children should be taught from a young age as to what is expected, so by the time they reach the age of 12 good dress practice is the norm for them.

We are against folkloric traditions that extend to celebrating the Prophet's birthday, especially as his exact birth date is unknown. We abhor incantations like the wearing of charms, which are used superstitiously as a means of protection. This is a baseless tradition of no worth. We disagree with decorations in mosques, which we believe should always be built and maintained as plain and simple in nature. We believe imams should be better qualified and we are against imams coming from abroad to the UK who aren't fluent in English, and feel this practice needs to be looked at because imams from abroad who don't speak English find it hard to adjust to a new environment and new customs. **Abdul Haq**

Sufism

Sufism is a sect within Sunni Islam that stands out because of its difference from other types of Islam and sects found within the different branches of the faith. In some cases it consists of spiritual thinkers and dancers known as whirling dervishes. It is a mystical form of Islam known for its tolerance and pluralism. Sufis display devotion to Islamic saints and shrines, which is often viewed by extremists as apostate. Sufism is mainly found in Turkey, Egypt and Sudan but there is a small number of Sufi-oriented mosques in the UK.

The whirling dance emulates the rotation of the planets around the sun and is mesmerising to watch. Sufi Muslims use music and dance for devotional purposes, which are otherwise absent in other mosques. Music and dance are used as means of a connection to the divine. Sufis believe that this was perfectly acceptable in the Prophet's time and do not understand why there are Muslims who object to this practice now, as there is no reason, from their perception, that it is not permissible.

Historically, there was an emphasis in Sufism on giving up worldly things in order to get closer to God. Some believed that salvation could be found through poverty – bringing about inner purity, leading the human spirit to achieving a greater intimacy with God. In current times, Sufis may not necessarily endorse poverty by giving up worldly goods, but Sufis maintain their devotion to music and dance in their mosques, and continue to believe that humility brings people closer to God.

Sufism concentrates on the spiritual side of Islam. If you lose your spiritual side, then things go wrong. Religion without spiritualism is like a body without salt. It is the essence of all religions. Sufism follows all of the other practices of Islam and it was only 10 or 15 years after the Prophet's death that prohibitions began to be placed on spirituality within Islam. Before that, when the Prophet was alive, there were no restrictions, so I think it is safe to assume that if there were to be prohibitions against Sufism in Islam, they would have been there from the beginning.

Sufism believes in wisdom, compassion and love for all of creation. Spirituality in religion is more important than rules, although of course rules bring balance. Muslims believe there is only one God, so it is important to feel connected to God through prayers and meditation. God represents harmony, unity and peace, and it should be with these qualities that you face your Lord. And when you face God, you must remember that he is watching you, so therefore it's important that you bring perfection to every action.

Sufi Muslims believe that you must present well before God, like you would before a king or a queen, by dressing appropriately before going to the mosque. As well as being concerned about your own appearance, it is important to be concerned about the appearance of the mosque. Sufi Muslims keep all their mosques in a good state of repair as a sign of respect to God. Islam is a religion that values respect, and this respect starts with your creator, followed by loving the Prophet Muhammad, followed by obedience and mercy towards our elders and young people. The harmony of chanting praise to God is indeed a gift from Him. But people are free to remember God all the time, whether they are sitting or out walking. It's between each individual and God how they form that connection.

How can you hate anything that God has created? God gave freedom to everybody irrespective of their race, colour or religion. God gave freewill to everyone. When people lose their spirituality, they fill this vacuum with their ego. The ego allows them to become proud and arrogant. They lose respect for others and start believing that others are bad and need to be punished. The ego is like a poison, and people who believe in their ego more than anything else place this poison in the honey.

The poison in the honey these days is terrorism. We live in a world where terrorists kill people, but once upon a time Muslims would feel guilty for stepping on an ant, such was the respect for God's creation. The ideologies behind this extremism have only started to bear fruit in the last 20 to 30 years, although I appreciate its conception was during the last century – Shaykhs who are full of ego and consider themselves better than God. They are only small in number but very dangerous. They are worshipping themselves. They are educated to hate and sometimes their hate is far greater for other Muslims they disagree with than it is for non-Muslims. This dirty extremist ideology is mingled with corrupt politics by those who control the holy places of Islam, which gives them political leverage around the world. But they are not the sincere, real followers of Islam, although for now, it would seem that they are unstoppable. But even they are beginning to wake up to the harm that is being done, even in Saudi Arabia where suicide bombers have showed their ugly evil in recent years. They gave birth to this dragon and groomed it. They were like an over-indulgent parent who lavished money on the child. They were able to control it at first, but little by little the dragon began to grow another head before bringing destruction far and wide. Now it is outside of their control and slowly they are beginning to realise their folly. They are like mushrooms around a tree. They have no roots and therefore will eventually disappear. The tree, on the other hand, will stay. Destruction is easy. Construction is hard. It only takes one or two people to destroy a building in a few seconds that took hundreds of men to build over several years. We need to develop better strategies to curtail and stop their activities. After all, prevention is better than treatment.

A person must remain humble with their actions done for God alone. On the Day of Judgement there will be three types to watch out for with regards to their ego. The first are scholars who were consumed by how clever they were. The second is the generous man who has given money and gifts to others so that they would praise him for his generosity. And then the third are the martyrs who saved others to make themselves look good for their actions. The moral of this is: do not seek praise from anybody. God will praise those with a humble heart whether they are a scholar, a kind person, or a martyr who has made sacrifices. God is most forgiving and merciful. The Prophet once said that nobody can enter paradise without their own good deeds. He even pointed out that it wouldn't be possible for him either unless God thought he was worthy of this reward for his good deeds – deeds that are done through humbleness and that are unconditional. **Imam Al Rawi**

IMAMS

The title Imam is most commonly used for Islamic clerics, prayer leaders and preachers. They are the equivalent to priests in Christianity. The title Maulana is mainly Indo-Pak and is used for esteemed Islamic scholars. The title Shaykh, which is an Arabic word meaning the elder of a tribe, a revered old man, or an Islamic scholar, is also used.

The average wage for an imam in London is between £32,000 and £35,000 yearly. It is generally seen as a fairly low-paid job (with minimum qualifications) despite its role and responsibilities and the fact that you are on call 24/7. An imam's main role is to lead the congregation in prayer and to teach ordinary Muslims in their community about the Qur'an and Hadith. But they must be leaders within their communities, not just for Muslims but also for non-Muslims to attain a better society together.

Muslims forget that the Prophet was an imam for everybody. He would never turn anybody away from the mosque. Imam's salaries are publicly funded. Some mosques are struggling to pay their bills. They are run by elders of the community, who form a committee. Some of the committee members won't value or respect the imam because they don't value the time and dedication that imams have invested in their education and the level of duty they carry towards their congregations.

Some imams should not be allowed to practise because they are underqualified, especially some who come to the UK from abroad. They are able to lead the prayers – that is about all – but that does not prevent them from starting to do things their own way. Many haven't finished their training before they come to the UK. They think they are experts and start espousing their own interpretations despite not being trained to 'qadi' level (a trained Sharia judge).

Women are not allowed to become imams because they menstruate. We protect their dignity because they would not be able to lead prayers while they were having their period. Everybody in the mosque would know that it was the time of their monthly cycle during absences, so we are giving them respect and dignity rather than taking away their rights. **Imam Khan**

Let's say a couple has four sons and one gets straight As in his exams – he will probably go to medical school. If another gets Bs, he is likely to become a lawyer or an engineer. If the third son gets Cs he will probably become a teacher, but the son who gets Ds won't have such a great choice. It's sons like these who become imams. There is no prestige in becoming an imam. There is no great deal of intelligence required. Most of them are incapable of thinking outside of the box; there is no blue-sky thinking available for them. They haven't got a clue how to solve a present-day problem: rather they constantly look for answers from the past, and in many cases are only equipped to deal with medieval opinion. Admittedly, imams are put into impossible situations where they are expected to preside over a community, but there is no such thing as a single Muslim community. There are communities. On average, most big mosques will see Muslims come to Friday prayer from over a hundred countries. Try getting all of them to agree on everything you say. It's an impossible job and this is very sad indeed because Islam has no culture. Islam is cultureless. It is Muslims who have culture and it is Muslims who bring problems to the religion, not the other way around. **Rifat**

A day in the life of an imam

I try and go to bed every night around 10pm because I need to be up to open the mosque for 6am. Morning prayers take about ten minutes. I study the Qur'an for six hours each day. The goal is to be able to recite the Holy Qur'an off by heart because on the Day of Judgement those who are able to recite the Holy Qur'an, in its complete entirety from start to finish, will be rewarded with automatic entry to paradise without having to account for any of their sins. In addition to this, God will allow them to choose ten members from their family ancestral lineage to join them in paradise – those who would otherwise be destined for hell.

I grew up in a strong Muslim family and was always surrounded by a strong Muslim environment. Most days after school I would go to the mosque to study the Holy Qur'an. I have always had a great devotion to learning about God and the Prophet Muhammad (peace be upon him). By the time I was in Year 8 at school, the imam encouraged me to start teaching younger children than myself. I would read parts of the Holy Qur'an to them as well as some basic books explaining Islam. I started off with classes of two or three but by the end this had grown to 30. From Year 10 onwards, I started to learn Arabic in earnest and also about jurisprudence (Islamic law). I am currently doing a scholarship in this and have an overseas tutor who I Skype for personal tuition.

The greatest challenge is this: to learn to recite the Holy Qur'an in Arabic, and every day I practise continuously by reciting aloud and memorising what I have learnt.

Being an imam carries responsibility. My role is to educate my community with Islamic teachings because an imam is responsible for their community. I offer classes at the mosque for all age groups so my days are filled up with teaching – this can be a group of youths or various groups of adults of different ages. I teach them the truth and never deviate from the purity in the holy texts. When extremism filters into a community, people ask who their leader is, and what he has said to fill their heads with this in the first place. I never preach hatred towards non-Muslims. I preach mercy. I am not a hypocrite who mixes with bad company outside of my role. In my view, imams need to be all DBS-checked (Disclosure and Barring Service) for their role because we often come into contact with children. If you teach them the wrong message, this is what they will carry with them. I have heard of imams who have sinned greatly by abusing their positions of trust, and those who have carried out sexual offences against children. It is this type of imam who brings shame to Islam.

My role is paid for by committee members (parishioners) of the mosque. I live alone in accommodation in the mosque. I have to cook all my own meals because I am not yet married. My parents will help me find a suitable bride. Some call this an 'arranged marriage' but in part it consists of an introduction to somebody they think would be compatible. I will meet my bride-to-be in a mutual family setting where we will share our goals and ambitions in life and get to know each other before we get married. In my spare time, which is sometimes very little, I like to occasionally play football with friends or a game of badminton. I also like watching programmes on YouTube about space and reality survival shows. *Bear Grylls* is a favourite. Other times I simply like to go for a walk or drop into Costa and have a coffee.

Births and marriages form part of my imam duties. Parents usually take their newborn babies to the mosque for a blessing. The imam will recite the Call to Prayer softly into the baby's right ear, and then into the left ear the Call to Prayer used in mosques for the congregation. As an imam, I officiate over authorised marriages by helping draw up contracts and arranging for two witnesses to be present. I often get people coming to me who are not in my neighbourhood, requesting that I 'marry' them outside of the legal process, but I refuse to do this and only carry out marriages approved by the government.

I also officiate at funerals. Good Muslims die in a beautiful manner with 500 angels greeting the deceased and each one holding a beautifully scented flower. The angels take the soul so gently from the body that the Prophet once compared it to a droplet of water falling effortlessly from a person's fingertip. Muslims are supposed to be buried within 24 hours after their death whenever possible. The coffin is taken to the mosque where prayers are held to seek forgiveness for the dead person from the Court of the Lord. After the person is buried and the grave is closed, two angels return the soul to the earth and each dead person is then asked three questions: 1) Who is your Lord? 2) What is your religion? and 3) Who is this man (after a vision of the Prophet Muhammad appears)?

A good Muslim will correctly answer the questions but before one of the angels shows the person their place in paradise, the other angel will show them a glimpse of hell, telling them that this is what they have been spared from, before showing them paradise. Their grave is then widened with the angels telling the person to rest and relax until the Day of Judgement. There is a large window the person can look through which provides a good view of the beauty and bounties of paradise – their grave acts as a small part of the gardens of paradise.

Muslims who have lived bad lives, though, do not have happy deaths. The angel of death appears with sharp dirty claws that digs into the person's joints and takes the soul from the body with the same force as it takes to hack a nail out of a piece of timber with a hammer. The angel will be accompanied by 500 angels, but they will disguise themselves, and each will be holding whips or embers. After the person is buried and the grave is closed, two angels return the soul to the earth and the person is asked the same three questions that were asked of the good Muslim, but instead of giving a correct answer to each question, he/she will respond with 'I don't know' to each one. One angel will then show the person a glimpse of paradise and tell them that this would have been their reward had they lived a good life, before showing them their place in hell. The grave is then narrowed with such a force that the person's rib cage is crushed. Their grave acts as the pit of hell until the Day of Judgement.

In order for a divorce to take place, a man has to say to his wife, 'I divorce you' three times. Once a man came to me after having told his wife three times that he wanted to divorce her but regretted his actions because he wanted to remain married to her for the sake of their children. He wanted to know if there was anything I could do – if there was any justification or interpretation of the rules that would help him skirt around not having to divorce her. I told him there wasn't because in the eyes of Allah, he was already divorced after having repeated his command three times, and he must therefore abide by his actions. The only way he could ever get back with his wife would be if she remarried and, having consummated the marriage at some later stage, got divorced. It is only then that they could remarry provided this was what the woman wanted to do. I have heard stories though of people manipulating the rules – of men getting their friends to marry their ex-wives and then quickly divorcing them with the intention of allowing their friends to remarry, but this is a very wrong thing to do because they are not abiding by the rules of Allah.

Every night before I go to sleep I recite the Qur'an and spare a thought for the souls who have not been saved. Every prayer is a supplication for those dead souls at risk of damnation on the Day of Judgement for their bad deeds, having not been forgiven by any other means. An example would include the deceased person's family contributing financially to build a mosque, where prayers recited are sent as a reward to the deceased.

Sometimes I wake up at 3am and when this occurs I take

advantage of this wonderful opportunity that the 'third' part of the night provides. This is such a beautiful, peaceful time – people are asleep, animals are asleep and even plants are asleep. Muslims can take advantage of this time to build a connection with God. You are making a little sacrifice in foregoing your sleep to worship him. God has said, 'Is there anybody who wants to be forgiven? Come and join with me. Any prayer you ask for will be answered.'

The Prophet Muhammad (peace be upon him) used to get up regularly to pray at this time and often stood for so long that his ankles would swell. Once his youngest wife Aisha said to him, 'Oh Prophet, why are you praying so hard? You are already guaranteed paradise.' She knew that as God's Final Messenger, his soul was without blemish. The Prophet replied, 'Should I not be a grateful servant for all the bounties and blessings that God has given me?'

I am not special. God chooses who he wills. The Prophet (peace be upon him) once said that if a person has so much as an atom's worth of pride in his/her heart, they will not enter paradise. A person should never think they are better than anybody else because in reality a beggar may be closer to entering paradise than them. **Imam Shammas**

CHAPTER 4

Women and Islam

PERCEPTIONS

Are women badly treated in Islam? Are their rights suppressed? Are they crying out to live free, liberated lives? These are questions that are frequently discussed by non-Muslims. There is indeed much curiosity about the treatment of women in Islam, which is often seen as being male dominated. People regularly query if women are secondary to men in the religion without considering that it might be unfair or discriminatory to make assumptions without knowing the facts.

> Some people construe Islam as being very backward. They assume that women have a poor quality of life; they stay at home to have children and cook. But they don't know that Khadija – the Prophet's first wife – was a businesswoman. The Prophet was one of the workers in her business when they got married. Afterwards, Khadija continued working in the successful business that she had set up in trading. She is often seen as a positive role model to a lot of Muslim women. **Nasreen**

Islam holds old-school values. You will find fewer single mothers in Islam than in other religions. Islam keeps families together. In society's fight for equality between men and women, we have lost what is important. Don't forget that women like a little chivalry. I love it when a man opens a door for me. I feel that if there is oppression against women in Islam, it comes from Muslims who don't know Islam well. The truth is we are not mindless, oppressed beings – it is not the teachings of Islam that are oppressive. I admit some women are brought up in negative village cultures, particularly in countries like India, Pakistan and Bangladesh, and are uneducated. What is not always generally known is that there are guidelines in the Qur'an about how women should be treated and they are put there for the benefit of women. **Saima**

The role of the mother is a big – very big and important – one to women, not a small one. Mothers spend a lot of time with their children. They breastfeed their babies. They don't rush to return to work after giving birth. There is value for full-time mothers in Islam. It is part of our core values and the pinnacle of womanhood to really to be a mother. This is viewed as a huge responsibility. Mothers are seen as the queen of the home. On the status of a mother in Islam, our Prophet stated, 'Paradise lies at the feet of your mother' (Hadith – Sunan an-Nasa'i).

The thing that needs to change to bring about a better treatment of women in Islam is people's way of thinking, which is a tremendous feat and a seemingly insurmountable task. I think the unfair treatment is mainly down to the culture and traditions of the patriarchal societies that govern countries across the Middle East and Asia. Again it is due to a lack of education. In these countries, the majority of people identify as Muslims, but typically their religious knowledge consists of a basic education at a mosque while they're young, and then cultural traditions passed down verbally, from one generation to the next. These oral traditions form the basis of many people's faith and it is a shame as they cannot see the disservice they are doing to their religion by following such cultural traditions alone and not pursuing a proper education in their religion. **Faria**

There are some Islamic feminists who defend the rights of Muslim women to think freely, criticising the practice that in Islam a woman's life is worth half that of a man, pointing out that a man can have four wives (under strict provisions), whereas a woman can only have one husband. Perhaps they miss the point that the Qur'an dictates this, and that therefore this is not a man-made rule?

Admittedly, life in the UK is much better for Muslim women than in some non-Western countries. A large number of young female Muslims now go to university and have professional careers. Most of them do not live under tyrannical rulings, unlike countries in the Middle East and the sub-continent. It's common to hear of *morality police* in countries like Iran, Afghanistan, Saudi Arabia and Pakistan, checking on women and chastising them if they are not dressed appropriately. In Saudi Arabia, women are not allowed to drive (this is due to change in 2018) and married women still can't travel outside the country without their husband's permission. In Iran, up until March 1979, women were allowed to be judges but that was stopped after Khomeini's Islamic Republic came to power.

There are few women in politics in these countries; the last, most notable, was Benazir Bhutto, who was the Prime Minister of Pakistan before being assassinated in 2007. It needs to be remembered though that women in the Western world worked hard to achieve equality, and in some areas still struggle for parity with men. It's not a question of everything being perfect for non-Muslim females. Women in the United States were not allowed to vote until 1920, and French women required their husband's permission to open a bank account until the 1960s.

What is needed is that Muslim males who abuse women's rights, that they are reminded to focus more on how the Prophet Muhammad practised fairness, equality and respect towards his wives based on Qur'anic revelations. I also believe that other issues,

such as socio-economic issues, poverty and illiteracy, also affect
the healthy atmosphere of women in any Muslim community or
country. Confusions between Islam and culture include people
believing that Islam does not allow a woman to leave her house
without a valid reason, and if she has to go out she must get
permission from her husband; or if a man hasn't eaten, his wife
must not eat before him; or if the husband calls his wife to bed
(for marital reasons) and she refuses, the angels send curses upon
her till the morning. There is nothing in the Qur'an that states a
woman has to walk behind her husband. Another great travesty
wrongly held against Islam is female genital mutilation. This
predominantly springs from East African countries like Sudan
and Somalia – it is not found in Asian or other cultures. This was
a practice embedded in cultural norms before Islam, where the
practice continues and does not have roots in Islam. This practice
has travelled, though, and that is why we have seen young Muslim
females subjected to this barbaric treatment here in the UK, and
it's wrongly getting blamed on Islam.

The Qur'an teaches men to be fair and equal to their wives.
The Hadith, too, is also full of fairness and goodness to women.
Did you know if a woman has a job, her salary is hers to keep?
She is under no obligation to share it with her husband. He alone
is responsible for the financial running of the house, including
paying all bills. A woman has the right to name a dowry from her
husband of her own choosing before she agrees to marry him. The
importance of education was also something the Prophet spoke
about by saying that parents get double the reward if they educate
their daughters. **Javed**

Culture has much to do with how women from countries of the
sub-continent are treated. Age is also a factor that impacts this.
I know those from Pakistani, Bangladeshi and Indian cultures
who expect women to stay at home, care for the children, cook
and clean, and do the shopping and cooking. They are not allowed
to work or wear make-up. But a new generation of Muslims are

emerging and once the current older generation have passed away, I believe we will see more and more women in these countries going out to work and having more non-Muslim friends. Things are definitely changing. **Hibbatullah**

WOMEN'S RIGHTS

In 2016 the Gatestone Institute reported that according to a survey conducted by ICM for the Chanel 4 documentary *What Muslims Really Think*, 39 per cent of Muslim men thought their wives should always obey their husbands. However, some Muslim women I spoke to in my own interviews dismissed this as a cultural attitude that has overridden the Qur'an, and they questioned whether this was a case of some cultures deliberately interpreting the Qur'an in line with their own values. The word 'obey' is often regarded as contentious, although theoretically it is just an expression of a woman honouring her husband in marriage. But it is not intended to imply that men are exempt from responsibilities and do not have certain duties towards their wives. There is a Hadith in which the Prophet used the word 'obey':

> *If a woman prays regularly five times a day, fasts the month of Ramadan, guards her chastity and obeys her husband (it will be said to her) enter paradise from whatever gate you want. (Hadith – Ahmed)*

There is also another which advises men to be good husbands:

> *The best of you are those who are the best to their wives. (Hadith – Tirmidhi)*

The Prophet tells us that a husband's treatment of his wife reflects a Muslim's good character, which in turn is a reflection of the man's faith. How can a Muslim husband be good to his wife? He should smile, not hurt her emotionally, remove anything that will harm her, treat her gently, and be patient with her. Being nice includes good communication. A husband should be willing to open up, and be willing to listen to his wife. Mutual respect in a marriage is very important.

The Prophet used to do his own chores. Isn't it selfish for a man to expect his wife to work constantly at home and raise a family but never to give her any help? She deserves love and kindness and if it's not given to her, then the bond between the man and woman weakens. The Prophet once said that irrespective of how good a man is, if he does not treat his wife well then he did not have value in his eyes. **Raza**

There are differences in Islam with regards to property rights between men and women. For instance, if a woman owns property in her own right, she does not have to share it with her husband. Yet the law regarding inheritance can seem unfair. If a father died and left behind a son and daughter, the son would inherit two shares of his property, whereas his daughter would only inherit one. However, the daughter's share is hers alone, whereas the son must use his share to help take care of the family, including his sister, if she is unmarried. If she is married then she is under the care of her husband, who is legally obligated to provide for her. When a woman gets married, she has the right to demand a dowry (a gift in the form of a sum of money or land or gold which is hers by right to do with as she pleases), but men cannot demand the same.

Muslim women I spoke to believe that it was the Prophet Muhammad who was responsible for raising the rights and standards of women in his lifetime, and that he made it abundantly clear that disrespect towards women goes against Islam. There are, though, literalists who interpret the Qur'an incorrectly by imposing rules on women that were applicable under certain conditions during the era in which the Qur'an was written. Indeed, life for women in the region that is now Saudi Arabia was very harsh during the Prophet's lifetime. The treatment of women throughout history in that territory has not been favourable to their interests. Non-Muslims, who favoured sons rather than daughters, used to kill their daughters in various ways. Some were buried alive; others were drowned or were thrown from mountain peaks. But the Prophet did everything in his power to educate people against these evil practices. The fact that he was a father to four loving daughters may have developed his understanding and great compassion in an era that was so cruel and devalued women so much.

> Women are actually liberated in Islam, which gave rights to women before any Western state ever did. Women had control over their own money, their own inheritance, years before we reached equality in the modern world – although as women we still get paid less in senior posts. Islam is freedom for all women. It has empowered women since its inception in the seventh century with many rights and protections, long before they were afforded similar luxuries in the West. Contrary to popular belief, in Islam women are not inferior or unequal to men, and a study of the Qur'an and Sunnah will enlighten those looking to learn more about this. **Umar**

There are many Hadith which support respecting women in Islam. It is related how once a party of the Prophet was running late during a journey. There were women in the caravan as well. When the camel drivers tried to quicken the pace to make up for lost time, the Prophet heeded them by saying, 'Mind the crystal', which was a euphemism he used requesting that the women be treated gently and respectfully in this instance (Hadith – Muslim). There was another time when the Prophet and his wife both fell off a camel. His companions rushed to his aid, but the Prophet instructed them to go and tend to his wife first before him (Hadith – Bukhari).

Once a man came to the Prophet and asked him, who amongst the people is the most worthy of my good companionship? The Prophet replied, 'Your mother.' The man asked 'And after that, who?' The Prophet replied again, 'Your mother.' The man asked again, 'And after that, who?' The Prophet replied a third time, 'Your mother.' It was only after the man asked a fourth time that the Prophet replied, 'Your father' (Hadith – Bukhari).

> Islam gave women special attention, with respect and rights that were not given before, nor were they given a long time after, in Europe and other regions in the world. However, bad practices against Islamic teachings do occur in some Muslim countries due to ignorance, misunderstanding and often corruption in governments. But this also happens in non-Muslim countries as well. **Abbas**

> So much perfection is given to women's rights in Islam that nothing else comes close to this kind of equality between men and women. Islam emphasises that God made males and females in different physical structures for a reason. Females bear the pain of childbirth and afterwards carry out the main role in the upbringing of children. The male has to work and provide for his wife and children. Women are allowed to work, but there should not be a need placed on them to financially contribute to the running of the family home. That is the man's responsibility. In addition to a dowry received before marriage, couples enter into a prenuptial agreement whereby men have to agree to an outright financial settlement if the couple divorce. However, even if they stay together, the man must make this agreed payment in instalments throughout the marriage, which is for his wife's personal use. To not give the money as agreed is seen as a breach of this covenant and against the rules of Islam. **Ratiq**

HEAD DRESS

The covering of women in Islam gives rise to discussion and contention in equal measure. Some non-Muslims think women in Islam are forced to cover themselves, believing this to be unnecessary, unjust and against their human rights. Muslim females, however, do not voice any concerns about having to cover themselves. To them, covering their head is part of their religion and something that is normal and routine. There is no evidence the practice causes discontent, and neither does there appear to be any desire to change the interpretation of the guidelines given by the Qur'an on the matter, which does not specifically mention hair covering.

> *O messenger: convey to your wives, your daughters and the women of the believers that when they go out they shall wrap around themselves their cloaks or shawls to cover their cleavage so that they may be recognised as righteous and modest women and avoid being stared at. God is Protector and the Most Merciful. (Qur'an – 33:59)*

There are five main types of clothing that Muslim women wear to protect their 'modesty':

Hijab: This covers the hair and neck.
Khimar: This covers the head, neck and shoulders.
Chador: This is a full body cloak but allows eyes or face to be revealed.
Niqab: This covers the body and face, showing only the eyes.
Burqa: This covers the entire body including the face and eyes.

The burqa as well as the niqab in particular attracts attention, with many sections of Western society viewing it unfavourably. There are politicians and even some Muslims who view it as a symbol of female oppression and say that there is no conceivable religious, cultural or ideological reason that can justify concealment of female identity in public. The burqa is also cited as preventing integration, because people are unable to see the person's face, which is viewed as a barrier to communication and social interaction.

> I feel offended when people comment on female oppression without any knowledge of how empowering covering can be for a woman in this day and age. In a time where women are treated

as second-class citizens, sexualised for the pleasure of men and advertising corporations, having a way to shield oneself from such discrimination is a saving grace. I, for one, practise wearing modest clothes and a head scarf, which has given me confidence in a society where women are judged by the clothes they wear and the way that they act, less so than by their personalities or intellect.

Islam teaches men to respect women by lowering their gaze and acting modestly to them. Similarly, women are taught to be modest in their appearance and manner and not send the wrong message to men, but instead leave this privilege of revealing outward beauty to family and spouse only. This is the beautiful way in which my religion empowers women, and it is absolutely ludicrous to lobby for change to my attire based on a few people's opinions – who have no idea how this has changed the lives of millions of women in this country alone for the better. **Sairah**

However, only a minority of Muslims wear the burqa, with the hijab or khimar being the two more preferred types of covering. There are of course Muslim women who wear modest clothing but prefer not to cover their heads. This is acceptable within the terms of the Qur'an, although some cultures might disagree and frown upon the practice with a degree of ridicule.

Covering of the hair can be a controversial topic in Islam. I am not against the scarf in any way: I believe women should dress how they feel comfortable; it's a matter of personal preference. I am against narrow-minded views, such as 'Women who don't cover their hair are not really Muslim', and even a silly old wives' tale that when a woman appears in public without covering her hair the devil is urinating on her head. It's absurd. It is true that the Qur'an does say that a woman must wear hijab, but it does not specify what a hijab is and therefore this is a matter of interpretation. To wear 'hijab' is to be modest. Being modest can be interpreted in a number of ways, from the way one dresses to one's personality and character. I find that with strict Wahhabi interpretations of Islam, women are increasingly being judged for what they wear.

For me it's simple; Islam is spirituality and just because I don't choose to cover my hair, as many Muslim women choose not to do, doesn't make me or them any less Muslim. **Jawaria**

Girls usually start covering up between the ages of 11 to 13, around the time the time of puberty. They see their mother and older sisters dressed in a particular way and are usually quite pleased to follow their example. It is often viewed as a rite of passage, viewed philosophically as being simply what Muslim women have to do. But ultimately, Muslim women wear a head covering because they want to and would feel awkward or out of place without it. It makes them feel comfortable. The use of nail varnish, make-up and perfume are allowed within terms of modesty, but over-usage is frowned upon.

I was walking down the street and noticed a young attractive woman, who was pushing a buggy, being ogled by a group of nearby builders. She looked embarrassed. I felt so sorry for her. Muslim women are covered for protection from what that young woman experienced.

When men look at me, they look at me as a person and not at my appearance. I choose to look good for my husband. I don't need to impress anybody else by how I dress or appear in public. In Islam, there is differentiation between how a person is externally and internally, with a much greater value placed on the latter. It is the duty of every Muslim mother to teach their sons that when the time comes for them to marry, they must choose behaviour and piety over physical beauty, because outward appearances have never been our principal reason for existing. **Naima**

SEGREGATION

Mosques are generally empty of women. As you will have read in an earlier chapter, one reason for this is that women tend to pray at home, especially if they have young children to look after. But what about women whose children have grown up? Or grandmothers, who are devoid of child-raising obligations? Why aren't they attending the mosque on a daily basis? Is the mosque viewed mainly as a man's place of worship where women are honoured guests? Some women do attend their mosque, mainly for Friday prayers, but the overall number of women who attend is tiny in comparison to the number of men. Women are segregated in mosques and never mix with men. In their own quarters they listen to the imam via an internal loud speaker. Imams claim that the reason that women are kept separate is more for the benefit of men than women, because it is men who are most unable to pay attention to their prayers if distracted by a member of the opposite sex. Is this an old-fashioned and sexist view that should be consigned to history? During the Prophet's lifetime he allowed men, women and children in one section of the mosque for prayers, but he divided everybody up into different categories and rows. The first row was for men, the second for children and hermaphrodites, and the third for women.

> *The Prophet said in a Hadith, 'The best rows for men are those at the front. The worst are those at the back. The best rows for women are those at the back. The worst are those at the front.' (Hadith – Muslim)*

Segregation between the sexes is the norm in mosques across the world, with few exceptions. Babies and very young children stay with their mother, but older male children will accompany their father in the main hall of the mosque. This is not seen as discriminatory or sexist in Islamic circles because it is generally known that women would feel uncomfortable coming into the main hall. On the whole Muslims accept not having as many women coming to the mosque as men. But maybe there is further wisdom behind this, too, as this interviewee pointed out:

> Why men go to the mosque and not women is because the Prophet said that the reward men get is 27 times more than those who pray at home. Women get this reward automatically by praying at home. Women can lead the prayers in their own section of the

mosque in private away from men, but all four Schools of Thought are in agreement against women leading the prayers in male congregations. Also, using a mosque as a social environment is never recommended. Prolonged social interaction between the sexes at the mosque is frowned upon. Segregation also prevents distraction, which is the main wisdom behind this; however, the Prophet did say, 'Do not prevent your women from going to the mosque – although their homes are better for them.'

There is also social segregation required when male visitors come to the home. When males visit a home – particularly those from sub-continent countries – the hostess will prepare delicious food, but when the male guests arrive she will scurry off into another room away from view, so as not to be in the company of male visitors. Traditionally couples never invite other couples to their homes, in order to avoid meeting in this manner. Other cultures, though, may interact more freely, especially those who are Turkish, Egyptian or from North Africa, but the rationale behind Islam's dislike of such encounters relates to the avoidance of adultery. Anything that leads to sexual desires and adultery should be prohibited – therefore men and women mixing in these types of social gatherings is discouraged. Mingling in the workplace and public places is allowed because the same degree of social interaction, which could lead to sinfulness, doesn't occur. **Haider**

The Qur'an gives two further warnings against wilful desires, inappropriate clothing and social interaction between women and men that need careful consideration:

O Wives of the Prophet! You are not like any other women if you are righteous. So be not soft in speech, lest he, in whose heart is a disease, should feel tempted: and speak decent words. (Qur'an – 33:32)

And say to the believing women that they restrain their eyes and guard their private parts, and that they display not their beauty and embellishments except that which is apparent thereof, and that they draw their head-covers over their bosoms, and that they display

not their beauty and embellishments thereof save to their husbands.
(Qur'an – 24:31)

Even the Prophet himself was not rendered exempt from these rules, and had first-hand experience of the need to keep his distance in random situations with women who were strangers.

> The Prophet was travelling on his camel in Medina once when he came across a woman travelling into the city. He offered her a lift on his camel and told her he would take her there. The woman refused and told the Prophet that her husband wouldn't like it and may get angry or jealous if he found out. The Prophet accepted her reason and left the woman to carry on her journey by foot. (Hadith – Bukhari) **Shahi**

YOUNG FEMALE MUSLIMS

I asked some young female Muslims if they felt their generation of Muslims would change the way Muslim women are seen in the world. They were outwardly confident that so much change has already taken place while remaining respectful to previous generations without feeling the need to criticise or blame.

> Modern Muslim women are different to their parents and grandparents. Women with degrees are less likely to take long-term maternity leave other than the statutory amount to raise their child. Although they recognise that careers can be pursued at anytime while your child only grows up once, they are prepared to look at compromises like working part-time. This is in contrast to older generations, who stopped working altogether after they had children. **Mateen**

> Young female Muslims take pride in the way we look. In Arabic-speaking countries, particularly in the Gulf and Middle East,

women tend to wear a lot of black. You also see this in East London. There is nothing in Islam that stipulates that women must wear black. It's entirely their choice, although cultural factors have crept into the equation. My hijabs and clothes are in a wide range of colours and styles. You can be fashionable and modest. And I love shoes! **Heera**

There is a great sense of sisterhood in Islam. Women look out for each other. There are many opportunities for getting together. We often meet at each other's homes for tea parties, when several generations of a family come together. There is a great sense of belonging, being loved and cared for at these gatherings. Everybody knows each other and is kind and protective of each other. There is that lovely feeling of never being alone. **Farida**

There are many examples of how female Muslims are oppressed in Saudi Arabia, Africa and in countries of the sub-continent. In Saudi Arabia there are restrictions for women exercising or going to the gym, because this is viewed as immodest. Dress codes are imposed, with many women forced to wear the hijab or burqa without choice. Female genital mutilation is carried out in barbaric fashion, even though there is nothing in the Qur'an that advocates this practice. Then there is the chauvinistic hierarchy of male-only Sharia Councils and Courts where women are banned from holding positions.

Of course, women need to speak out about injustices to Muslim women, but I think they are too scared. I think Saudi Arabia is the world's biggest bully, which has power over Muslims in the West. They fund many Sunni mosques and because of these financial strings, imams do not speak out and would do anything in their power to prevent others from doing so. But what also needs to be taken into consideration is the alliance between the UK and Saudi Arabia. On one hand we would look foolish challenging them on human rights when on the other hand we are quite happy to sell them arms, which they use to kill innocent Muslims in Yemen. It is hard under these circumstances to speak out against oppression, but I agree that something needs to be done. I think Muslims don't perhaps pay enough attention to it and maybe we should be braver and ask for more media coverage of when Islam is damaged by practices that are not congruent to its teachings. This might help raise greater awareness and shape change for the better.

I think young Muslims in the UK are doing their bit to raise greater awareness and education of what Islam is and what it is not. There is a constant drip feeding of this that has spilled over into social media. I myself have set up an Instagram account for women. I research topics ranging from motherhood and young mothers, to wearing of the hijab and sisterhood in Islam, and have developed a good following for this. I think the tide is definitely changing and that within the next few generations female Muslims will have greater autonomy over their lives. But this will be a gradual process rather than by some revolutionary means that bring instant change. **Raheela**

MOVING FORWARD

Returning to the beginning of this chapter when I questioned if women were treated unfairly in Islam, I can confirm there is nothing in Islamic teachings – either in the Qur'an or the Hadith – which stipulates that women should be treated as secondary to men. Furthermore the Prophet spent his life improving the conditions of women in Arabia. It's a great pity that future generations did not follow his example.

Cultural backwardness and tribal customs in sub-continental countries, taken with them by immigrants to other countries, has much to answer for regarding poor treatment of women. This has often been construed as Islamic, but this is not true. The perpetrators happen to be Muslim, but their practices are cultural and man-made, as opposed to Islamic.

When will things change? I think they are already changing in small measures. It is not unusual to see women writing books about human rights and the treatment of women in Saudi Arabia and other oppressive countries. Further exposure of this kind will go some ways to bringing about change –thanks to women brave enough to speak out about injustice and inequality, and refusing to succumb from pressure to stay silent.

Here in the UK, it is the norm for young women to go to university and pursue professional careers. They are not turning their backs on Islam as a result of this and remain committed Muslims, but they are slowly changing the landscape of the role of women in Islam as lived by their parents and grandparents. The traditional practice of staying at home and raising babies while their husbands go to work is no longer the prevailing scene amongst married couples, particularly those who are second- or third-generation migrants and who have professional careers. Well-educated women have different values, thoughts and aspirations to previous generations, and are not afraid to express them.

Segregation between women and men will continue in Islam under the traditional clergy. There won't be a sudden surge any time soon of women attending mosques on a regular daily basis, although they do attend sometimes for Friday prayers and for special occasions. You will see in a subsequent chapter that arranged marriages are still common practice in Indo-Pak Islam. In the main, there is no strong opposition from women to these customary arrangements, although many steadfastly refuse to be forced to marry someone against their wishes.

The definitive point of determining whether women are poorly treated in Islam must come from educated female Muslims themselves and not be relied upon from perceptions offered by non-Muslims. Overall, it might be reasonable to say that further improvements can be made in countries and cultures where Islam is the main religion of the people. Perhaps, the best way of ensuring these changes is to focus on the Qur'an and to also reflect back on how kind and respectful the Prophet was towards women, and how he fought for their rights long before anybody else ever did.

CHAPTER 5

Sharia Law

There will always be new problems and dilemmas in the world – so if the answer can't be found in the Qur'an or Hadith or if a consensus of the scholars is not available on the matter – then an analogy is determined based on something similar. An example of this is God prohibiting intoxicants. He never specifically went through a list of what these are but Muslims interpret this as a deterrent for alcohol use but it can also be equally applied to illicit drugs (e.g. cannabis, cocaine).

There are some 55 countries in the world that are predominantly Muslim, with only four of these – Saudi Arabia, Afghanistan, Pakistan and Iran – considered Islamic states. Sharia law is considered by traditionalists both a legal code and God's divine law consisting of Islamic scholarly interpenetrations of the Qur'an and the Hadith, which show how the Prophet lived his life and how he preached. Sharia stands for being just and being humane, with many Muslims believing that it provides the best system of judgement for everybody.

The origins of Sharia law can be traced back to when the Prophet lived in Medina. People, including Muslims, Jews and pagans, used to come to him for advice about how to resolve disputes. He would ask them what law they wanted to apply in their case – whether it be Mossiah (law of Moses), or the law of Islam (based on the Qur'an), or whether they wanted him to apply common sense to the situation and judge by that. These days in Islamic jurisprudence, an Islamic judge (known as a qadi), may use a form of 'theocracy' in his decision-making wherein he feels guided by God in his sentencing.

Sharia law is very broad. It regulates public conduct, private behaviour and private beliefs. It covers every aspect of a person's life, for example family matters, worship, marriage and the keeping of the law. Its core essence is about preserving the good practice of Islam, and it holds as key several basic principles that deal with religion, preserving life, marriage, divorce, inheritance, property, politics, economics, banking, business law, contract law, honour, intellect, social issues and the punishment for criminal offences.

Sharia law, in respect to crimes and punishment, is complex and is rarely practised the same in any two countries. All Muslim countries, including the four Islamic states, operate a system of Sharia law courts and secular courts – both for Muslims and non-Muslims.

The Sharia law itself cannot be altered, but the interpretation of Sharia law can be given some flexibility by imams, and this is a reason why it is practised differently in different countries. This situation has led to criticism that in some of the Muslim countries Sharia law has become a state-administered means of cultural control, which does not follow the correct teachings and fails to give people the rights and protections the Prophet had intended. When practised in accordance to the Qur'an and Hadith, Sharia law is deemed just and fair because if there is even the slightest suspicion of wrongdoing or dishonesty on the part of the accusers, the advantage goes in favour of the accused.

A man takes a white jacket to a tailor and asks him if he can dye it black. The tailor tells the man that he will do this, that it will cost £10 and will be ready for collection in a few days. When the man returned to the tailor to collect his jacket, he was shocked when the tailor said to him, 'What jacket? You never brought a jacket in to me to dye.' The man walked away feeling upset.

A few days later, he received a telephone call from the tailor telling him that he had his jacket. The tailor felt terrible guilt for depriving the man of his jacket and that he could not live with his deceit. On first reflection, was this a straightforward case of theft?

In Sharia law, the situation would be explored from different viewpoints before a decision would be made. The true intentions of the tailor would need to be established. Was it his intention to keep the jacket before or after he dyed it? If he decided afterwards, then it would be ascertained that he dyed the jacket for the purpose of the customer's intention and therefore no crime took place. The customer would be asked to pay the tailor £10 for his services. **Dr Ramzy**

TEN KEY FACTS ABOUT SHARIA LAW

1. Sharia is the law of the Qur'an and literally means 'A path to life-giving water'.
2. Sharia is composed of five main branches: adab (behaviour, morals and manners), ibadah (ritual worship), i'tiqadat (beliefs), mu'amalat (transactions and contracts) and 'uqubat (punishments). These branches combine to create a system for society based on justice, pluralism and equality for every member of that society.
3. The Qur'an does not promote any specific form of government, but requires that the form people choose must be based on justice or 'absolute justice' as well as participatory governance.
4. Most Muslims don't want a Sharia takeover. The Qur'an teaches that religion must not be a matter of the state. Sharia is a personal relationship with God.

5. Sharia obliges Muslims to be loyal to their nation of residence.
6. Sharia cannot be forced on others and only applies to Muslims.
7. Sharia law champions absolute freedom of conscience and freedom of religion. For example, the Qur'an goes as far as to oblige Muslims to fight on behalf of Jews, Christians and people of other faiths and to protect their churches, synagogues and temples from attack (Qur'an – 22:41).
8. There is not a single Sharia-compliant nation in the world. All countries with a form of Sharia have ignored the fundamental tenet of justice inherent in Sharia law, and have instead used Sharia as an excuse to gain power and sanction religious extremism. In fact, the most Muslim countries in the world are countries like the UK and America, because they guarantee freedom of religion, freedom of speech, freedom of expression and freedom of thought – all hallmarks of original Sharia law.
9. Islam was the first religion to champion the educational and economic rights of women. The Prophet Muhammad remarked how it was the duty of every Muslim to acquire knowledge.
10. Sharia teaches Muslims to remain united as one community, as that is the best protection against violence and discord, which is why leadership matters.

THE ETHICS OF SHARIA LAW

There are five foundational goals (Maqasid al-Shariah) contained in Sharia law, which is intentionally designed to preserve the following key factors considered necessary to live a decent and honourable existence:

- Religion/Faith (din)
- Life (nafs)
- Lineage/Progeny (nasl)

- Intellect ('aql)
- Property/Wealth (mal)

A Jewish man once accused Ali (fourth caliph and son-in-law of the Prophet) of stealing one of his shields. Ali was innocent of this but there was ambiguous evidence provided to the court, by which the court ruled in the Jew's favour. The man admitted afterwards that he had lied and only brought the case before a Sharia court to test its honour. He was so impressed with its fairness and the fact that the Court sided with him and not Ali that he converted to Islam. **Jamal**

These are the principles that Muslims must adhere to privately and in public to ensure that they are living good, moral lives. Every Muslim is subject to this set of rules and ideals. In essence, these are the principles that separate good, devout Muslims from those who do not practise the faith sincerely. The following outlines the do's and the don'ts contained within the religion:

- Forbidden (haram): Eating pork, eating of food sacrificed to an idol, adultery, fornication, stealing, fraud, rape, using drugs, drinking alcohol, lying, gambling (even buying a lottery ticket), gossiping and slandering, eating animals that prey on other animals, or that die of natural causes, or are killed by strangulation.
- Must be performed (fard): Carrying out the five pillars of Islam (declaration of faith, praying five times daily, fasting during Ramadan, paying Zakat and undertaking hajj if able to afford it). This also involves looking after your parents and obeying them, having belief in the five articles of faith, and raising your children in accordance with the teachings of Islam.
- Despised (makruh): Smoking, eating snails (escargots), eating the meat from in-between cows' hooves, having smelly feet/ socks while in the mosque, eating smelly food and then going to the mosque, not praying on time without a valid reason,

laziness, overeating, over-indulgence in wealth, being too miserly with wealth, having dogs as pets (in the Far East).

- Recommended (mustahab): Additional prayers during Ramadan, giving extra Zakat and making extra fasts outside of Ramadan, sacrificing wealth for the sake of God, spreading the word of Islam to others, performing hajj as a representative of those who may not be able to perform it, reciting the Qur'an, marrying and having children.

- Allowed (mubah): This is wide-ranging and encompassing. Every person can choose their occupation, political affiliation and hobbies and interests according to their inclinations and talents. They are free to choose what type of foods to eat (with the exemption of haram foods). Men are allowed their own choice of clothing and can wear gold jewellery.

THE CRIMINAL ASPECTS OF SHARIA LAW

The Qur'an only stipulates punishment for three crimes – murder, theft and adultery. All other punishments are derived from the Hadith.

Murder

> *O you who have believed, prescribed for you is legal retribution for those murdered – the free for the free, the slave for the slave, and the female for the female. But whoever overlooks from his brother (i.e. the killer) anything, then there should be a suitable follow-up and payment to him (i.e. the deceased's heir or legal representative) with good conduct. This is an alleviation from your Lord and a mercy. But whoever transgresses after that will have a painful punishment. (Qur'an – 2:178)*

The Qur'an (5:32) has the following to say on murder, which illustrates how important it is to protect the sanctity of life:

Because of that We ordained for the Children of Israel – that whoever kills a person – unless it is for murder or corruption on earth – it is as if he killed the whole of mankind; and whoever saves a person, it is as if he saved the whole of mankind. Our messengers came to them with clarification, but even after that, many of them continue to commit excesses in the land. He who kills a soul unless it be (in legal punishment) for murder or for causing disorder and corruption on the earth will be as if he had killed all humankind; and he who saves a life will be as if he had saved the lives of all humankind.

In Islamic countries where Sharia law is practised, the punishment for murder is the death penalty, although this is not automatically upheld for every conviction.

Capital punishment in Arabia during the initial period of Islam was exceptionally rare; in modern Saudi Arabia there are hundreds per year. Such a high frequency itself alludes to the misuse of power and a cherry-picked approach to Islamic law. Such methods do not lead to a greater good and instead allow elitist dictators to suppress and oppress the poor. In Saudi Arabia, European expats are never charged with capital punishment. It's always the poor Pakistani or Yemeni worker. **Jaziba**

Honour killings

These have no basis in the Qur'an but are known to take place in some Muslim families, including the UK, where the action of a family member is thought to have brought shame and disgrace upon a family's honour. This usually occurs as a result of an illicit relationship or sexual indiscretion. Fathers have murdered their daughters, and brothers have taken the lives of their sisters if it is believed they have had sex outside marriage.

Blood money is allowed in Sharia law, provided the victim's family accepts it. But even if they don't and the person is due to be executed, the victim's family can stop it from going ahead at any point, even up until the point the sword is drawn ready to execute, by telling the court that they have forgiven the murderer without requesting any blood money in return. The fact that the murderer had to go through the ordeal believing they were going to be beheaded is sometimes deemed enough for the victim's family to stop the execution from going ahead. They may feel the murderer has suffered enough.

Islam believes it is better to forgive and is more desirable because the victim will receive extra blessings from God as a result. The Prophet never took revenge on anybody; even when somebody murdered one of his daughters he forgave them. He was the perfect example of forgiveness. In poor countries, depending on financial circumstances, other punishments for murder – like a suspended death penalty – can include the murderer being made to promise to look after the children of the victim by ensuring they are housed, clothed, fed and educated up until the age of eighteen. The court can routinely check that the murderer is carrying out his promise and if he is found to have reneged, the court will reinstate the death penalty. **Asif**

Honour killings take place because of the shame and dishonour that young couples cause to their families by having sex before marriage. The woman is seen as soiled. It is better that she and the man that she has had sex with get married. This is the ideal outcome, but is not always possible. Yes, you do hear of cases, even here in the UK, when women have been murdered by their fathers and brothers because of the shame they have brought to the family honour. Parents of these girls know the disrepute will mean that no other man will want to marry their daughter, hence the intense anger this brings.

Honour killings are terribly wrong and only intensify pain and suffering. Thankfully this only occurs in rare cases and is usually carried out solely by male patriarchal types of character. Education around the teachings of the Qur'an can prevent these occurrences. Mosques, too, have a role to play in this, and should consider excommunicating people (a process called takfir) who have fallen below the standards expected from them as means of punishment. **Zahid**

Theft

As for the thief, the male and the female, cut their hands in recompense as a penalty (for what they reaped – a deterrent) from God. God is Mighty and Wise. (Qur'an – 5:38)

This is one of the punishments in Sharia law that is perhaps the hardest to accept and needs modern instead of medieval application. It is here God's cruelty is mulled over and questioned. People question would he really sanction somebody's hand being cut off for having stolen something? Could this crime not be dealt with by some other type of punishment – lashings even? For many people even thinking about amputation in these circumstances is too chilling to contemplate. And yet in some Muslim countries – notably Saudi Arabia – it still takes place. And it is carried out without an 'apology', because those who implement the law view the thief as being worthy of the punishment, because it is something derived directly from God. The opinions of those who see amputation in these circumstances as barbaric and inhumane are simply discarded.

> Sharia brings peace and harmony into society. It covers all aspects of life. Take stealing for example. This is a very bad thing to do. If a thief is caught red-handed stealing money and does not have a just reason, they will be punished by having their hand cut off. Losing a hand is a very bad thing for a person and to some people this may look brutal. But there is a reason why Allah devised this rule. It deters people from stealing.
>
> During a recent trip to Saudi Arabia, I was surprised to see shops left open without any staff in them while they went to pray.

It also proved how trustworthy people are when they know that theft is a bad sin to commit. Having a hand cut off for stealing does not excuse repentance, which must be sought from Allah, and if the person does not intend to steal again, Allah will forgive them. **Haroon**

Some Muslims believe that although amputation of the right hand is a draconian measure for acts of theft, it is also good for society, acting as a deterrent. The crime rate is low in predominantly Muslim countries. Amputations rarely occur and usually only take place in Saudi Arabia because the Sharia judge would want to know why the person stole in the first place; not everybody commits the same crime for the same reason. If, for example, it was proven that a poor man stole to feed his children, then no action would be taken against him. The next interviewee thinks otherwise though.

Amputations occur from time to time and are usually only ever done against a poor person. The corrupt business people get away with theft all the time. Those who are rich and from a high clan: they get away with financial dishonesty. This is not Sharia because it is not fair and Sharia law is supposed to be based on fairness to everyone.

The Prophet made it quite clear that Sharia was about equality in society, and said that even if Fatima, his own daughter, stole something – he'd have her hand cut off. Making an example of a poor person who steals is just propaganda towards Sharia. It is not following Sharia law in the correct way. Lashings would be a more humane punishment. This would act as a deterrent not to thieve. **Masood**

Adultery

The adulteress and the adulterer you shall whip each of them with a hundred lashes. Do not be swayed by pity from dispensing this

punishment in accordance to God's law, if you truly believe in God
and your accountability to him. And let a group of believers witness
their penalty. (Qur'an – 24:2)

Adultery is taken very seriously in Islam. Muslims view it as breaking
down the fabric of society and family life and see it as something filthy,
immoral and dishonourable. Although lashings are the prescribed
punishment in the Qu'ran, there are some Islamic countries, mainly
Saudi Arabia, who go beyond this and have used the death penalty.

During my research Muslims pointed out that the prescribed
punishment for adultery in Christianity and Judaism is much harsher
than the lashings contained in the Qur'an – and one even quoted the
Bible to back up his claim:

> Have the Christians and the Jews deliberately accepted some of
> the Ten Commandments and rejected some? Perhaps you should
> ask a representative of the Anglican Church, the Pope and a
> rabbi where they stand regarding the commandment 'Thou shalt
> not commit adultery.' Is the Sharia of Moses and Jesus exempt?
> According to the Old Testament, Jewish law and morality went
> hand in hand as a deterrent to prevent the committing of the
> crime. Unlawful intercourse with a woman betrothed to another
> man was adultery, because the betrothed woman was deemed as
> inviolable as a married woman. The punishment for this crime
> was as mentioned in Deuteronomy 22:22: 'If a man is found
> sleeping with another man's wife, both the man who slept with
> her and the woman must die. You must purge the evil from Israel'
> – and in Leviticus 20:10: 'If a man commits adultery with another
> man's wife, with the wife of his neighbour, both the adulterer and
> the adulteress are to be put to death.' **Taimoor**

Four witnesses need to testify in a Sharia court that they have actually
seen the adulterous act take place. Hearsay and allegations are not
acceptable, and people found making slanderous comments without
proof risk being punished themselves. There is a requirement for

four trustworthy people of known integrity to have witnessed the act fully from start to end with no doubt about any details or persons involved.

Even though Sharia law is designed only for Muslims, it does not mean that if a person goes to an Islamic country where it is widely practised and commits a crime that they won't be dealt with as severely as a Muslim committing the same offence. For example, if a non-Muslim male commits adultery in Saudi Arabia with a Muslim woman, he could receive the death penalty (hanging), although this has rarely occurred. However, non-Muslim couples who are unmarried and living in countries like the United Arab Emirates have been jailed when the women have become pregnant. **Nadir**

There is a huge difference between religion and culture, and often these are intertwined and this causes confusion to the Western world – and sadly there are not enough liberal Muslims to preach the difference. Stoning to death is an extreme where culture and religion have come together. It is also down to interpretation – many Muslims today are taking the literal meaning of words, not understanding the contexts in which they apply. Also, Islam is perfect, the followers are not, and this is key! **Omari**

LASHINGS

Imagine picking up a newspaper one day and seeing three photographs under a headline relating to a young woman receiving lashes for having had sex outside marriage. You take a closer look at the first photograph and see a male court official standing on a platform that resembles a boxing ring; he is dressed in a brown uniform with a hood over his head concealing his identity. He is the person responsible for administering the punishment, and he is holding a piece of animal hide as he stands prepared to deliver lashings to a young couple who have had sex outside marriage, and who must now receive divine punishment for having committed this sinful deed.

In the photograph, there is a petite young woman dressed completely in white. This includes her headscarf. She is kneeling down in front of the court official in preparation for her beating. Her face is uncovered but she has placed her hands across it, maybe to conceal her identity or humiliation. This makes you imagine how frightened she must have felt, how humiliated, how lonely, how vulnerable and totally hopeless – while a crowd of people, mostly men, gathered around observing the punishment.

The next photograph shows the young woman collapsed after receiving some of the lashes, crouched in pain as two female wardens try to hold her upright so that she can be examined by a doctor to determine whether or not she is strong enough to receive more lashes – or to stop the punishment on medical grounds.

There is a rule that states that the arm of the court official is not allowed to go up high, preventing it being brought down with extreme force, but whether or not this is always adhered to is not clear.

The third photograph shows the young man who had sex with the young woman. He is tall, handsome, with black wavy hair. He is dressed in a green tobe and is being held by two male wardens, each holding one of his arms as he is being led up onto the platform to receive his punishment. His face is not covered but his handsome features are marred by his frightened stare. Like the young woman, he too will receive up to 80 lashes. If either of them was married, the punishment would have been 100 lashes.

Stories and photographs like these have become more regular in the media in recent years. Countries such as Indonesia regularly carry out lashings on young people found guilty of having sex outside marriage. This leads me to wonder how so many of these young people have been found out, given that Sharia law requires a minimum of four witnesses to have seen them having sex, and who are willing to testify before a Sharia court. According to the law, if it is proven that the witnesses have lied, they will also be lashed.

I showed a similar newspaper article, about a young couple who were flogged for having pre-marital sex in Indonesia, to a selection of Muslims and non-Muslims and asked for their reactions and opinions.

Responses from non-Muslims

Beating a woman is an awful thing to do. It seems inhumane and worrying that this still happens in today's world. It's tragic that this happens and that it is seen as entertainment, and it is also hard to comprehend what kind of act would deserve that as a punishment as it should never be done to anyone. **Samuel**

I was horrified to think this was still happening in some parts of the world, under some ancient Sharia law. It belongs back in the past where it started over 1000 years back. It shows how Islam could take precedence over any country that accepts their principles over that country's own laws because of political correctness. Any country that practises this torture should be sanctioned by the UN for allowing this form of brutality. **Janet**

I disagree with any law that allows this type of punishment. I think that religious-based laws should only be allowed if they do not cause physical harm, and only then if the followers of a religion are willing to receive a punishment as part of their own beliefs. It should never be forced onto anybody, whether they are Muslim or part of some other belief or non-belief. I think these punishments portray a version of Sharia law, as practised by some conservative Muslim countries, in a negative light in comparison to Western liberal values. **John**

My initial reaction was one of disgust. As much as I appreciate people's rights to have faith and belief in a religion, this personally highlights to me that religion causes so much upset and segregation. For those who follow this law, they are only assisting in causing a divide in the world. God would not want anybody punished with a whip. I think Sharia punishments are an absolutely horrific and inhumane punishment. **Hayley**

This is barbaric and out of date with current times. I appreciate it's a law attached to a religion, but the world is evolving – society's expectations change, and even things that happened in this country many, many years ago would not happen now. This law and punishment has not adapted through historic change, and therefore must be seen as unacceptable. **Helen**

Responses from Muslims

If the lashes cause pain to that extent then that was not the intention, but it may be the shame that was more painful? However, in a promiscuous world, this act is now rarely seen as a crime, let alone a crime worthy of such punishment. But the misery that illicit sex can cause and the ill effects on society are all too evident. So what is the answer? Should mankind continue on this downward path or do we attempt to prevent it? If it is a crime then it warrants punishment as a deterrent and this is appropriate, but perhaps not to make such a spectacle of it. **Zahid**

I'm a firm believer that Islam is a religion that promotes morality, fairness and justice, and has a set of guidelines that promotes a way of life that prevents promiscuity – while recognising that humans are fallible and need guidance. I feel the West in particular today has broken down the barriers of morality, and promiscuity is rife, causing marriage to be no longer important, other than pictures at a church or a pretty venue.

Islam has laws to prevent social breakdown, including sex outside of marriage. However, before any Sharia judgement is made, a proper trial is required, for which the Qur'an states you need four separate witnesses, and if four witnesses are not brought forward then those making accusations should be flogged.

Rules for flogging include the court official holding a Qur'an under the arm so the strike is not hard, because there should be no tear of the skin. Also, floggings are not to be seen by the public but should be witnessed by a select few to confirm the punishment has been carried out. **Ahsan**

I fear we are becoming a people without respect for those outside of our nation, yet we expect others to recognise our ways of living while completely rewriting their natural order to be deemed as 'acceptable' to living amongst us. It begs the question, why then do we not show such appreciation the other way around?

Why did this punishment occur? We must keep in mind that it is the laws prescribed in the Qur'an and by the Prophet, which are used as a deterrent from immoral or criminal behaviour. It is a reminder that family is of utmost importance, that the institution of marriage is still recognised as a sacred union of two souls, hence the extremely low divorce rates in such states. We cannot allow this to be destroyed by people's promiscuous habits, because if there are no repercussions it is far easier to make a decision to commit these acts. **Faiza**

Allah created Sharia law to prevent great injustice in society. It may look very barbaric but you have to look at the consequences of promiscuity. Sex outside marriage insults the institution of marriage that Allah specially created for everybody. There is a quote in the Qur'an that states: 'Among his signs is the fact that he has created spouses from among yourselves, so that you may find tranquillity with them; and he has put love and mercy between you. In that are signs for people who reflect' (Qur'an – 30:21). And there is another that says: 'They (your wives) are your garment and you are a garment for them' (Qur'an – 2:187). Islam enjoins that a wife and husband should have the most intimate and loving relationship, which can never be had with random sex outside marriage. I believe in Sharia law and would love to live in a country where it is practised correctly because I think it would be so safe to live there. I don't, however, think it is practised correctly in situations like this in Indonesia, because it would be practically impossible to have four witnesses who'll have seen the couple actually having sex. More often than not lashings like this take place as a result of gossip and innuendo, and that is not the correct basis of administering Sharia law. **Kausher**

I agree entirely with the basis of prevention of crime. However, due to the strict penal process in Islam for proving crimes, these types of punishments were seldom actualised throughout Islamic history. There were literally a handful of cases throughout the 20 years of the Prophet's life. Why? Because Islam provides many mechanisms for the prevention of crime at the elemental level. Physical punishments are the last and final measure. So, although I agree with the preventative approach that Islam condones, if lashings were to become commonplace I would not agree with it as this would imply a failed penal system. **Sadia**

SHARIA COURTS

When it comes to sentencing in Sharia courts the onus is on the court judge (the qadi). Qadis are usually male, although change is slowly creeping into Sharia courts in some countries, with Israel being the first to appoint a female qadi in 2017.

The Sharia qadi (judge) first consults the Qur'an for guidance, followed by the Hadith, or they use common sense in cases in which there are no clear precedents to enable them to reach a rational decision. However, for Muslims, Sharia law often presents a tough conundrum. In instances where the law differs between the Schools of Thought – for example, the Hanafi School states there is no punishment for those who commit homosexual acts, but the Maliki School states these acts are punishable by death – Muslims must decide which form of Sharia law they accept. Furthermore, between the various groups of Muslims – Sunni, Shi'a and Ahmadiyya – there is no overall precedent as to how Sharia law should be practised. Differences, like the above example concerning homosexuality, are blamed on questionable elements creeping into the Hadith, because no punishment for this was outlined in the Qur'an.

There are aspects of Sharia law that are seen as crude and outdated. The whole of society has changed, with most of the world having modern rights and values. These were not in place at the time of the Prophet.

I have seen it misused in Iran, especially in areas of employment where there are loopholes in the way it should be practised. Some employers expect employees to work ten-hour days and pay them poorly, with no holiday entitlement. This is in striking contrast to a country where employment legislation has set rules regarding the treatment of workers. However, there are aspects of Sharia law that are good. Lashings for certain offences are better than having to go to prison. Tell me what would you prefer – a hundred lashes or five years in prison? I think most people would endure the physical pain and get it over with rather than going to prison for five years. **Akbari**

There are some other aspects of Sharia law that are controversial, mainly concerning women. Examples include:

- A divorced wife loses custody of all children over six years of age, and of younger children once they exceed that age.

  This sounds harsh given the emphasis placed on motherhood in Islam. It raises the question as to whether this was first put in place for financial reasons, believing that women would not be able to support themselves without a husband. While this might have been the case in the time of the Prophet, it no longer has validity in today's world. It could be viewed as concerning pride, with men believing their ex-wives would remarry and that their children would be raised by another man. The other side of this question is to ask how many single fathers are Muslim. This is a religion that places a high value on marriage, so it is unlikely a male with children will remain single for long. Remarrying will entail his children being raised by his new wife and not their mother.

- Testimonies of four male witnesses are required to prove rape against a woman.

This seems deeply unfair and biased against victims of rape. Where this rule originated is unclear. It isn't found anywhere in the Qur'an and it's inconceivable that the Prophet, who was a champion for the rights of women, would impose such a cruel ruling unless, arguably, there were a lot of women who wrongly accused men of rape.

Equally cruel is that some states, mainly Muslim countries although not exclusively so, insist on victims marrying their perpetrators in the cause of 'protecting their honour', avoiding scandal and unwanted pregnancies. However, change is on the horizon, with some countries like Morocco outlawing this sexist practice.

- A man can marry an infant child and consummate the marriage when she is nine years old. They can enter a contract of marriage (waiting until maturity when she is able to consent to sex).

Today this is very controversial, viewed by many as child abuse and paedophilia. But in the time of the Prophet a man in Arabia was allowed to marry a child, though requested to wait until she started menstruating, around the age of nine, before consummating the marriage. Child marriages are less common now, though they are still practised in remote parts of Pakistan, a country that does not have a legal age of consent between married individuals. In other countries, such as Afghanistan, the minimum age of marriage is nine for girls and ten for boys, which is seen by the Western world as leaving children wide open to all forms of abuse and manipulation.

* * *

There are also various inconsistencies in Sharia law in the areas of blasphemy and apostasy.

Blasphemy

Blasphemy is considered by some Muslims to be so great a crime that it is beyond man to punish, and therefore should be left entirely to God. Being blasphemous towards God is deemed more serious than being blasphemous to the Prophet. Muslims readily point out the story of the Prophet forgiving a man who was blasphemous towards him, and even offered one of his shirts as burial clothes when the man died. That aside, the death penalty is imposed in countries like Pakistan, Malaysia and Indonesia, which take a harsh Sharia view of blasphemy; although most people found guilty of the crime are imprisoned and their sentences extended as means of delaying execution.

Scholars have pointed out that there is no punishment outlined in the Qur'an or Hadith for blasphemy, and they argue that the reason why some countries take such an extreme view of the crime is that they confuse it with treason. There are examples in the Qur'an and Hadith where harsh punishment was administered to individuals who committed treason, betrayal and hypocrisy by pretending to be Muslim.

In February 1989 the Ayatollah Khomeini, the spiritual leader of Iran's 50 million Shi'a Muslims, issued a fatwa (death sentence) on the author Salman Rushdie for blasphemy in his novel *The Satanic Verses*, which had been published a few months previously. Rushdie's novel had apparently insulted the Prophet Muhammad by exploring, in fictional terms, a controversy deeply rooted in Islamic history that some verses of the Qur'an were the work of the devil, although there is no specific evidence to support this claim.

The announcement on Radio Tehran read as follows:

In the name of God the Almighty, there is only one God, to whom we shall all return. I would like to inform all the intrepid Muslims in the world that the author of the book The Satanic Verses, *which has*

been compiled, printed and published in opposition to Islam, the
Prophet and the Qur'an, as well as those publishers who were aware
of its contents, have been sentenced to death. I call on all zealous
Muslims to execute them quickly, wherever they may find them, so
that no one will dare to insult the Muslim sanctions. Whoever is
killed on this path will be regarded a martyr, God willing. In addition,
anyone who has access to the author of the book, but does not have
the power to execute him, should refer him to the people so that he
may be punished for his actions. May God's blessing be on you all.

Around the world there was a mixed response. While some heeded
the call to kill Rushdie, so much so that he was forced for several
years to go into hiding with police protection, many found it an
overreaction that cast a spotlight on a novel that might otherwise not
have garnered so much attention. Sunni Muslims felt affronted that
a Shi'a leader had called for 'all zealous Muslims' to execute Rushdie
and his publishers, considering that Khomeini, who was the leader
of a minority group in Islam, had no moral authority to issue such
a fatwa.

The fatwa against Salman Rushdie was eventually lifted but
fatwas, which are basically religious rulings, still get issued in the
UK and across the world against Muslims who have committed a
misdemeanour. These decrees are expediently handed out by senior
imams to anybody seen to have broken a rule considered contrary
to a teaching in Islam, for example, a woman leading the prayers
or somebody who has deviated from Islamic teaching in terms of
immodest dressing, or alcohol and drug misuse. Admittedly, these
are far less serious than blasphemy. Only the State can issue a fatwa
calling for somebody to be killed for bringing a great shame to Islam.

Apostasy

Some countries, particularly Pakistan, Saudi Arabia and Indonesia,
take a dim view of apostasy – a Muslim abandoning their religion in
favour of another faith. This is viewed as a major aberration and sin,

and the punishment of death is declared upon anybody who leaves. Islamic scholars, however, say that this does not warrant the death penalty, or indeed any lesser punishment, and that Muslims who decide to leave the religion should do so without repercussions. They say freedom of will in religion must be respected, because imposing punishment on anybody who commits apostasy goes against a basic tenet of Islam; it is clearly stated in the Qur'an (as previously mentioned) that there is no compulsion in religion.

There are no statistics that provide a picture of how many Muslims commit apostasy – or of those who have lapsed in their faith and remain 'Muslim' in name only.

There are Islamic channels in English and Urdu where you have programmes on peace talking about killing people for apostasy. They completely ignore or twist the Qur'an, which states there is 'no compulsion in religion'. The truth is there is no punishment for apostasy.

If one of my children left Islam and joined another religion, I would be very sad, but most of all I would be angry at myself for failing as their father to properly make them believe in the religion. If a parent can't instil that in their children, they have failed.

I have also seen arguments on these Islam channels about blasphemy, with some preachers saying that this also should be punished by death. How can anybody consider themselves a peaceful person if they start ordering somebody's death?

But these sorts of programmes make good television. The dollar speaks and as a result there are preachers who are willing to come out with this sort of stuff because they know it will get them noticed. The Prophet never ordered anybody's death for any of these things. People may infer that he did but there is no proof. **Naweed**

I could never understand why I had to believe in the 12 imams or why I had to cut the top of my head each year and be covered in blood when it was Husayn's anniversary. Neither could I understand why people had to dress in black for 40 days to acknowledge their sadness. But they weren't sad. They just had to do what everybody else was doing. And I was just the same. I hated living in Iran. People are so two-faced – lovely to your face but their hearts are full of badness. They see the worst in everybody. They see sin everywhere. They are obsessed by it, and the police and government are so corrupt. If they find you have a girlfriend, they will force you to marry her. They will jail you for drinking alcohol. A woman not wearing a hijab will be stopped and arrested. But getting arrested and being spared jail is easy if you have money. Bribes are expected, almost obligatory.

My first interest in Christianity came through the son of my cousin. I was in their house one day when I noticed a copy of the Bible. I picked it up and started reading it. Something sparked my interest in Jesus, and I began researching him more and more. What he had said and done fascinated me greatly. It was only when I came to England that I was freely able to leave Islam and become a Christian. If I had done this in Iran, they would have killed me. I have found peace in my new religion and do not regret my decision.

My family, except for my mother, disapprove and won't speak to me, or if they do, it is usually in a tense, judgemental manner. But I don't care because that is the price I have paid for my freedom to practise my belief. Having said that, I believe in God the same way I have always done. Since leaving Islam, I have tasted pork but dislike it. My food is no longer halal. I occasionally drink whisky but prefer beer. I have female friends, although I have yet to have sex. I go to church weekly and feel a great sense of peace once I enter the door. On the rare occasion I have missed going, the week has not felt the same. People at my church have made me so welcome and this has increased my sense of belonging here in Britain. Their warmth and friendliness are totally unconditional. **Khazin**

SHARIA COUNCILS IN THE UK

Self-appointed Sharia councils were first introduced into the UK in the 1980s. Currently there are over 85 Sharia councils, which means there is a council in nearly every area with a sizeable community. These self-styled councils act as mediators, resolving disputes between members of the Muslim community, almost entirely in matrimonial matters. The main reasons for divorce in Islam are cultural differences and general incompatibility; bad habits or behaviour in conflict with Islam, for example, the man drinking; family interferences from in-laws; and domestic violence, although this is only noted in a small number of cases.

Financial disputes are also heard in Sharia council settings, but these, like matrimonial divorce settlements, do not have any legal authority. In the case of divorce, the Sharia council looks for a financial settlement by calculating who put what money into the matrimonial property. After a settlement is worked out the couple can go through the official UK court system to be divorced and get their decree nisi. Legal courts usually decide in accordance with the Sharia council agreement, provided it is both reasonable and fair, and both parties agree to its terms.

One criticism of Sharia councils is that only men are allowed to sit on them. Some Muslims have considered that it would be permissible to have women on councils, who may be able to carry out certain duties, such as being advocates for women who appear before the councils.

The overwhelming majority of cases heard by Sharia councils are divorce suits. Some Muslim women have spoken in the media saying that a British civil divorce does not count in the eyes of Islam, and that any woman who embarks on a new relationship will, without also having obtained a divorce through a Sharia council, be committing adultery. This has led to media criticism which claims that the rights and safety of Muslim women in the UK have been sacrificed, with some Sharia councils (which have charitable status) becoming a business, often charging up to £800 per divorce. This has led for calls for stricter regulation as to how such councils are structured within the framework of national legislation, so as to ensure good practice is carried out across the country. Councils that did not adhere to the regulations could then be challenged and fined.

Will Sharia law expand in the UK?

Younger Muslims do not generally appear to be enthusiastic supporters of the implementation of Sharia law, and generally do not support those who advocate its practice.

> Britain is not a Muslim country, so how could we have Sharia law? It wouldn't be possible or fair on the people. Muslims in this country follow the rules of Britain. The rules of this country are good, and Muslims live very good lives here. They are well protected because the laws of this land are fair and decent.
>
> When Muslims apply their own life rules (i.e. their own moral codes of Sharia), they can live in perfect harmony with the judiciary and legal elements. Muslims have the same freedom to make a will in the UK and the State, upon their death, will carry out the wishes of the person, as described in the will. As a result some Muslims have their wills drafted according to Sharia principles. **Hamid**

> There is a vanguard pushing for it in Britain – a small minority who believe that the world should have a single universal legal system. I don't believe in Sharia councils because I feel they are a Trojan horse in our midst.
>
> My greatest fear would be around judgements. Would the Sharia courts use correct Islamic teachings and guidance? We know that the punishments they give homosexuals in some Muslim countries are not correct. We know about the way the punishments are delivered without the mandatory four witnesses for other crimes, and we know that issuing fatwas for blasphemy

is not correct. We know there are cultural pressures put on women to stay in marriages.

I do not trust their judgements because I know them to be wrong. So, the greatest fear for me if Sharia law was expanded to Muslims living in the UK is: would the elders try to impose cultural rules, values and punishments in the name of Islam that have no foundation in Islam?

Strict regulations would have to be imposed on these Sharia courts if they were introduced (even though there isn't the slightest hint that this will ever happen in the UK) because it's like Islamic schools: the government lets them exist without regulations and waits until there is a scandal before suggesting that they should be regulated, which isn't the best way to go around things. You have to ask if it would be the same if Sharia courts were allowed to come into existence.

Very few Muslims are demanding Sharia law in the UK. For those who seek this, you need to look at their lives. They are usually those who are disillusioned with the West. They are politically motivated and hate Western interference in Muslim countries, which they regard as unjust. They also tend to be isolated in their own communities and do not mix easily with non-Muslims. And just like young disillusioned non-Muslim youths who get preyed upon by the far right, these young disillusioned Muslims get preyed on by extremist groups – because it is here, and not in ordinary everyday Muslim communities, that you will find a small number of Muslims who believe that Britain should be an Islamic state. **Tahir**

ISLAMIC BANKING

Muslims seeking to take out a mortgage are more likely to go to a high-street lender than seek a loan from any of the Sharia banks located in major UK cities. This is because, comparing the long-term overall cost of mortgages, Sharia banks are more expensive than mainstream capitalist high-street banks and building societies.

Sharia banking is viewed as a break away from capitalism. Charging interest on loans is banned in the Qur'an because you are not allowed to profit from the need of another. Nowadays, you see loans being given from a rich Europe to a poor Africa with high interest rates payable on them. How can this be ethical?

The Islamic system was intended to be pure and not to charge any interest. Although it holds true to this value and does not charge any interest, the problem lies in high administration fees being applied to loans, which makes taking out these loans more expensive in the long-term than conventional high-street banking. The latter is deemed the lesser of the two evils with those seeking a mortgage. I know I wouldn't take on an Islamic mortgage. I have been advised to steer clear. My friends share in this view.

Islamic banking has failed to impress young people living in the UK. It resembles a square peg in a round hole and can be left open to non-scrupulous practices if left unregulated. It was deemed more attractive to older Muslims, who were often advised – and still are – to avail of this type of banking as recommended to them by imams. But in fairness to Islamic banking in the UK, it needs to be viewed in a more general context. There is no country in the world that adheres fully to Islamic banking. Instead this runs alongside conventional banking in every country. **Khobaib**

CHAPTER 6

Sex, Arranged Marriages and Sexuality

SEX

Sex and Islam can be a contentious subject. In addition to pre-marital sex being a big taboo, every form of intimacy prior to marriage is frowned upon, so unmarried couples must abide by the rules including no holding hands, kissing or touching. Islam is a religion where men as well as women have their own kind of 'hijab' in the sense that the Qur'an advised that men should not ogle but cast their eyes down when they pass a woman. Yet it is also a religion in which celibacy is abhorred, and regulated polygamy permitted. Muslims men can have up to four marriages at the same time, if they have the financial means to support their wives, but the Qur'an says one is best (4:129). Women, on the other hand, as previously mentioned, are only allowed one husband at any one time.

Young people have a difficult time in Islam because they are not allowed to have relationships or to date before marriage. Contact between males and females is usually monitored, which entails a male never being alone in a room alone with a female who is not a relative, and vice versa. Ultimately, Islam strictly adheres to rules about sex that could be considered outdated in today's world.

Imams continuously warn their congregations against lust and illicit desires. I could easily write this chapter and tell you that sex before marriage is strictly forbidden in Islam and try to convince you that the majority of young men and women refrain from all sexual activity before marriage. Some do, but based on the interviews I conducted I can tell you that many Muslims do engage in pre-marital sex, finding the temptation too great not to succumb to.

Young Muslims know that sex outside marriage is not easy to keep secret, and that it is greatly frowned upon in Islamic teachings. Despite strict religious upbringings, young British Muslims are not alienated from modern day culture. Sex is everywhere in society and the media. There is sex education in schools. They are surrounded by peers experimenting with sexual activity. The temptation for kissing, touching and oral sex is too powerful to dismiss, although these acts are seen as secondary and somewhat detached from sexual intercourse.

This situation is far from that of all young Muslim people. For many fear and guilt either prevent or put a stop to sexual experimentation, Islamic teachings never being far from their minds. The experiences of others vary. Overseas students coming to the UK sometimes avail of sex with 'white girls' as a coming-of-age experience, treating them with distain and disrespect and are often boastful about the number of conquests they make during their time in the UK. Young refugees and asylum seekers are usually very surprised by the culture they encounter upon arrival in the UK, perhaps having previously seen few women in their lives without a hijab. They see women in revealing modes of dress they have never previously experienced, resulting in testosterone-fuelled young men becoming curious to experiment sexually and seeking outlets to do so. Because sex outside marriage in Islam is sinful, a lot of sexual activity is secretive. The guilt of disobeying Islamic teachings is often comforted, at least in the short term, with the justification that God will forgive these human weaknesses.

MASTURBATION

Ask any imam if masturbation is allowed and most likely they will tell you that it is wrong and not permitted – but not everybody in their congregation might agree.

Masturbation is natural. Isn't it reckoned to be not healthy not to do it? It doesn't hurt anybody. Having sex before marriage is the difficult part. I broke up with my girlfriend when the time came for us to have sex. I couldn't go through with it. We did things to each other, but I couldn't bring myself to have full sex with her because of my upbringing in Islam. Masturbation is different though. It is my only outlet until I get married. I don't think Allah is that bothered whether men or women masturbate because, as I said, it's not hurting anybody. I also think masturbation should be allowed to those who marry late in life, for example a man who does not get married until he is in thirties will need this outlet. **Bashir**

It's a sin. Men who masturbate are killing the souls of human beings. The sperm is wasted when instead it could be used to impregnate women. Masturbation draws men away from their maker. God is clean. Masturbation is dirty. The Prophet recommended that men control their hormonal desires by fasting. I do this, as well as engaging in football and other sports, which helps me to calm my hormones down and to avoid feelings of fornication. It's best to use your physique in meaningful ways rather than useless ways, so it's important to keep busy with school, football and praying. **Amir**

Masturbation isn't allowed in Islam. The Prophet viewed it as an act of self-harm and it leads to having even more sexual desires than would be usual. The thing non-Muslims need to know about Islam is we see the problem from the beginning. We don't let the problem grow. We don't tend to prolong sexual desires to the point that they become harmful to us. We get married early, because that way we don't veer off the main path – which prevents opportunities and temptations to have sexual relations that are sinful. This is deemed the best way. Everybody has urges and desires. It's only natural. That's the nature of human beings. But life is a test. God is merciful, though, to those who fail the test, provided the sinner shows remorse and repents. **Khalid**

* * *

Thinking about the dilemmas faced by young Muslims left me wondering if, by Western standards, unconventional attitudes towards masturbation, as well as being expected not to engage in sex before marriage, lead to frigid and sexually repressed young men and women. It also led me to question if young people feel pressured into entering marriage at the earliest convenience, even an arranged marriage, so that they can experience sex.

I didn't have any girlfriends before I got married. I was friends with girls, but this just meant being friendly with them at college and later when I started working. I did not want to try and see or date girls because I knew nothing could ever happen between us. And that was not just Muslim girls, because I knew I could never bring a non-Muslim girl home to meet my parents. Marrying somebody outside Islam would have been considered unthinkable in my family. The advantage of not having had girlfriends before I married is that my wife is the only woman I have slept with and there is absolutely no jealousy between us. We both invest in our marriage. Of course, I know of Muslims who secretly date and have sex with lots of girls before they get married. So much of this goes on – but mainly in secret though, shielded from family scrutiny. **Suleman**

I don't go to parties and I avoid girls. Of course I want to get married one day, but I will only do that when I am ready to make that commitment. If I were to meet a girl I liked, I would make an appointment with her father to ask his permission to meet his daughter.

Dating is permissible in Islam, but this should be done in a controlled environment, like meeting the girl in her home but keeping the room door open so that a parent or other family member can supervise. There is a Hadith which states that whenever an unmarried man and woman are alone in a room together there is a third 'person' present, i.e. Shaytan, the devil, who is ready and waiting to tempt them. I wouldn't enter into any marriage blindly because I would also need to get to know the parents of the girl I was interested in marrying. I would need to be satisfied that they were of good character and that they had a good relationship with God. **Akram**

Some young men can't control themselves. They will have sex before marriage – especially those who convert to Islam. This would be common for them to have pre-marital sex. Men come to me with their problems, be it an addiction to pornography, or occasionally when somebody has contracted a sexually transmitted disease. I advise them on how to discontinue immoral sexual practices by avoiding temptation as best as possible. Sometimes, this might include telling a man to marry the woman he is having sex with, if he has become emotionally attached to her. I have also married a small number of Muslims to non-Muslims and they have ended up being very happy together. **Imam Begum**

* * *

Marriage is seen as fulfilling a major duty in Islam because the Prophet according to Hadith equated marriage as half the religion. Therefore it is seen as a duty for every Muslim to marry, and those who don't are severely frowned upon. Muslims believe that sex should always be behind closed doors. All types of intimacy should be in the bedroom and should never be done in front of anybody. There are other guidelines about physical contact including not giving a kiss or a hug to anybody of the opposite sex who is not a family member.

Some Muslims also said that this is also to show respect for women as well as preventing any type of elicit sexual arousal.

Males are allowed to marry once they are physically, mentally and financially prepared for the task. Most, after the age of 18, are mentally prepared to take on the responsibility of a family, though the man should have the financial means to support his wife and children. Although sex is allowed to be enjoyed in Islam, it's often seen in terms of procreation, not pleasure, with couples often praying for God to grant them a righteous child. Some also pray before sex, requesting that there are no complications during sexual intercourse.

Islam doesn't frown upon sex. Maybe some Muslims do but that is a separate issue. Islam expects people to be responsible and not to engage in either pre-marital sex or sex outside of marriage.

Yes, there are some Muslim males who will have sex before marriage. Some might even say this is quite prevalent. Those who do have pre-marital sex either don't know the rules or choose to ignore or reject the teachings. Unfortunately, those who don't observe the rituals of Islam give it a bad name. Ultimately, Islam encourages marriage and procreation. It expects people to be responsible in their sex lives.

Humans are naturally built to have sex. To suppress that would result in more damage than good. Muslims are generally socially conservative people, and some, both men and women, find it difficult to integrate with members of the opposite sex. That is why many participate in arranged marriages or avail of a marriage introduction agency attached to their local mosque.

There is nothing which suggests that Muslims who have not had sex prior to marriage are disadvantaged. There are many books available to Muslims written by Islamic clerics that explain how to sexually satisfy your partner. **Mobeen**

While there is nothing in the Qur'an to prohibit contraception, it is still not routinely allowed in Islam. Some orthodox Muslims frown upon its usage because they feel it devalues the natural process of a married couple having children at God's will. There are other Muslims, particularly younger ones, who ignore or disobey the traditional guidelines. Contraception is only supposed to be allowed though in the following circumstances:

- A woman is physically weak and would be unable to sustain pregnancy.
- A woman is away from home on a journey with her husband for a lengthy period.
- When there is discord between the husband and wife and divorce seems likely.
- There is fear of older siblings being subjected to any form of difficulty if another child is born.
- There is a need to space out children in order to give them adequate and equal attention.

ARRANGED MARRIAGES

Arranged marriages are still commonplace in Muslim communities with the greater majority of people meeting their spouses this way.

I'm an accountant and I got married recently. I was 28 and it was an arranged marriage that had been several years in the planning. I think I was about 25 when I asked my parents if they would help me find a suitable bride. They told me they had somebody in mind who might be suitable.

My parents and I travelled to meet the girl and her family. Men were placed in one room and women in another room. I was a little nervous, but I was made to feel at ease from the beginning. The girl's father talked about life in general along with some politics and sport, and asked me questions about my job.

Over the course of the first half of the evening – even before I had actually seen my then-prospective bride – I made up my mind that I would marry her simply because I thought they were such a lovely, warm and welcoming family. Luckily, when I met the girl, we liked each other.

The only contact we were allowed to have before the wedding was via text messages and phone calls, but that was only after the engagement. Before that, it was no contact other than when I visited her house or when she visited my house, always with both our families present. The meetings were purely to get to know her and her family, and to assess our compatibility. **Arif**

I asked Arif to tell me three advantages and three disadvantages of arranged marriages.

Advantages:

1. The potential spouse will be of the same religion and community so therefore will essentially be pre-approved, whereas if you were to find your own spouse there is a chance you would meet someone who does not share the same belief system as yourself. It would potentially be very difficult to find a partner who is of the same religion, as that would rarely be the first thing you would ask when you met someone.
2. With arranged marriages, the whole family unit is part of the process. This means you don't need to introduce your spouse to your family as it's already happened through the process.
3. With our arranged marriage, because it was set up through our parents, it meant we didn't have to do anything! Everything from initial meet-up to engagement preparations was handled by parents. All we had to do was decide whether or not we wanted to pursue the marriage.

Disadvantages:

1. It's difficult to really get to know the potential spouse when family are always around.

2. There may be added pressure from family members to rush into decisions. Luckily for us, that wasn't the case – both sets of parents left the choice up to us.

3. There is always a risk that personalities change drastically after the wedding, and this may not be within your expectations.

I think the age of 25 to 26 is the optimum time to get married. My parents will probably talk to me about marriage after I've graduated. More likely than not, I will get married to someone from Pakistan. But let me clear up a misconception here. My parents will probably choose a girl that they like for me, but they will not force me to marry her if I don't think she is compatible. Hopefully, whomever they chose will be to my liking. I want to be able to please my parents because Islam places great emphasis on respecting your parents and elders. But they wouldn't want me to be unhappy and therefore they would understand if I rejected the girl they chose for me to marry.

There is of course nothing that prevents me from finding a girl myself and taking her to my parents for approval. However, if they disapprove, I would be sad but would let her go, because to do otherwise would be disrespectful to them. I know my parents would choose a well-educated girl for me. There are many of them in Pakistan who speak good English because they have gone to good schools and have been well educated. They are also more Westernised than previous generations and know more about other countries and faiths. This leads me to think that whomever I marry will not have too many difficulties integrating into the British way of life. **Maqbool**

I'm 19 and got married recently. I married the son of my mother's childhood best friend. It was an arranged marriage. I wanted to get married young and had asked my parents to find me a husband. After I was introduced to my husband for the first time, I wasn't sure that we were suitable for each other and told my parents that

I had changed my mind. Then I changed it back again and allowed myself to get to know him better.

He was still living in Pakistan, but we were allowed to Skype each other. He spoke very good English and was well educated, having completed a degree in engineering. Over a period of six months we continued to get to know each other, before deciding to get married. I think my husband has integrated well living in the UK. He was totally supportive and relaxed about me wanting to go to university. We are now in love and very happy together.

I am so much luckier than one of my friends, whose parents practically pushed her to marry. They arranged for her to meet a man they wanted her to marry. She wasn't keen on the idea but went ahead with their plans by meeting the man in a restaurant for a meal. Her father and brother sat at another table close by to keep an eye on them while her mother sat outside on a windowsill. My friend didn't like the man and refused to marry him.

Young Muslim women are becoming strong in their opinions these days and won't accept things in the way their parents and grandparents did. We would never tolerate meeting your husband for the first time on your wedding day. I have heard of horror stories of women from previous generations going to the airport and meeting their husband and then being taken to marry them later that day. This was totally lunacy, but having said that, women stuck it out and the divorce rates were much lower than today. But times have changed. The concept of forced marriages or marrying somebody at short notice wouldn't work now. Values have changed so much. Women are far better educated now.

Islam permits us to marry our first cousins, known as consanguinity marriages, because this is something the Prophet allowed, but far greater awareness around the risks of genetic conditions are taken into consideration these days. Women go and have genetic testing beforehand for advice on the risks of their children having a disability if they were to go through with the marriage. Common sense is also prevailing, whereby families know that marrying cousin after cousin within the same family network is not a good thing. **Saba**

ISLAMIC MARRIAGES

Islamic marriages are not recognised in the UK or Europe under civil law. Muslims can get married under Islamic law (known as nikah) in the UK, but if they do not also marry under civil law, their union will not be legally binding under the Marriage Act 1949. This leaves couples, women in particular, vulnerable in matters of divorce settlements, being unable to argue their case in a court of law. As a result, women often fear homelessness and loss of assets, and can be left with little power to escape an abusive or unhappy relationship.

Several Islamic marriages take place in the UK each year where couples do not follow the ceremony with a civil law marriage. There is nothing to stop a male Muslim from marrying up to four times in Islamic ceremonies, although the law of the UK does not recognise Islamic marriages, and only allows for one wife under its civil law.

The nikah religious ceremony is not recognised under UK law, and large numbers of women believe they are protected by the law when sadly they are not. As a result, women and children suffer disproportionally to men when these 'marriages' fail, leaving partners with little or no financial settlement.

There is concern regarding Islamic marriages about the use of the word 'talaq'. If a man says this word three times to his wife, which means 'I divorce you', then they must divorce. Women, too, are allowed to divorce their husbands – this is known as 'khula' – but if they do so they must repay him the dowry they were given; however, if it's the man who chooses to divorce, then the woman keeps her dowry. Implementing the word 'talaq' three times is now prohibited in Pakistan and is subject to review in India, where Islamic marriage is recognised by the state. Men have been known to use the word in a fit of temper, only to regret it later.

INTERFAITH/MIXED MARRIAGES

Mixed marriages are allowed in Islam, although Muslims are usually only allowed to marry 'People of the Book', meaning they must be either a Christian or Jew, or members of faiths who believe in the same God – as opposed to, for example, a Hindu or Sikh.

However, Orthodox Muslims are against women marrying outside their faith to people of other faiths. There appears a fear – a myth – that if a Muslim woman marries a Christian, for example, that her husband will force his religion upon her, although evidence of this happening remains unclear. Others fear women marrying outside Islam will prevent them from retaining an Islamic family surname and therefore will affect the progeny of the offspring. It is acceptable, although not always met with approval, for Muslim men to marry women from other faiths who believe in God. Wives, in this instance, are not required to convert to Islam, but the expectation is for children produced by the marriage to be raised as Muslim.

This is understandably a difficult task when the children's main caregiver is not Muslim, so women in this situation usually convert to Islam, either before or after they marry. Liberal Muslims on the other hand take an altogether different view. They say the Qur'an does not state that there is anything wrong in a Muslim female marrying a non-Muslim. During my research for this book, I was invited by a liberal imam, Dr Taj Hargey, to witness him conducting a wedding ceremony between a female Malaysian Muslim to a Finnish Christian. His requirements for marrying the couple were that they both believed in one God, one humanity and one destiny. During the ceremony, various verses from the Qur'an were spoken including these:

Surely, all those who believe, and the Jews, and the Christians, and the Sabians, whosoever believes in God and the Last Day and does good deeds, they shall have their reward from their Lord, and there is no fear for them, nor shall they grieve. (Qur'an – 2:62)

O Humanity, We created you from a single male and female and made you into different peoples and tribes so that you may know and recognise one another and not despise each other. Verily, the most honourable amongst you in the sight of God are those who are pious and righteous. Surely, God is all-Knowing and all-Aware. (Qur'an – 49:13)

Surrounded by family and friends, Dr Hargey wished the couple a lifetime of happiness, harmony and good health – a life where the husband is not the boss of his wife but where they would be equal partners: a life where love and laughter were ever-present. The couple were encouraged to never stop touching each other intellectually, emotionally and spiritually.

After the ceremony we all sat down to a beautiful meal where alcohol was allowed for non-Muslims. There was a relaxed and easy atmosphere in the room, which saw two cultures merged together in mutual respect. Integration is mentioned several times in this book, but for me this wedding and the coming-together of Muslims and non-Muslims was the best example of what it should look like – the retaining of cultural identity while associating with people whose cultural identity and faith are different. What I saw was respect and acknowledgement of differences, but at the same time everybody got on well with each other and enjoyed themselves.

Interfaith marriages are on the increase in the UK. Muslim women are incredibly well educated and are doing far better at university than some men, and are going up the career ladder. Many are doctors, barristers, dentists, teachers or architects. They find it difficult to find a husband that matches their income and social standing. Some marry men who they have been to university with or who they have met at work. Their personalities just click and this leads to love. Of course, this goes against the grain, and many other Muslims disapprove of this type of union, without considering the facts.

Take 100 postgraduate Muslim women and 100 random Muslim men. Out of these 100 men, 25 will be in prison (mainly for petty crime as opposed to extremism), 25 will have low-paid jobs (shelf stackers, workers in take-away shops or taxi drivers), 25 will be 'players' (i.e. inveterate womanisers) – and the remaining 25 will be postgraduate professionals.

So what does this mean? Well, 25 fortunate women will meet 25 eligible fellow Muslim professionals and they will be able to get married. That's great; however, it leaves 75 women who will not be able to marry the 75 ill-suited men for the reasons given. This is a huge problem. That's the stark picture of what is actually the reality of the current situation. Other Muslims will not tell you this.

Muslims on the whole dislike washing their laundry in public – and would never discuss this with a non-Muslim – but equally many are in denial of the situation or feel it is disloyal to talk about difficult issues in Islam, as if they were being disloyal to the Prophet. By not discussing issues and not being open they are hypocrites who are preventing change and improvements. If anything, the Qur'an (4:135) advises against hypocrisy: 'O you who have believed, be persistently standing firm in justice, witnesses for God, even if it be against yourselves or parents or relatives. Whether one is rich or poor, God is more worthy of both. So follow not (personal) inclination, lest you not be just. And if you don't distort (your testimony) or refuse (to give it), then indeed God is ever Aware of what you do.' **Dr Hargey**

Families play a big part in mixed marriages. It really comes down to individual families and how educated they are. My mother is a doctor and my father an engineer. I was lucky that my family are practising Muslims and are open-minded people. They follow the Qur'an, which clearly states that Muslims can marry People of the Book. Disagreements only occur when there is a lack of knowledge of Islamic teaching. I come from Afghanistan, where a high percentage – maybe up to 70 per cent of the population

– is poorly educated, both in their religion and in non-religious academia. I came to Britain when I was 17. I am not ashamed of my story. I arrived as an asylum seeker from Kabul under the bottom of a lorry. I spoke hardly any English. My wife, who is a year older than me, was my next-door neighbour at the time. Because I spoke little English I used to ask her to help me with things. She was always helpful and over time we became good friends. She stood out from others on the street where I lived. Others used to mock me because of my accent or tease and try to fool me because of my lack of English, but my wife always took time to explain things properly. Eventually, I asked her to be my girlfriend. Within six months of meeting her, we got married – first by an Islamic marriage ceremony followed by a registry office marriage two years later. We went on to have six children and have always been very happy together. I am an extremely lucky man.

Some speak of overcoming cultural difference when they arrive in a new country, but fail to acknowledge what they went through before they came here, or indeed their journey in getting to safe territory. You realise that when you live through an ordeal of this kind, you are ready for any challenge. So adapting to a new country and culture was easy for me. I love Britain and feel totally at home here, although I wasn't too fond of the food when I first arrived! But that has changed. My wife and I keep everything balanced. She likes British food so we split the menu in our house with a combination of English dishes and continental dishes. We often dine out with her family. They are very considerate people, and since my wife converted to Islam, they always suggest that we go to halal restaurants for meals.

My wife decided to convert to Islam about four years after we were married. At first she wasn't keen to embrace Islam and that was fine with me. As a Muslim, I was always straight with my wife because for the relationship to work I always believed in honesty. We had come to a mutual agreement that our children would be raised as Muslims and that pork would never be eaten in our house. But over time my wife became interested in Islam without me persuading or forcing her into anything that she didn't want. In fact, her conversion was fuelled by interest that her family showed in the religion. We had lots of discussions and debates about Islam with her father and other family members. I love my children dearly. The older ones are fluent in English and in my language – Persian. The youngest is two years old. None of the children were planned. They just came as God had intended; however, before my youngest was born, my wife commented to me one day that she missed the sound of a baby crying in the house. So as you can imagine, one thing led to another (at this point Abdul smiled warmly) and we had another baby. **Abdul**

HOMOSEXUALITY

Many Muslims simply refuse to face up to the facts with regard to homosexuality and their faith. They fail to consider that when the Prophet first founded Islam he had around 100 followers, most of whom were men. Amongst this group several would have had homosexual desires. Yet there has always been an intrinsic, it must be assumed, denial that there are gay Muslims, resulting in the majority of LGBT Muslims living in fear of coming out to family and friends, fearing that this could result in violence, unwanted medical consultations, or being forced into marriage. Lives are therefore often lived in fear and in secret. Is this really necessary? Gay and lesbian Muslims I have spoken to have told me that there are no verses in the Qur'an that unambiguously condemn homosexuality. It is therefore considered that reports from the Hadith that denounce homosexual and transgender people are of dubious authenticity.

Sarder (2012) points out that in the Prophet's household his wives had male servants who were effeminate. There were eunuchs and gender-ambiguous men within his circles and who attended his mosque. As mentioned already there is also no evidence that the Prophet ever adjudicated a case involving homosexual intercourse, such that Sharia courts have based their 'Fiqh' (expert in Islamic law) judgements on the opinions garnered from the Prophet's companions or later generations of moralists.

How do Muslims reconcile being gay and being Muslim without constant guilt? Ali (2016) states that some Muslims leave Islam entirely, while others choose to separate sexuality from religion, considering themselves to be Muslim but acknowledging that their sexual acts are not acceptable in Islamic ideology. Furthermore, the fear of recognition and retribution are deemed too great to remain within their communities.

On the other hand, there are no self-proclaimed gays in Muslim-majority countries. In many Muslim societies, gays are comparatively free to do what they like, provided they do not publicly assert their homosexuality.

The Prophet Lot and homosexuality

Great importance is placed on the story of the Prophet Lot (referred to as 'Lut' in Islam). In the Qur'an Lot was the nephew of Abraham and, like him, a sheep herder. They left Egypt and went to the city of Sodom, on the western shore of the Dead Sea. The city was deemed an evil place because of robberies and murders routinely taking place. It was also considered an immoral place where men had sex with men instead of women. God asked Lot to tell the people of Sodom to give up their indecent behaviour, but their sexual practices were so entrenched this proved difficult. Lot even offered his daughters to men who came to his house inquiring after some male visitors who were staying at his house. Homosexuals are often referred to in Islam as Lot's people. With regards to Lot and homosexuality, the Qur'an covers this in many chapters, including: 7:80–84; 11:77–83; 11:88–95; 15:51–77; 26:160–175; 27:54–58; 29:24–35.

The majority of Muslim countries have anti-homosexuality laws. There are five countries where sodomy is punishable by death (Iran, Saudi Arabia, Sudan, Yemen and Mauritania) although no such executions have reportedly been carried out since the early 2000s. Predominantly Muslim countries where lengthy prison sentences are imposed for homosexual acts include Algeria, Kuwait, Lebanon,

Libya, Morocco, Oman, Qatar, Somalia, Tunisia, Syria and Bahrain, where sentences of ten years or more are passed.

It's interesting to reflect that up until the 1960s, gay men who were persecuted for their sexuality in Europe often went to countries like Morocco, where they could freely express themselves. Another irony is found in Iran, which carries out more gender reassignment surgeries each year for transgender people than any other country apart from Thailand. However, all trans people in Iran are 'forced' to have surgery, whether or not that is their wish. Ignorance of the differences between trans and gay people prevails in Iran; sometimes if gay people are found having sex they are instructed to have gender reassignment surgery to avoid risking execution.

In 2009, a Gallop poll looked at European attitudes towards homosexuality amongst Muslims. It found that 35 per cent of Muslims in France found homosexuality to be 'morally acceptable', against 78 per cent of the general public. Nineteen per cent of German Muslims considered it acceptable as opposed to 68 per cent of the general public. In the UK, none of the Muslims interviewed admitted to finding it acceptable, against 58 per cent of the general public who did (the Gallup Coexist Index, 2009).

In 2017, a survey commissioned by Channel 4 television amongst a random sample of 1081 Muslims found that 18 per cent of British Muslims agreed that homosexuality should be legal, as opposed to 52 per cent who disagreed (Channel 4, 2016).

> My family ignore that I am gay because in Palestine being gay is a crime. I couldn't be myself in front of family members; I'm always trying to live someone else's life to protect myself. I'm not happy in my life and am trying hard to keep my real me closed and secretive, because I trust nobody.
>
> In real life, I don't have LGBT friends, but on social media I have many. We exchange our experiences and we try to support each other. In my country we don't have the chance to meet LGBT people without the fear of being caught. In my society they judge

you about the way you look, your clothes style and even the way you speak. So we don't have the freedom to have LGBT friends in public.

Islam is strictly against being gay, but I really believe that it's not my fault that I'm gay. I don't have a problem with Islam. I'm not expecting to see change in the way it views LGBT people, but I really hope the Muslims become open minded and at least try to accept others without judging them. **Faisal**

Here are some entrenched views from non-LGBT Muslims.

Procreation is between a man and a woman

In Pakistan, it is not the tradition to openly talk about this type of issue. I was 19 when I came to live in Britain and had to ask a friend about the meanings of 'gay' and 'lesbian'. He laughed and asked how it was possible that I didn't know.

My mind has never been drawn towards these things. I believe God gave us sexual organs for procreation and anything that doesn't match with this is going against nature. Same-sex relationships are not about desire. I think there has to be something not right in their lives to have these issues.

I would ask the person to remain busy to keep their minds away from having these types of desires; if they didn't like my instructions, I would pray for them because when all is said and done what they are doing is between them and Allah, and not for me to become their judge. **Mazin**

It's bad for society

Being gay is part of a dirty lifestyle. If all men were gay they wouldn't have had the opportunity to come into the world and neither would the next generation. I believe being gay is against God, the Qur'an and Hadith. If somebody told me they were gay,

I would follow the advice of the Prophet in such matters. First you advise the person against such activity and draw their attention to the Qur'an and Hadith. Hopefully, the person would change but if they didn't, the Prophet said that you should pray for the person thereafter, because there is nothing else you can do. **Razia**

Condemn the act and not the person

There is a general abomination for gay sex acts in Islam, as opposed to gay people. Every young man should be given a copy of the Qur'an and given tuition on why it is forbidden. People often have debates and question if homosexuality is caused by nature or nurture. I believe it is caused by nurture, because nature is not responsible for people to automatically become gay; rather I feel it has more to do with society and the way people are raised. It has become difficult to publicly speak about it these days unless you wish to risk being called a homophobe, which stifles debate. I dislike nastiness towards gay people though. This is totally uncalled for. I was friends at school with somebody who was gay. Others were abusive to him and called him a 'poof', but I could never do that to him because I felt sympathy for him. **Dinar**

Between the person and God

Punishment lies with Allah. The punishment lies with God and not man because God is merciful first and foremost. I heard a story about the Prophet once who recalled a story about a prostitute. One very hot day the woman was out walking and she saw a dog dying from thirst. In order to save the dog's life, the woman took off a stocking and went to the well where she filled the stocking with water and allowed the dog to drink from it, saving its life in the process. This one kind deed was enough to forgive the woman for her prostitution and saved her from hell. (Hadith – Muslim) **Idris**

* * *

Group questions and answers

This was a scenario that I presented to a group of young Muslims to test their reaction:

'You have a friend – he's 20, lives at home with his parents and siblings, attends college and likes sports. On the surface everything looks okay. But your friend has a secret. He's struggling with his sexuality and is frightened that his family will find out. To complicate things even further, he has fallen in love with another male at college.'

Here were some of their responses:

1. I would ask what happened to him, especially as our upbringing would have been similar. What happened to make him like this? Should he not know as a Muslim that this is wrong? I would ask him why he was betraying us. I think our friendship would suffer.
2. I always think logically. I would be thinking how I could help to fix him. I would ask him, do you believe in Islam and do you believe in God? I would ask him if he felt he was born this way or if he created it.
3. I don't know much about homosexuality. I have never known a gay person. I honestly wouldn't know what advice to give to him but would direct him to the imam for some guidance. I think I would carry on being his friend though.

What advice would you give to somebody
who was Muslim and gay/lesbian?

Islam supports the right of every human being; we value everyone – regardless of gender, ethnicity, religion or sexuality. So if there was someone who was Muslim and gay I would say, first and foremost you are human and you have morals – be good to the world, your relationship with God is your own. Also, it should be noted, Islam despises the act of homosexuality, not the individual – and that can be checked against the Qur'anic verses. **Jahiz**

We are told it is forbidden and I agree that we should stay with this biased view because it is the general view of the Muslim population. We don't target gay people. We leave them to their own devices, but Muslims believe that family is one of the most important things in our religion.

I do not think that Muslims should judge gay people by something they are doing. Just like the Prophet Muhammad once said, you should not hate alcohol, just the effects of alcohol; you should not hate gay people, and it is just their sexual behaviour that's wrong. There is no compromise for gay people in Islam. They have to either change their behaviour or leave Islam. The religion is quite clear on this. **Ehan**

If somebody came to me and told me they were gay, I would advise him against this decision. It is a sin just like gambling; being an alcoholic and committing adultery are sins. I would ask him the reasons why he has chosen this and encourage him to leave it behind, but ultimately this is something that is between Allah and the person. As an imam, I cannot stop him from being a Muslim. I would not refuse him coming to pray in the mosque, but neither would I hold back from telling him that it is bad to be homosexual. **Afsa**

What advice would you give to a Muslim in a same-sex
relationship but who still attended the mosque
and joined in prayer with other Muslims?

The person should struggle with themselves to repent for good and not to return to practise it. They may fail a couple of times, but they should not give up. They would benefit highly by conducting regular daily prayers, while asking Allah almighty to help them stop falling into this desire. They would need to avoid seeing their partner and avoid attending places or shops that may stimulate their attraction to their bad desires. They also need to make friendships with new people who are straight. **Fadi**

Tell me what you would do if somebody came to you
in the mosque and told you they were gay?

Having feelings of homosexuality is okay. I accept that people may be born that way. But gay people must suppress their feelings. This is the vital point in Islamic teachings and that is to not act on homosexual feelings.

If somebody came and told me they were gay, this would be a good thing. It would show that they have guilt and that they are acknowledging that something is wrong. I can work around that, as opposed to them having no remorse and loving how they feel. That way there is nothing I can do to change that love. But when they are unhappy about how they feel I can help them to repent and to change. I can tell them that a man was not created for another man. I can give them practical advice on how to live their life to free themselves from their affliction. They need to avoid bad company and environments that would lead to a sin. They need to avoid other gay people so that this removes temptation, and not go to places where they will get aroused. They also should try to get married. **Jawarin**

Here are life stories of gay and lesbian Muslims.

Ejel

My story is typical to that of many other gay people. I realised I was attracted to men around the age of 13. I kept my feelings to myself and although I suspected my parents and sisters had guessed my sexuality, it was not until around the age of 30 when I actually told them. My sisters were fine with it but I experienced a muted response from my parents, who I would describe as socially conservative Muslims.

I come from a working-class family, and I'm third generation Muslim living in Luton, Bedfordshire, from a Bangladeshi and Pakistani background. I've attended the same mosque all my life and have told the imam, whom I have known for many years, that I was gay. He appeared fine with it and blessed me, but added a few words of advice before asking me to never talk publicly about it. But this isn't always possible because of my LGBT activist work in London, which sometimes attracts media attention.

I would estimate that 200 people out of a congregation of 1000 that attend my mosque know that I am gay. Most of these have known me all my life and are either people I went to school with and/or who know my family. Although I never discuss my sexuality with them, I know they accept and respect me because they never shun me, and there is never any awkwardness between us.

I'm probably the exception. I'm lucky that my congregation has been understanding but there are strict rules regarding bullying, and most mosques don't tolerate bullying of any kind and expect their worshippers to adhere to these principles. And maybe I have acclimatised them to the idea that somebody can be gay and Muslim. But you have to remember that not discussing sexuality amongst peers is the norm in our culture, because on the whole Muslims tend not to talk about personal things like sex.

Life, on the other hand, has not always been plain sailing. Because of my activist work, I have been challenged in my home area by fundamentalists who are opposed to homosexuality. They have even come to my home, where they shouted and argued with me, and refused to accept any other point of view than theirs. I've had many taunts directed at me including, 'You'll go to hell – repent now – you're going against Islam.'

These fundamentalists take a very literal interpretation of the Sodom and Gomorrah story, which isn't unique to just the Qur'an, as the story hails originally from the Hebrew Bible (Old Testament). But fundamentalists are never easy people to debate with, and on one or two occasions I was physically struck across the face and head when I tried to discuss with them that they needed to view the Sodom and Gomorrah story in the context of its time. I know people like this will never accept gay people because their prejudice is too deep to change. But I am happy in my life.

I have a partner who I love and who loves me. He is a non-Muslim but is understanding of the difficulties that arise in Islam about homosexuality. Neither of us wants to get married. My biggest difficulty with this would be that our union could not have an Islamic blessing. I'm quite a traditionalist at heart and value rituals that acknowledge who we are as people. At the moment my religion is unable to provide this endorsement. This aside, I practise Islam in every other way and I am dedicated and proud of my religion.

I am a Sunni Muslim and drawn principally to the Hanafi School of Thought because in Hanafi there is no specific punishment for homosexuality. In fact, Hanafi disagreed with the death penalty for homosexuals, while other scholars had accepted it – after their interpretations from the Hadith – and formed the view that homosexuals should die by being thrown off mountains or by stoning.

I know I am a good person and that I am not sinning against God. I am reconciled with Islam and myself. I don't have any internal conflict because I view being gay as merely a part of human nature, and knowing this allows me to be at peace with myself and God.

Sarwat

Before, I was ambitious, hopeful and strong. I would like to think that I am still brave but I'm now suicidal. My life seems to get worse each day. I am losing hope for anything good to happen in my life and that I will never be free to be with the woman I love.

I knew I was attracted to other females from the age of 12, but

I didn't tell my family because if I told them they would probably have killed me or my mother would probably threaten me that she would commit suicide if I didn't change to the way she wanted. I heard her threaten my brother with this when he was seen talking to a non-Muslim girl who she feared he might want to marry.

This pressure has existed since I was in primary school. I hate it all. I hate tradition and I started hating religion because of the way it controls people. And I hate myself for being who I am, because of the way my parents wanted to raise me as a good, heterosexual Muslim girl.

I like women who act mature and independent and who are brave and willing to do anything for love. They don't have to be Muslim, but I prefer when they are from a similar background to mine because they understand me better.

I met my girlfriend online two years ago. At first we were just friends before we decided to start a long-distance relationship. I loved the way she speaks about her life. I love her mind, her thoughts – everything about her. But I could see how much love and care she needed, although I loved how pure she is and how she never wishes bad for anyone. She actually reminded me a lot of myself, but her family are like mine – narrow-minded and traditional. They would persecute her if they were to find out about her sexuality. Our relationship at the moment feels perfect, but it is so sad and painful that we may never be with each other and share together the wonderful affection that had grown so deeply between us. Almost all of my close friends know about me because I would rather not be friends with someone who I could not be my true self with.

I don't think of God that much anymore. Once upon a time I was really religious but not anymore. Maybe one day, Islam will accept LGBT people – maybe in 30 years when all of us who don't have freedom have died. I don't care about Islam anymore because I believe it shouldn't be forced on anyone. I was forced to wear hijab since I was 14. My priority now is myself – my freedom and how best I can find a way to be with the woman I love. I would go to hell for this woman and I know she would do the same for me. It is the only true feeling I ever felt. We plan to meet as soon as possible so that we can spend some time together to share our love. I wish we died in each others' arms before they separate and kill us.

Nazir

I'm not a devout Muslim but I practise certain elements. I pray twice a day rather than five times. I attend my local mosque every Friday and I complete Ramadan every year without fail. I also plan to complete the hajj one day. While I don't drink alcohol or eat pork, I am not that bothered if I eat other meats that are not halal.

Growing up gay and Muslim in South Africa was not a big problem for me. At school I encountered minor bullying, with some boys calling me a 'fag' because I didn't play football; however, I tried to hide my sexuality by fabricating stories about me fancying girls. As for my family, I never told my parents or grandparents. Not even my sisters – all of them somehow assumed that I was gay but none of them asked me any questions or put pressure on me to conform. It was something that was just left unsaid without there having been any awkwardness, except once when my mother referred to a local non-Muslim hairdresser who was gay as being 'bad luck'. That comment really hurt.

During my early adulthood, I was conscious of having a secret that I could not freely share with others. For a time, I could not reconcile with being gay, but neither did I want to go into the deep end. By that I'm referring to some gay Muslims you hear about who go to the extreme and reject Islam because of their sexuality. Some go completely off the rails by rejecting their families and start drinking alcohol or taking drugs. I had no inclination to go to such extremes, and chose the middle ground. By that, I mean I have chosen to stick with my faith but still be a practising homosexual.

The Qur'an is very clear on the subject of homosexuality. Muslims believe it is wrong and will say that 'man was not made for man' and 'woman was not made for woman'. I've listened to imams giving sermons and denouncing homosexuality in their reference to sinful acts, but not singling it out by itself, rather grouping it together with other sins like adultery or drinking alcohol and taking drugs. However, during one of my last trips home to South Africa I was encouraged to hear an imam deliver a sermon mentioning gay people and saying they should be welcomed into the mosque. It was lovely to encounter this softening of the strict stance that mosques and imams as a rule have about homosexuality.

I know that we are light-years away from Islam ever truly accepting homosexuality. In fact, it may never happen. But I think we can be hopeful that one day more mosques will become welcoming and that this will mean that gay people will feel less alienated.

What does God think of me being gay? Oh, I think God is absolutely fine with it. He gave free will to everyone, didn't he? Wasn't it only a matter of time that people would start experimenting with their sexual urges? It even happens in the animal kingdom. Provided nobody gets harmed, I cannot see there should be a reason for concern. And besides, there are plenty of people in the world who can procreate. I don't feel in the slightest that God disapproves of me.

It's natural for me to be gay. I didn't choose it, but I am now reconciled to the fact that there are things I can do and there are certain things that will never be part of my story – like a wife and children. I'm not ashamed of what or who I am, and I am now at complete peace with it. I feel free from the terrible pressures that some married Muslims get caught up in, particularly gay men from Middle Eastern countries, who are married but engage in extra-marital affairs with men, with their wives none the wiser. People from those countries who visit the UK hardly believe how free we are over this side of the world to be openly gay, to be in relationships and even be allowed to get married to people of the same sex. The cultural difference is the complete opposite to what they are used to, with many shocked that gay people can even demonstrate affection in public.

Razia

Ten years ago when I was 12, I told my mother everything after she caught me talking to a girl. She hit me and told me I needed to change. I was angry with Allah for making me this way when I was a little girl. I said to my mother, 'Don't blame me, blame Allah.' And I blamed him more and more for all the pain and threats that I received from my mother at first.

To be in love is something that can't be explained. When I love someone I love insanely in a way that people think is crazy. I feel alive and safe – nothing can break me. I like all women. I don't have a type as long as she's a woman. Her religion doesn't matter as long as she accepts and respects me for being Muslim.

Growing up was a lonely time. I only came out to one friend and that made me lose her. She was my best friend and like a sister to me. I think my mother must have thought I had changed, because she stopped talking about it for several years until a few months ago, when she caught me with a woman and went into a complete rage. She told all my family that I was a lesbian.

My family tell me that they hope I find a nice man and get married and have children. They use the words 'Allah yoster Allah', which means something along the lines of 'May Allah cover your honour and protect it.' As if I'm not already honoured. My family are also pushing me to go out more so that the mothers of unmarried men will bring me to their attention and bring their sons out to meet me and gauge my suitability as a bride.

The pressure gets worse every week. My greatest fear is that they will force me to marry and that I will have to live a life of hell emotionally every day for the rest of my life.

Lately, though, I have made peace with Allah and now believe that if it were forbidden then why would he create any girl or boy this way when they can't understand anything? I was born this way and I now feel proud about this. I also believe that if the Prophet was in our time he would accept me exactly the way I am.

Iqbal

I am the eldest son in my family. The anticipation of my parents for me to get married was sky high. I decided in my late teens that I could never tell them and that the best thing for me was to leave India and settle in another country. Here I would be able to have a new life and have a boyfriend. Being gay in India will never be easy. It's impossible to have a free life. Having said that, it is more about culture than about Islam. I don't know what it's like to be gay in a strict Islamic country, but it is definitely taboo in India, even amongst Hindus and Christians. There is something intrinsic about it because family status is so important, with being gay severely frowned upon.

Every trip home to visit my parents, they asked me when I was going to get married. I lied and lied, telling them that I was too busy and too career orientated. Most men in my culture get married before their mid-twenties so the clock was ticking. My parents persevered, prompting me to lie again by saying that I was infertile and didn't want to marry if I couldn't have children. This didn't deter them. My father said, 'That's not a problem, we will help you get that sorted.' During the next visit home, they even started planning an arranged marriage for me, and when I balked at this they told me that there was something wrong with me and that I needed to see a psychiatrist, whom I agreed to see.

I told the psychiatrist exactly what the problem was. At first he seemed to understand and was sympathetic to my dilemma, but said I needed to tell my parents, although he knew they wouldn't understand. In the end, I left it to him to tell them.

He changed his tune afterwards and together with my parents they prompted me to have shock therapy in the belief that it would 'cure' me. I still remember the words of the psychiatrist: 'If willing, you can change.' I declined the treatment because I knew it wouldn't work. There was no need to believe that it would work because I was perfectly happy the way I am. Finally, my parents stopped pressuring me and have now come to terms with it. They no longer ask if I'm ever coming back to live in India to settle down. We get along fine now whenever I visit. They appreciate the financial assistance I give them to assist in their retirement.

I was born Muslim but I don't practise Islam; I believe in one God and say prayers every morning and every night. As a child growing up, I went to madrassah (Islamic school). Here I first became aware of homosexuality with the story of Noah's Ark and how this was one of the main reasons why God decided to wipe out the human race, because homosexuality was out of control. But I don't believe that was the reason at all.

I see myself as one of God's children. I believe God loves his children and that he loves me. I know being gay is a sin in Islam. That's one of the reasons I don't go to a mosque any longer. To be honest, it is easy for me not to go – because I don't have to be fearful of the imam or other Muslims telling me that I need to change because of my sexuality. Besides, I don't want to feel the odd person out. I jokingly say that gay and straight men should not be mixed together in a mosque anyway. Everyone knows that the reason men and women are not allowed to mix together is because of the fear that the men cannot be trusted around women with their sexual urges. But what about the men being all together? Can all of them be trusted together? I don't know how I would be able to concentrate on my prayers if I was beside a handsome man.

My advice to any young gay Muslim growing up is: be yourself and put yourself first. I know by my own experiences how intense everything can be in life. This often means having to put distance between yourself, your family, friends and community. I've had to cut cords and lose friends because if I hadn't, I wouldn't have been able to achieve the degree of freedom and contentment that I currently have in my life. I'm now piecing back together people in my life that I 'lost' in the process by contacting them on social media and telling them that I'm gay. They were all accepting of it, although none of these friends were Muslim.

* * *

If you ask whether Islam will ever fully accept homosexuality, the answer is an emphatic 'no' in this age, but the same probably applies to most other world religions. Islam, however, may soften its stance in a few decades' time, in the sense that homosexuality may no longer be condemned as severely as it is at present. In time the countries mentioned earlier in this chapter may either decriminalise it or abolish the death penalty, but this will take time as the prejudice is deeply rooted. An imam told me that the things God considered to be the worst are referred to time and time again in the Qur'an, examples of which are lying, adultery and causing disorder on earth, whereas homosexuality is mentioned much fewer times, which could indicate that less importance is placed on it than those of other 'sins'.

Muslims are more and more exposed to gay people in their communities, although many may still denounce homosexuality and erroneously connect it to paedophilia. Parents are less inclined to kick children out of the family home if they are gay. There are the occasional horror stories about exorcisms, mainly carried out by imams reading passages of the Qur'an over the person. There are still some misguided views that people have of homosexuality as some type of mental illness – that is what is referred to as jinn – an evil spirit living inside you. The concept stems from ignorance about people with mental health problems, who are also sometimes subject to exorcisms, but in the case of gay people it is their parents who basically are unable to accept that their child is gay, and treat it as a 'test from God'. Thankfully, these types of scenarios are dwindling in number.

Muslims are also hearing far less about it in the mosques. Imams can't publicly say discriminatory comments against the LGBT community any longer. This is in sharp contrast to ten years ago when imams would preach against it, but these days they don't want to get into trouble so the subject has gone 'underground'. These days imams are more inclined to say 'You must respect the dignity of the person, but don't respect the action.' As a result of this, there is less talk in Islamic circles about hating gays or discussing punishment for gay people, which shows a promising change from when imams had no restrictions from preaching on the subject.

Things are definitely improving. Admittedly, it is still very difficult to be gay and out in Muslim communities, but those who are brave enough to be so are acting as role models for other gay Muslims. The biggest shift, though, is definitely coming from younger Muslims who are far more integrated into society than their parents and grandparents. They have fewer hang-ups about homosexuality because they mix with gay pupils at school. It's also nearly impossible to go to university and not come into contact with LGBT activist groups, and if you are Muslim and part of a student union group for human rights, it pretty hard to start discriminating against gay people if you are campaigning for equality and justice for other groups who face discrimination and injustice. **Imitaz**

CHAPTER 7

Converts

I once read an article about how a convert will catch Islam tightly and never let it go. I understood this to mean that those who convert to Islam embrace it so fully they never leave. Based on anecdotal evidence I gathered from imams, it is estimated that in Britain, a third of converts are black and two-thirds are white.

The majority of converts are male, with female converts tending mainly, although not exclusively, to convert as a result of marrying a Muslim. It could also be argued that some of the young females who are radicalised into becoming brides of jihadi terrorists are also converts, although their reasons for becoming Muslim are presumptively less honourable than those who have made a rational, informed choice about embracing Islam.

For some, mainly orthodox Muslims, the word 'revert' is preferred to 'convert' because they feel everybody arrives on this earth as a Muslim in a natural state called 'fitrah' – an Arabic word which has no exact English equivalent although it has been translated as 'primordial human nature', 'instinct' or 'common sense'.

There arc people who come to me who have had Christian backgrounds interested in converting to Islam. They discover the unity of Allah is very straightforward in comparison to other religions. They also discover that the real Islam is unlike the media portrayal. There are mixed marriages in Islam as well though. It is not the purpose of a husband to convert his wife and he must not force her. If she decides to continue being a Christian, he must respect her wishes. **Tamam**

Liberal and progressive Muslims disagree with the term 'revert' and feel the word 'convert' fits the description better because it is closer to the truth.

I detest that word 'revert' because it was first coined in Saudi Arabia by a group of Muslim fascists. It belongs to fundamentalism and has a deluded belief that everybody is a Muslim deep down. It doesn't make sense that somebody who is leaving one religion to become a Muslim is reverting back. How can you revert back to something you were never part of or knew anything about in the first place? People are born into Christian, Jewish, Hindu and Muslim families. It's as simple as that. This word 'revert' suggests exclusivity and is part of a false ideology that people are going back to what they are naturally, rather than becoming something they have never been before. Where in the Qur'an does it state that people who change their religion are 'reverts'? It doesn't state it anywhere. **Dameer**

Converting to Islam is a big step for any man or woman, and often involves far-reaching changes to both identity and lifestyle (e.g. no promiscuity, immorality and no longer being allowed to eat pork or drink alcohol). In addition to adopting rules regarding food and drink, there is the need to adopt an Islamic name. Uncircumcised men are recommended to have this procedure done after converting, although this is not mandatory. But having said that, most, if not all, are circumcised by Abrahamic tradition. There are also changes to dress codes, especially for women, who will mainly be expected to cover themselves with a hijab, or at the very least, will be expected to dress modestly. Social relationships with family members may change, especially if there is opposition or rejection from close loved ones about the decision to convert. Likewise, changes around social gatherings (e.g. mixing with members of the opposite sex, or the avoidance of parties with alcohol, or pubs, bars and nightclubs) may affect relationships with friends. In light of politics within Middle Eastern countries that are ridden by conflict (Syria, Afghanistan, Iraq and Yemen), differences may also arise concerning how war and the political landscapes of such countries impact upon Islam and Muslims. Occupational changes may become a factor too, because being employed in a profession that is not in alignment with Islamic values is forbidden (e.g. working in a pub, a nightclub or a betting shop, or being employed as a particular type of masseur).

Converts to Islam, though, can sometimes make uncomfortable statistics – 16 per cent of Islamic-related offences in the UK have been committed by converts to Islam, and 32 per cent of UK converts have been linked to the now-banned UK-based Islamist and political terrorist organisation Al-Muhajiroun, which was led by Anjem Choudary (a well-known Islamist in the UK who was later imprisoned). This was the group that infamously burned poppies and chanted 'British soldiers go to hell' during an Armistice Day commemoration in 2010. Admittedly, most of these statistics are based on those who converted to Islam in prisons. Conversion in British prisons, when life has reached its lowest point, results in converts often accepting a very fundamentalist, angry and resentful version of Islam, colloquially known as 'Prislam'. According to Stuart (2017) religious converts have been disproportionately involved in Islamic-inspired terrorism, with some having commonly researched terrorist-related material on the internet prior to, or as part of, their offending. Three-quarters of those committing acts of terrorism were previously known to the authorities through a variety of terrorism and non-terrorism-related channels, including connections to crime.

The murder of Fusilier Lee Rigby close to his army barracks in southeast London in May 2013 will stand out in many people's minds because of the barbaric methods employed by his attackers – Michael Adebolajo and Michael Adebowale, who used knives and a machete to decapitate him. Both murderers were recent converts to Islam and had been radicalised by Anjem Choudary.

Ultimately, people convert to Islam because they are looking for meaning in their lives at a time when there is increasing dissatisfaction with Christianity in the UK and other Western nations, with many countries, including the United States, becoming increasingly secularised. This situation has led to people exploring Islam in closer detail and finding in their search a religion that brings peace, justice and equanimity to all aspects of a person's life, as well as bringing rejuvenation to their spiritual life.

STORIES FROM CONVERTS

The remainder of this chapter features the stories of men and women who have converted to Islam. Here they explore their preparation, anticipation and desire to fill something their heart had most desired, and which they found in Islam. My research concluded that the majority of people in the UK convert to Sunni Islam followed by a small number choosing the Ahmadiyya community, with hardly any becoming Shi'a Muslims.

Imran

Before I converted, I was a Catholic but non-practising. I knew little about my religion. My family weren't religious. Anytime I did go to church, I was confused about the Eucharist and could not understand why the body and blood of Christ was meant to wash away my sins. I turned away from religion and remained switched off until one day I got speaking to my neighbour who was a Muslim. I could see he was a good person doing his daily prayers. We had some really good conversations about Islam, which I found interesting. He gave me a copy of the Qur'an to read along with some other booklets. I was living with a girlfriend at the time who didn't have anything nice to say about Islam and who didn't want me to convert.

After I had studied Islam for a while, I became friendly with another Muslim at my workplace. We struck up a good rapport and he soon became aware that I was drawn towards Islam. One day he asked me to pray with him and I did. From that moment onwards, I knew that I was going to convert to Islam and thanked God for the gift he had given me. I was spared telling my girlfriend of my decision, but rather curiously, when I went home that day after making up my mind to convert, she had already packed and left without saying goodbye. I was sad at first because I loved her, but I know deep in my heart that I was about to make the best decision of my life. My mother understood my decision to convert and was supportive, but my father and grandmother were less so. They had developed in their minds a fixed idea that Islam was bad and dangerous, based on reports in the media, and were for a time frightened that I would become an extremist.

Since converting, I study Islam every day and my knowledge of the religion now is very good. I have learned that following God is the fastest way of becoming close to God. I believe every man and woman in the world needs to discover God and to have a connection with him. I believe that good values come to those who start following God. You simply become a much better person naturally.

After my girlfriend left and between marrying my wife a few years later, I managed easily without sex. I manage without alcohol also. It's easy, really. People look towards sex and alcohol for ecstasy but never find it. I have found my ecstasy in my religion.

My wife is expecting our first baby. It was her father who introduced us. He approached me in the mosque one day and asked me if I would be interested in marrying his daughter. My wife and I are good together and we are very happy and excited about parenthood. We recently purchased our own home. Really, everything has become so calm and serene since I converted, and so many good things continue to come into my life. I view these as blessings from God and I pray and thank Him for all of his goodness every day. I am currently at the happiest point I have ever been in my life.

Bahir

I was born in Jamaica but came to Britain when I was little. My parents were Seventh-day Adventists. From an early age, I became interested in religion. There were a few things about Christianity that I didn't understand or agree with: the Trinity didn't make sense to me; Christ dying on the cross for the sins of mankind made me doubt. I disliked rap Gospel music because I couldn't see any value in it. I also couldn't understand why people did things, like getting up early, believing that this would please God. I couldn't understand why some people seemed to make up their own laws that had nothing to do about God. I couldn't understand how people bowed to kings and queens but didn't bow to God, who created them.

At school, I loved debating issues in RE classes and would ask my teacher many questions about God. It was here I noticed discrepancies in the answers I was given about Islam in contrast to what my parents had told me. I began doing my own research online and in the school library. Having cleared up some more misconceptions, I decided to go one day to my local mosque. It was Ramadan at the time; the mosque was packed with people, but there was something about it that made me relaxed and at ease. My quest for more information about Islam was fulfilled by the Shaykh, who helped me understand what Islam stood for; before long, I decided to make my declaration of faith.

I was 11 at the time. I wasn't pressurised in any way to do this. It just felt right for me. But I kept it secret from my parents and didn't tell them for another four years that I had become a Muslim.

They were fine about it, although my mother felt a little depressed because her religion is everything for her. I knew she would have to accept that Islam is everything for me. My life does not revolve around Islam, rather Islam revolves around my life. And that is the way it should be for all Muslims.

My life has changed for the better in so many ways since becoming Muslim. The friendships and brotherly companionship I have received from friends I've made at my mosque is priceless. It brings with it so much meaning and joy into everything I do.

In some ways, I have grown up in my mosque. I feel happy and contented here and know that I don't need nightclubs, music, alcohol, parties or girls to feel fulfilled. I'm already fulfilled because Islam offers tranquility. Every time I listen to the Qur'an being recited, I feel peace within my heart, knowing that I am listening to the very words of God who created the world, and I feel humbled that he narrated these words so that the likes of me could hear them.

Alongside my college studies, I have a job where I am saving up to go to Egypt because I want to learn Arabic. I am good with languages and it's my ambition to learn Arabic so that I can recite the Qur'an. I am really determined to achieve this goal.

With Islam, the doors for forgiveness are always open. The reminders in the Qur'an that God is compassionate, merciful and forgiving brings reassurance and strength to those who feel pressured by life. Islam has the answers about how to function properly as a decent human being and gives you examples of how to live your life with purpose and direction. I know that one day, when I am an old man looking back on my life, I will realise how becoming a Muslim at 11 years old was probably the wisest decision of my life.

Fatima

I came from a Church of England background. My parents were Christians in name only. I did religious education at school, but that was all I knew about religion and hardly anything about Islam before I met my husband. He aroused my interest. I started watching debates on YouTube about Islam and Christianity, and comparing the Qur'an to the Bible.

I've read the Qur'an in English once. I would like to read Arabic, but I listen to the Qur'an being recited in Arabic on CDs. My husband did not force me to become Muslim. I chose to. He taught me how to pray in Arabic and what to say. I don't say any Christian prayers when I pray, like for example the 'Our Father'.

My husband has taught me other things too, like how everything is available to Muslims. There is a solution in Islam for everything. You pray to Allah for answers. People read and do research and most of all they pray to Allah for answers. Non-Muslims, on the other hand, take drugs or resort to alcohol when they have problems.

My parents were fine with me marrying a Muslim and said: 'We're happy as long as it's what you believe in.' Friends I knew from school treated me similarly and said to me, 'If you're happy how you are, we're happy.' I have never encountered any hostility from anyone.

Our Islamic wedding was a quiet occasion. There was just myself and my husband, the imam and two male witnesses in the mosque. I didn't invite any of my family or friends because I wanted it to be between me and my husband. A short time afterwards, we got married in a register office, where my parents and family and my husband's parents and family attended. My husband hired a limousine. It was a lovely occasion. We had a party afterwards.

I have worn the hijab since I got married. We are told we must be covered from the head down to the ankle, and that only our face and hands should be shown. I'm happy with this. We are for our husbands only to see. I don't see the point in being Muslim if you keep your hair uncovered or if you wear a scarf and your hair can be seen underneath it. You see women wearing a scarf but they will be wearing short sleeves, which are not good. I even wear the hijab at home because it makes me feel safe. I feel protected that I can't be harmed.

My children are my life. All four of them are happy and healthy and I love them dearly. My life is taken up with my children and husband. I occasionally go to the mosque and talk to the other women there. At first they mistook me for being Turkish because of my skin colour. They are friendly and kind to me.

My life has changed since I've become Muslim. I am generally quite shy, but these days I notice I am less stressed and feel more relaxed. I observe the rules in Islam of not being alone in the company of any man that I am not allowed to marry. Over the years people have learned not to shake my hand or try to hug me. If there is any awkward encounter where I feel somebody might try doing this, I usually stand back from them.

I don't visit my parents or any of my siblings at Christmas. I'm against what they are celebrating. Christmas for them is about fun and not religion, and they all drink alcohol. I don't want to be part of that.

We have our own festivities like Eid, which we celebrate twice yearly. I celebrate with my husband, his mother, his brothers and sisters and their children. We always have a good time and eat lots of good food, which I help to prepare. These get-togethers are always enjoyable and a great time to celebrate life and to be thankful for all the blessings that Allah has bestowed upon us.

Tabeen

Before converting to Islam I had been looking for spiritual answers for a long time. I wanted to know if God existed and to understand the purpose of existence and creation. Deep down, I think I was looking for a more beautiful and peaceful life.

I went to a Christian school followed by university. I had an amazing job, good friends, a lovely lifestyle, and I wanted for nothing. But still I yearned to find out who I truly was and to discover if there was more to life than just living and then dying. I questioned whether that was all there was to life. Surely not.

Western religions didn't offer me any suitable answers. I became a Buddhist for two years, and while this was satisfying, it wasn't fulfilling enough because there was still something within me that prevented me from becoming the person I felt I was meant to be. Simply, I knew I wanted something more than what I had, but I couldn't quite put my finger on what that was. However, that all changed, and although the circumstances of my conversion to Islam may look like a conscious decision, I can now see it wasn't. I continued looking for answers and kept reflecting on whether God had stopped speaking to people, what his relationship was with people, and whether he could be communicated with. And I also wondered if my prayers could be answered. Shortly afterwards, they were.

One day I was in a café and struck up a random conversation with a group of Muslim students. We got onto the subject of the ego and exchanged philosophies around how to best understand your ego and become self-aware. Little did I know at that point that this was the start of my journey towards God.

I made friends with the group and we met up several times afterwards and discussed Islam, God and the universe. Sometime afterwards, I went away to the countryside for a weekend and while I was walking in a field one day, I had a revelation which from that moment onwards changed my life. It was like a person being told all their life that their parents were dead and then suddenly finding out that they are actually alive. And then the person goes to meet them and the intense emotion that this brings is everlasting and powerful. That's what it felt like at the precise moment that I decided to convert to Islam.

Converting to Islam was not that difficult for me because I felt I had journeyed towards it and I wasn't rejecting my past in the process. In fact, I still believe in Buddha as a Prophet of God. On a practical level, I didn't drink alcohol anyway, so this wasn't an issue. I was also used to fasting as a Buddhist. I meditated five times a day, which I replaced with praying five times daily. I used to do charity work with homeless people, so valued giving something back to society.

When I told my parents, who weren't particularly religious, that I was going to formally accept Islam as my religion, my mother said to me, 'I trust you because whatever you do, I am happy with it.' My father was a little more hesitant and questioned my decision. He asked me why I could not remain being a spiritual person without committing to a particular religion. He wondered if it was a sensible decision for me to accept a religion that had rules and structures. It's sometimes difficult to reassure people with answers to their questions but, over time, my father saw the change in me, and how happy and settled I had become, and I guess with that his previous anxieties disappeared.

Islam is a very patriotic religion. It teaches you to love your country. I certainly love Britain. I feel a strong duty and obedience towards Britain. Islam teaches you that if you want a beautiful country around you then you must invest in this and become part of its fabric. Islam also teaches you self-acceptance. I see so many people walking about sprinkled with pain on their faces. Their pain is deep. It's a yearning for something more meaningful than what they currently have. Of course, they often fill this quest for greater depth to their lives by diets, fashion, building muscles or getting tattoos. They are simply focusing on the wrong stuff. None of these things brings lasting fulfilment – a fulfilment that I can confidently say I have found in Islam for the past six years.

My advice to anybody thinking about converting to Islam would be to do it because it's wonderful. It really is transformational because you become the person you are destined to be. You will understand how important life is and you will begin to live your life to a higher degree with God's presence and love.

True Islam is life-changing, but if you convert for the wrong reasons – be it for popularity through extremism and radicalisation, through marriage or political gain – then this will never lead to a true spiritual endeavour. There is a special word we use in Islam that is called 'kalima', which means 'Do it for God.'

Another way of looking at it is to say that you only get what you put into it, but if you enter with a true and willing heart, then you instantly start the journey towards God and, in turn, you also become your true self. This will be somebody who values humankind and whose qualities include kindness, gentleness, humility, honesty, dignity and self-worth. I try to live my life by these qualities because I want to live in a world where people listen to their hearts, not a world filled with hate, violence and aggression. Those traits will only serve to move you away from Islam – not towards it.

Damilola

I grew up in the UK. My parents are Nigerian. My mother is a devout Christian and my father a non-practising Muslim. I was raised in a Christian environment because mum is Pentecostal, but I also had friends at school who were of other Christian denominations.

Before I converted to Islam I attended a Methodist Church for nearly two years. That satisfied me for a time because I liked their message of following the 12 disciples and doing good in the world. I read the Bible from cover to cover. But despite liking Methodism, I was still searching for something more – something deeper within myself that was still not satisfied.

I love reading and read up on the major religions of the world. I watched documentaries, anything that meant devouring knowledge and learning more about life, spirituality and myself. Then one of my best friends committed suicide, leaving me devastated and empty within. I couldn't find any comfort in Christian teachings that eased my pain. I was left feeling that my friend had gone to hell. I felt lost without hope.

After I finished my degree in philosophy, drama and media studies, I still felt I had not found what I was looking for in life and continued to explore for more meaning – to expand on philosophical freedom – more than what I had seen on offer in Christianity. I went to a Sikh temple and learned about Sikhism, which has connections to both Hinduism and Islam, although obviously very different in some aspects. But I was blessed with a liberal mindset. I was blessed with a quest for new discovery. Slowly, through my exploration of Sikhism, I gradually became drawn towards Islam for some unexplained reason. I even turned to my father for advice, even though he had not practised Islam for the majority of his adult life. Nevertheless, he gave me advice to follow my heart. And this I did. Soon afterwards, I went to my local mosque and made my declaration of faith, which in Islam is called the 'shahada' – bearing witness before God.

After I converted, the feeling was incredible. Inner peace flooded through me. I was quickly able to deal with my friend's death by getting it into perspective. I began to learn that although suicide is a major sin in Islam, God is so merciful. I discovered that my friend will be given a chance by God and that eternal damnation is not definite for everyone who commits suicide. My friend never encountered Islam. Before he committed suicide, he wouldn't have known the extent of what he was doing was wrong. I am convinced that God will forgive him.

There were lifestyle changes that I had to make to my life. After converting there was no more clubbing, no more interaction with girls, or certainly no longer in a sexual sense. I swear less. I have become more conservative and have become better at communication. I am also more respectful to my family and friends. I was already circumcised, which was one less thing to worry about.

The problem with youth today is they don't aspire to be anything. They lack purpose. There are those who end up with no qualifications and no hope, trapped in inner-city poverty and gang culture. And some of these young people are Muslim. They may have good hearts and good intentions, but they can also be easily swayed. While some are prepared to listen, their education comes from the wrong kind of teacher. This is not a time to be brain dead. We must awaken the intellectual side of ourselves. But above all, we must seek peace – peace within ourselves as much as peace in the broader world. This starts in your own country. I'm very proud to be British and very patriotic towards my country.

Islam is about freedom of speech. Islam believes in freedom of choice, but the basic principle is to respect the law of the land. Religion can be dangerous and divisive and the greatest danger with Islam is when it is not explained properly. The Qur'an is full of metaphors. In a way it is an algorithm because it contains hidden stories with deep meaning that need deep analysis.

It's hard to defend Islam when the illiteracy rate is so high in large Muslim countries – as a result of education not being valued in some cultures. There are millions of young Muslims, particularly girls, in countries such as Nigeria, Afghanistan and Pakistan, who never get the chance to enter a classroom because prejudice, violence and poverty prevent this from happening, which is a terrible injustice in the world.

CHAPTER 8

Extremism and Radicalisation

If you look up the meaning of extremism in a dictionary, you will discover it entails steering ideals and views to the limit. In Islam, extremist ideals and views are expressed by those who hold beliefs that most ordinary Muslims think are unreasonable and unacceptable. Those who become radicalised in the religion consist of individuals or groups that have come to adopt increasingly extreme political, social and religious ideals and views that reject or undermine Western values and freedom of choice. Taking this a step further, Islamism is defined as a political ideology that sees Islam as a complete sociopolitical system, and as such, advocates an expansionist 'Islamic state', or caliphate, within which state law is derived from Sharia. Set against this concept in the UK, terrorism is defined in accordance with the Terrorism Act 2000 as: 'The use or threat (of action) designed to influence the government or an international governmental organisation or to intimidate the public or a section of the public for the purpose of advancing a political, religious or ideological cause' (Stuart 2017). Figures from the right-wing Henry Jackson Society tell us that there are 3000 committed Islamists in the UK who want to do harm. However, the Centre for Security and Intelligence Studies at the University of Buckingham fear there could be as many as 10,000.

There are several Islamic terrorist groups in the world, including: Boko Haram in Nigeria; Hizb-ul-Mujahideen in Kashmir; Al-Qaeda and the Taliban in Afghanistan; Islamic State – Sinai Province in Egypt, formerly known as Ansar Beit al-Maqdis (Supporters of Jerusalem); and Al-Muhajiroun, a banned Islamic terrorist group based in the United Kingdom, which is known to have 'cells' within the country linked to international terrorism, homophobia and anti-Semitism. These organisations are officially unrecognised Salafi jihadist proto-state and militant groups who follow a fundamentalist, Wahhabi doctrine of Sunni Islam. They are against Western education and believe that warfare should be used to spread Islam.

One of the biggest Islamic terrorist forces until its gradual decline in defeat in recent years is the Islamic State of Iraq and the Levant (ISIL), also known as the Islamic State of Iraq and Syria (ISIS), and by its Arabic-language acronym Daesh. ISIS, like other Islamist terrorist groups, has a uniquely twisted and fanatical view of the world, and has obsessions with patriarchy, intolerance, sadism and murder. ISIS, in particular, has recruited broadly all over the world, and in doing so has scooped up petty criminals as well as confused and frustrated young men with only a basic knowledge of Islamic teachings. It is a hugely well financed organisation with thousands of supporters and sympathisers spread across the world, including here in the UK.

REASONS FOR EXTREMISM

Poor interpretation and misintrepetation of the Qur'an features heavily in the mindset of Islamic terrorists, but this alone is not the sole reason behind extremism and radicalisation. After speaking to several dozen Muslims, including imams, this section comprises of the other main reasons why some Muslims are drawn towards radicalisation and extremism.

1. Some young people lack a sense of belonging, and feel rootless and are lacking in purpose. They get offered a place amongst those who are already radicalised to come and join them. This is an attractive offer to some young people who were born in Britain but don't feel British – and to those who feel ostracised by mainstream society due to factors such as poor integration, unemployment and a general disillusionment with the Western world.

2. Some young people feel alienated from society and think that they are unable to fully follow their religion in Britain. They are told by hate preachers (often on social media) and in some mosques that by living in this type of Western society, which isn't predominantly Muslim, they are hypocrites. Young converts to Islam, who are part of gangs in cities, are told that they should go instead to ISIS and fight for the true cause.

3. Jihad is seen as a desire and yearning for adventure, an exciting thrill for ill-educated young men. There is an innate attraction towards jihad, which is seen as something that is macho and full of bravado. It is seen as something only for the physically fit and emotionally strong. This is often coupled with a sense that in taking an extreme path a young person is doing something superior for mankind, which can never be achieved through ordinary day-to-day living.

4. Some young women see nice-looking men on internet recruitment posters with captions inviting them to become brides of paradise where martyrdom will never separate them from their handsome husbands. Young women of a particular vulnerable mindset fall for this allure and freely abandon their families to go and marry a jihadist, under the false illusion that they are going to experience their romance fantasy.

5. There is a general ignorance about Islam, where young, inexperienced people who have never read or understood the Qur'an are affected by what they see on certain Islamic TV channels. They watch programmes that often give a biased view of world politics and Islam. Their minds become confused

as the truth and lies become inseparable. Overall, these are people who are completely ignorant of Islam and its meaning.

6. For other young people, sincere intentions to make a difference are formed after they become emotionally aroused by horrific scenes on the internet, for instance, of young children sucking on the bosom of their dead mother. This makes them think, 'I have to go and help these people,' but they lack insight into considering the long-term consequences of their actions.

7. Pulpit preaching by radical imams espousing Wahhabism (the ultra-conservative brand of Sunni Islam) is designed to brainwash young and impressionable people into terrorism. Their biased views and ignorance of the teachings of Islam and misinterpretations of the Qur'an are coupled with a hatred for non-Muslims. Those vulnerable to radicalisation become consumed by the hate-filled ideology of Wahhabism and are brainwashed into believing that they have a religious duty to enter into jihad in order to please God.

8. There is a belief that all of the laws in the Western world are wrong – that they are 'shirk' (man-made and godless), with the voting system and democracy viewed as being in opposition to God's system. Islamic radicals believe that Muslims are losing hold of their faith by committing shirk. Therefore, fighting for the sake of the establishment of God's supremacy as expressed through a global Islamic State is seen as the ultimate goal of goodness.

9. A quest for martyrdom is sought by those who have taken its concept out of context from the Qur'an and the Hadith. Here Islamic extremists believe that those who are martyred will go straight to paradise and that there will be 72 virgins waiting for them. Martyrdom for some means becoming suicide bombers in the belief that causing havoc and revenge upon non-believers is an automatic pathway to paradise.

10. Prisons play a big part in the developments of jihadi networks. They are full of Muslim gangs consisting of damaged individuals who like to boast to each other with rhetoric, for example, that

they are the biggest and strongest amongst their peer group, which entices competition to prove who is the most violent. Poor regulation of prison networks only further escalates the problem of radicalisation and extremism. According to Acheson (2016) Muslims make up 15 per cent of the prison population in England and Wales (out of 86,000 prisoners), which is disproportionate given that Muslims only comprise of 6 per cent of the population. In high-security prisons, one out of five prisoners is Muslim, although jihadists returning from Syria and Iraq have boosted this figure. However, it is felt that some prisoners have been coerced into converting by the pressure placed on them by extremists.

11. A large percentage of imams are out of touch with their individual communities and have repeatedly failed to produce a narrative that counteracts terrorism, allowing the problem to grow rather than decrease. Often, acts of terrorism are met with silence in mosques run by imams who speak poor English, are elderly and who themselves are not well-integrated into society.

12. There may be personal issues which signify traces of psychopathic behaviour, or some who are mentally ill. Others may have problems with drug and alcohol misuse and be known to the criminal justice system before becoming radicalised either in the community or in prison.

ISIS, a linear product of the illegal 2003 Anglo-American conquest of Iraq, first gained global notoriety in early 2014 after they committed unspeakably barbaric killings and beheadings (redolent of ancient civilisation) of anybody, including other Muslims, whose Islamic ideology differed from theirs. The Yazidi non-Muslim people of Iraq and Syria were particularly singled out by ISIS because their beliefs were considered idolatry and devoid of monotheism, with women from this community repeatedly raped and held as sex slaves. ISIS want jihad, like other extremist sects, to become 'the so-called sixth pillar of Islam' and have political aspirations to create an Islamic caliphate based on an extreme, literalist adherence to Islam's sacred scripture. They want, based on their distorted interpretations of the Qur'an and the Hadith, to implement God's law in every aspect of life and live in a world without colonial borders.

Muslims who didn't agree with ISIS ideology were and are dismissed as traitors and disbelievers and sometimes murdered. Many believe that ISIS are a death cult, having a fatal attraction to those predisposed to kill and be killed. Others believe they are 'born again' Muslims whose duty is to bring back jihad. They place far more value on idealised versions of the afterlife than they do on fearing death. With mesmerising audacity, the ISIS flag contains the sacred words universal to all Muslims ('There is no God but God'). The flag also features the seal of the Prophet – the ring that the Prophet designed to reach out his hand to mankind in representation of engagement and dialogue. This is essentially the hand of friendship, the very opposite that ISIS offers the world with their grotesque, perverse and twisted ideology.

I believe there are three factors that tend to promote radicalisation. The first is poverty, when young people have no homes, no jobs and no dowry to get married, often resulting in sexual frustration. Secondly, segregation plays a part, with young men and women isolating themselves from other cultures and British values because they don't feel valued or heard. Thirdly, and perhaps the highest cause, is poor governance. Hate preachers calling on British Muslims to martyr themselves for jihad, which of course is a complete violation of what Islam is really about.

But Islamic terrorists have no understanding of their religion. They have no real knowledge of Islam and become radicalised after watching hate preachers on YouTube espousing their vile spiel. The acquaintance with Islam of those who do the radicalising is shallow and superficial. These young people who become brainwashed haven't read the Qur'an and have little or no knowledge of its teachings. They revolt against society, are often involved in petty crime and delinquency, and become part of gangs in prison. Remember, these hate preachers and the misguided people they brainwash are responsible for the distortion of Islamic teachings. They are killing humanity and must be held culpable and responsible for their actions. **Said**

NORMATIVE ISLAM VERSUS EXTREMIST IDEOLOGY

Normative Islam prohibits any form of violence against civilians. It positively reinforces Islam as a peaceful religion. The overwhelming majority of Muslims in the UK are orthodox Muslims who practise normative Islam, whether they are Sunni, Shi'a or Ahmadiyya Muslims. Normative Islam encourages a balanced and comprehensible teaching of Islam and encourages members of Muslim communities to steer clear of extremism. It generally recognises that a large number of those involved in terrorism do not practise their faith regularly. Many lack religious literacy and are novices in the faith. The ideology of Islamic terrorists is at total odds with normative Islam. These terrorists believe that there is only one true form of Islam which draws upon Muslim scriptures, texts and books as examples of Islam during its early years. This pseudo-state wants all Muslims scattered across the world to forget about individual national identities and to adopt a radical form of Islam governed worldwide under a caliphate.

Islamic terrorists believe they are fighting for Islam, justifying their atrocities as obedience to God in their quest to protect Islam from Western corruption. They hold copies of the Qur'an, believing that they alone are carrying out God's will. They believe the murders they commit are serving an idea as well as conveying a message – the message being that they are killing in the name of God. They don't care what other Muslims might think about this.

Putting Islamic terrorism into context, it is estimated that less than 10 per cent of the terrorists in the world are Muslim. Research has shown that there is no typical jihadist. According to Frampton and co-workers (2016), people who are drawn to extremism come from a wide range of socio-economic backgrounds, religious upbringings and educational levels. For some, terrorism becomes their prime goal in life, often turning their backs on their families and communities, believing they have been chosen by God to enter into war. People question why the architects, philosophers, scientists, mathematical pioneers and poets that made the early Islamic empires so rich and diverse are not the true inspirations of young Muslims today, rather than this deranged leaning they have towards violence and terrorism. After all, the Islamic world once represented power, wealth and knowledge, while today 70 per cent of Muslims worldwide cannot read or write with the clergy doing little or nothing about it.

The state of Islam in the UK worries me because 90 per cent of Sunni Islam is now diluted with ultraconservative and fundamentalist and Islamic orthodoxy. As a result, Sunni Muslims have moved so far away from the original Islamic teachings. This is most notable in Muslims under the age of 40. It is going to be hard to bring them back. Ex-prisoners come to me with their problems and I usually know within minutes of speaking to them that they have picked up bad Islamic practices in prison. They come with high energy and say things to me like, 'We need to do something about Islam' or 'We need to deal with kafirs.' It boils down to their interpretations of the Qur'an because they have been given free copies of it in prisons which have been translated into English by publishers funded by Saudi Arabia. These same copies are often distributed free on the streets of major UK cities. Did anybody stop and ask why these are being given out free when a Qur'an costs at least £10 to buy on Amazon? They will have altered several passages to support their own interpretations. Muslims these days are not being taught that piety comes from within the person's heart and soul. There is far too much teaching these days about fearing Allah, and hardly any which tells about the love of Allah. This is almost overshadowed by everything else but this part is most important because it teaches you to have love for everybody. They need to be shown the chapters in the Qur'an that talk about righteous Muslims whose duty it is to strive for Allah in order to be good Muslims. There is nowhere that says killing is the way to achieve this. (Qur'an – 78:30–35) **Ebrahim**

God loves all human beings. Think for a moment: if you truly fall in love with somebody, you will want her love, her praise. You will give her gifts and you will ensure that she always gets what she likes. God loves his creation like this and more. How would it be possible that God would ever sanction destroying human beings and nature? Do you really think God would like somebody's actions if they did this? God will never love this. He will never approve of hurting innocent people. If people are told that God has instructed them to harm people, they are badly mistaken. **Maadil**

Some question if Islamic groups are ghosts from the past coming back to haunt humanity, given their behaviour resembles ancient civilisations. These Islamic radicals commit unspeakably barbaric acts, including crucifixions and beheadings of non-Muslims – as well as killing fellow Muslims who they perceive as being 'disbelievers' because of their ideological differences.

Perhaps these terrorist groups feel it's their right to inflict this suffering as a payback to non-Muslims for the past suffering inflicted on early Muslims? This may sound a ridiculous idea, but so much of their ideology does not make sense that it becomes difficult to fathom their logic – if there is a logic to it that can be unearthed.

Islamic terrorist groups believe that the sword wipes away sin. They believe God wants the violence they bring and that they are doing God's work and are implementing his laws. They believe Islam has been corrupted by the West, placing more value on laws made by man than laws made by God, failing to realise that laws made by God are better and universal. They seek to change this by returning to what they interpret as the supposedly true teachings of Islam as preached by the Prophet. They wish to establish a strong and stable caliphate without further delay in order to lay the foundation for future generations of Muslims to live happily and to bring order back to humanity. They believe it's their duty to conquer the world and eradicate the corruption that has entered Islam by the Western influences.

I believe the Prophet has a clean history. He set out to convert people to Islam, to believe in one God. That is what he presented to the people. Had there been any contradictions in his actions, he would not have achieved what he did. What you get through history books is just one side of the story, not the full picture. History can be very distorted. I'm not saying that all Muslims after the Prophet's time kept to the rule book. Those who lived immediately after him knew Islam well, but later Muslims may not have brought the spirit of Islam with them on their journeys and somewhere their practices became corrupt, with true Islam getting lost in this process. **Abid**

The Prophet had to flee from Mecca to Medina in fear of getting murdered after his uncle died. He was never involved in the massacre of non-Muslims. He put his armies together to fight bitter persecution from Jewish and other tribes. The Prophet was aggressively pursued to Medina by his aggressors. That was how the defensive war started. It is a cruel, false claim that the Prophet was a warmonger. He never initiated battle or bloodshed. He fought for survival. Muslims to this very day have to swim against the tide of falsehood that sees Islam brandished as a religion of violence. There is no licence in Islam for cruelty or to seek the blood of others. **Musa**

The name Sayyid Qutb comes up frequently in discussions about the origins of extremism and its poisoned ideology, with many saying that his written works have radicalised and sown seeds of hatred in thousands of hearts.

Qutb was born in Egypt in 1906 and was executed there in 1966 after attempting to assassinate the Egyptian president Gamal Abdel Nasser. Known as an author and extremist theorist, Qutb, who was influenced by the theologian Ibn Taymiyyah, wrote 24 books on Islamist ideology. These books were hard line but were used in many colleges and universities at the time. He also wrote a 30-volume commentary on the Qur'an while in prison.

Qutb was known too for his intense disapproval of the society and culture of the United States, which he saw as materialistic and obsessed with violence and sexual pleasures. Some of Qutb's followers think of him as a great thinker and martyr for Islam and as leading the understanding of Islamist ideology, although many Muslim scholars do not view Qutb as being amongst their own ranks. But he continues to have a faithful following and his writings are read and quoted by current-day jihadis. His ideological influences are also known to have made their way to the UK and have been used by hate preachers in their talks, with emphasis placed on radical practices of spreading Islam, including war and getting rid of leaders who stand in the way of jihad.

The question remains: did Qutb take jihad out of its correct context and think of it only in terms of warfare?

Jihad is a word that many Muslims feel needs to be reclaimed because it's meaning has become distorted, being wrongly associated with war, death and destruction. The word is often associated with depictions of young men and women joining ISIS or supporting this terrorist group by being directly or indirectly engaged in war against the 'enemy', whether this is Western governments, or non-Muslims or Muslims who do not agree with their ideology. But in the time of the Prophet, the word jihad had a different meaning, being divided into two distinct categories.

The first category of jihad is popularly known as lesser jihad. Lesser jihad allows self-defence with arms in a holy war. This is categorically only meant to be used as a means of self-defence. If Muslims are attacked, they have a right to defend themselves – but war is not allowed to be perpetrated in any other circumstances. The second category of jihad is known as the greater jihad and is itself divided into two parts. The first part of greater jihad consists of the internal challenges each person has when struggling with evil desires. Muslims have a duty to protect their honour – and prevent sin, especially promiscuity and fornication – and to know overall the differences between right and wrong while being obedient to God. The second part of greater jihad is to preach the message of the Qur'an by learning it and becoming free of misconceptions as a result of ignorance. This leads to a deeper connection with God, and to becoming aware that you were put on earth for the purpose of leading a holy and pure existence.

I was told a story about the Prophet and two types of jihad. Once his followers came back from battle boasting about their success – feeling proud that they had beaten their enemies – overjoyed at their achievements and thinking that the Prophet would be pleased and would heap praise upon them. In fact, the opposite occurred. They were silenced when the Prophet told them that what they had achieved was the lesser jihad and was not something they should feel proud about. He outlined to them what the greater jihad entailed and how this needed far more stamina, perseverance and loyalty to Allah than what could ever be achieved in battle. This was because the more difficult jihad is the personal fight each person needs to win if they are to take responsibility for their inward fight to control themselves against evil desires and actions. **Maashir**

MUSLIM VIEWS

The following extracts are extended views of imams and non-clerics as to how they view extremism in today's world – both the causes and its wider effects on humanity.

These people are no longer following the Qur'an. Instead they have become consumed by the toxic man-made theology that is lurking about the place. This forms an attraction offering young men and women excitement and romantic adventure in this life and paradise in the next.

We live in an age of secular bankruptcy. Here we have young people in dead-end jobs, or in occupations that hold no real meaning, rendering them with zero validation to live life to the full. The average British male wants a comfortable life consisting of a wife, two kids, house and car. These are viewed as disposable to those who have become radicalised. What they are looking for is a spiritual compound, and that is why they are drawn towards this violent wickedness where they are deluded into thinking they are battling for God, struggling for Islam.

They believe their death in holy war will mean that they go straight to heaven to 72 virgins and that they automatically bypass the Day of Judgement. So their attitude is 'Stick your comfortable job, house and wife because they are all disposable nonsense, which ends the moment you die.' What they strive to achieve is something great that will last for all eternity. Personally, I would ask them how they think that 72 virgins are waiting for them in paradise when this appears nowhere in the Qur'an. They need to be deprogrammed and only then will they realise they have been hoodwinked. They need to be shown the chapters in the Qur'an that talk about righteous Muslims whose duty it is to strive for Allah in order to be good Muslims. There is nowhere in this that says killing is the way to achieve this (Qur'an – 78:30–35).

We condemn their actions. We condemn them for the negative picture they give of Islam. Suicide is a major sin in Islam. The souls of suicide bombers will be continuously tortured until the Day of Judgement whereby they won't be able to seek forgiveness and they won't be able to repent. Only God is allowed to take your life away. Suicide takes away God's precious gift and once it's gone, the person cannot get their life back. Their soul lies in limbo for eternity. **Redwan**

They watch stories on television about Syria and Palestine and feel that they must do something to help. They question what other Muslim countries are doing to help and more often than not they decide to then take matters into their own hands.

A prime example of this was the killing of the soldier Lee Rigby. Nobody should just go and kill people. You cannot take the law into your own hands. Islam must always follow the law of the land and abide by its rules. Of course, there are appropriate steps you can take to voice your disquiet at injustices in the world by joining a peaceful protest and making your voice and opinion heard. But you cannot pick up a knife and kill an innocent person.

Imams get to know their congregations well and know those who may be at risk of radicalisation. We often read about young men and women in the UK who have become influenced by radical speakers, who they have discovered through social media and the internet. I'm lucky that I don't have any such people in my congregation, but if there was I would feel it my duty to inform him or her about the correct teachings of Islam and how it is firstly a religion of peace and that it advocates living a good law-abiding and just life. I would tell them about the teachings of the Prophet and how he faced many difficulties in his life but responded to difficulties and conflicts with an open and just heart. **Jalal**

Radicalisation and extremism have nothing to do with Islam. The media rarely portray this in its correct context. Young people who get drawn into terrorism serve their self-interest and nothing else. Any true Muslim would never be able to turn to violence. We say to each other, 'Assalamualaikum' which means 'Peace be onto you'. How can anybody turn their back on this, especially those who stand shoulder to shoulder with their Muslim brothers in the mosque during congregation prayers? How can they turn against the fundamental principle that Islam is about peace by turning to violence and carrying out the most barbaric and depraved acts of cruelty on individuals, cities and nations – to both their Muslim brothers and sisters and those from other religions? Why can't these people not keep to the Five Pillars of Islam and live peaceful lives alongside the rest of humanity? **Ziyaad**

The isolation comes from an inner conflict with some trying to balance religion and modernity. The Crusades and the end of the Ottoman Empire are regularly cited, along with a misguided sense of longing for a time when Muslims were united, which never really existed since the time of the Prophet.

Some Muslims forget that the medieval period was also a time of enlightenment – Muslim scholars rediscovering the works of the ancient Greeks, with subsequent developments in the arts and sciences, which ultimately informed the Renaissance in Europe.

Islam hasn't undergone an overhauling reformist period,

the likes of which was undertaken by Martin Luther. Instead Muhammad ibn Abd al-Wahhab is lauded as a reformist, who advocated a back-to-basics approach to a more orthodox Islam. The Salafists, too, brainwash the young with a purist doctrine that appeals to young people seeking identity.

Radical preachers who are political Islamists have a lot to do with it, with their teachings readily available online. The notion of jihad is distorted. The term merely means to strive or struggle against obstacles. During the Crusades it was attributed to holy war, but even in a war there are rules and regulations in Islam. Nevertheless, jihad is a spiritual concept asserting one's human rights.

The terrorists want to replace democracies with theocracies and implement a caliphate. The terrorists always refer to the Ummah (the global community of Muslims) and want to divide Muslims and non-Muslims, particularly those living in the West.

The Ummah actually included others from the Abrahamic faiths, such as Christians and Jews. Our worst enemies as Muslims are ourselves. Just look at sectarian conflicts around the world. You can only love others after you start loving yourself, and believing in a shared humanity that binds us all irrespective of religion. It is mainly Christian Europe that gives Muslims refuge from conflict. **Arshad**

Islamic terrorists are pure evil – killing of parents, children and innocent people. They are nothing but criminalised gangsters. Young people who join ISIS are generally inexperienced, and have disengaged from liberal Islam (groomed via the internet) or have become radicalised in prison.

At the moment, the water is so mixed. Take ISIS away, another terrorist group will form. Extremists make themselves independent from Islamic Schools of Thought. You must realise that most ordinary Muslims don't encounter people who have been radicalised. Islamist terrorists do not represent Islam. Their actions are not related to ordinary Muslims. I'm not sure why they think they represent us. These people are brainwashed from a young age, despite the Qur'an being against what they are trying to promote. The biggest jihad any person on earth has to fight is the jihad against themselves. **Nadeem**

I feel the media likes to highlight violence that distorts Islam. They would never highlight Christian terrorists in the same way. I do not associate myself with other Muslims who commit acts of violence. What they are doing is wrong, but that does not mean that I have to justify myself to people or publicly denounce their actions just because I am a Muslim. Besides they are often done by people who aren't proper Muslims. When I see the aftermaths of terrorist attacks on television, I usually switch channels because I do not associate myself with the people who carry out these acts. **Prabhat**

The Qur'an states that whoever kills even one life, it is as if they have killed the whole of humanity. Whoever saves a life, it is as if they have saved the whole of humanity. All human life is sacred and worth preserving (Qur'an – 5:32).

These completely misguided people who think that any type of violence is okay completely astonish me. Extremist groups seem to be insane people who simply can't be bothered to put any actual effort into living life and instead they like to scapegoat other people, rather than actually doing something good in life.

Normal, law-abiding people work towards goals, like taking care of their families or building their careers, but these insane and completely stupid people don't. The thought process of these deplorable people completely dumbfounds me. I doubt any of them have ever actually picked up a Qur'an and read it. Had they done so they would know that their thoughts and actions go completely against every single fibre of Islam and being a Muslim. **Shahzan**

Firstly, and most importantly, the people who carry out these acts and the ones who encourage them to do so, do not have proper knowledge of the religion of Islam. They select excerpts from the Qur'an to support their way of thinking and disregard the part that contradicts their actions.

Of course there are passages in the Qur'an that appear extreme when not read in the context that they are meant – this is common in most religious scriptures and a classic attribute of having been written so long ago when such views were the norm. But there are also passages that advocate peace and love for humanity, treating others fairly, and harsh punishment for those who commit murder and other bad crimes. The people who commit terrorist acts clearly do not have any regard for the above and possibly don't even have any knowledge of such guidelines, with their goal being to die a martyr. But it is said that the Prophet stated that those who go against these rules are not going to war for the sake of Allah but for themselves, in which case how can they expect to reap the rewards of martyrdom in the hereafter? The sheer stupidity of such actions and beliefs astounds me.

I believe that the recruiters for such activities and groups target young wayward Muslims with contentious and violent predispositions, who lack the intellectual capacity and curiosity to question the validity of what they're being taught.

Another factor which cannot be ignored is that it can stem from a lack of belonging in this society. Most likely, the ones that spew hate and are very anti-West have probably experienced discrimination of some sort which will have ignited, or contributed to, their hatred. They don't feel accepted, so they're easy targets for extremist preachers who emphasise that point a lot.

We are living in a period where violence is almost ever-present. Ongoing war between countries and within countries leaves a lot of people feeling helpless. For some, this can turn into anger and can make them susceptible to be preyed on and used by extremist preachers. Even in this modern age of technology – video games, the internet, the news on TV – we are constantly being bombarded with images and clips of never-ending violence. This is bound to have an adverse effect on the developing and susceptible minds of the youth because hate perpetuates hate, and violence perpetuates violence. **Mohibur**

Prisons have tapped into this with make-believe preachers delivering convincing arguments to vulnerable inmates who fall sway to it. Here, minds are filled with stories about racism and Islamophobia directed at Muslims as a result of the wars taking place in Syria and Afghanistan. They are told that the West is happy to drop bombs in Afghanistan and that Muslims should fight back against those who fight against them. Verses in the Qur'an are twisted to back up their arguments – as well as corrupting stories from the Hadith, which they also use as part of their evidence to convince impressionable people that they have a duty to do something about it. It doesn't matter that innocent people get killed because the killing of civilians is justified by them being told by the 'preachers' that the people who get killed deserve death for voting for the governments who continue to impose misery and suffering on Muslims. **Jahanger**

MISUNDERSTANDING THE QUR'AN

There are millions of Muslims across the world who subscribe to interpretations of Islam and the Qur'an that endorse humanity, tolerance, compassion and co-existence with people from other faiths or none. These Muslims firmly believe that Islam is a religion of peace and want to live alongside non-Muslims in loving and peaceful harmony. Then there is the opposite side of the coin: a minority of Muslims whose interpretations of Islam and the Qur'an contains a puritanical ideology that is anti-Western and advocates intolerance, inhumanity and violent jihad; they are opposed to democracy and human rights and have a deep yearning for a caliphate for all Muslims.

It would appear that there are gullible young people who are easy prey and ready to be brainwashed into an extremist way of thinking. Some will go to join the caliphate of war and terror in the hope of imposing strict Sharia law in Muslim countries, as well as dreaming of reconquering countries once occupied by Muslims before the Crusades. Terrorist groups sow disunity; they have a total lack of understanding and tolerance of other Muslims who interpret the Qur'an differently to themselves, to the point of outright rejection of them as fellow Muslims.

> Somewhere along the line, things have become skewed, with some Muslims being selective in what they read in the Qur'an, resulting in them leaving bits out or adding bits of their own. Then they are those who take notice of certain things but ignore other parts.
>
> Why do some people do it? There are those who have political motivation in mind. A desire for land, money and power, and to achieve these goals, they will use anything within their power to achieve their objectives, including violence and death. Take Saddam Hussein for example. None of those who were part of his Ba'ath party believed in God. They just used religion for their own political agenda. And some very naive Muslims believed in them to their folly. ISIS fighters won't have read the Qur'an. In fact, they will be as far away from the word of Islam as you can get. **Nashir**

The culture of the time when the Qur'an came into existence was both violent and barbaric, and witnessed centuries of fighting amongst the Arab tribes. Although there were some Jews and Christians in Arabia, paganism was at the root of the land.

The tradition of the pagans was to fight and they were renowned for taking revenge against those they viewed as a threat to their existence. These were times of continuous and persistent persecution, which saw Muslims constantly being tortured and murdered. This resulted in the Prophet going into battle against those who tried to kill him and his companions, and those whose quest was to eradicate Islam from Arabia.

It was the brutality of the pagans who tortured and brutally murdered Muslims for their faith that brought about what is referred to in the Qur'an as 'qital' (not jihad), which means to fight and go into battle in self-defence when others are trying to kill you. The Prophet declared that war was defensive in Islam if enemies of the religion initiated hostilities against them. All offensive wars according to Islam are unholy. And it was with this mindset that Muslims in those times went to war.

They had to endure harsh conditions, coping with very hot temperatures and a lack of water. They rode in windy deserts on camels and horses. Their diet consisted of camel meat, goat's milk, dates and barley, when there was enough food to go around. The Prophet placed special conditions on his people before going into war against those who wanted to harm Islam. His faithful companion, Abu Bakr, summarised various injunctions as instructed to him by the Prophet. These are contained in a Hadith:

> *Stop, O people, that I may give you ten rules for your guidance on the battlefield. Do not commit treachery or deviate from the right path. You must not mutilate dead bodies. Neither kill a child, nor a woman, nor an aged man. Bring no harm to the trees, nor burn them with fire, especially those which are fruitful. Slay not any of the enemy's flock, save for your food. You are likely to pass by people who have devoted their lives to monastic services; leave them alone. (Hadith – Bukhari)*

The first great battle in the early days of Islam was the battle of Badr in 642, which saw 313 Muslims fight a tribal army of a thousand and defeat them. This event is considered a defining moment in Islamic history, with many of the key protagonists of the pagan Quraysh tribe being killed. These were people to whom the Prophet once belonged to before Islam, but who turned their backs to him after he founded the religion and who persistently undermined him and had sought ways to kill him.

Extracts from the Qur'an

Key to correctly interpreting the Qur'an is not taking individual lines or phrases out of context. It is unwise and misleading for anybody to do so. Rather, in order to understand the full context of the verse, the preceding verse(s) along with those that follow immediately afterwards need to be read. The following extracts are taken from chapters with verses commonly referred to by some Islamic scholars as the 'war verses'. It is believed that these are the verses most misinterpreted by Muslim fanatics who radicalise ignorant young people into becoming jihadists.

Chapter 2: Verses 190–192

> **v.190** *And fight in the cause of God against those who fight against you, but do not transgress. Surely, God loves not the transgressors.*

> **v.191** *And slay these transgressors wherever you meet them and drive them out from where they have driven you out; for persecution is worse than slaying. And fight them not in and near the Sacred Mosque until they fight you therein. But if they fight you, you fight them. Such is the requital for the disbelievers.*

> **v.192** *But if they desist, then surely God is Most forgiving, Merciful.*

These verses must be read together to ensure context – rather than reading just v.192 and not reading either the verse before or the verse after it, to avoid misinterpretation. This verse is often quoted by Islamic militants or opponents of Islam to support the idea that the Qur'an supports war against disbelievers until everybody in the world embraces Islam.

Yet in context it is clear that Muslims were given permission by God to fight those who waged war on them. Verse 192 stipulates that Muslims should lay down arms as soon as their enemies stop fighting. A central message in these verses is that Muslims are only allowed to fight in self-defence when war was inflicted upon them. However, they were allowed to continue defending themselves until complete freedom was granted to them to practise Islam.

It was never the intention of the Prophet to impose Islam on anybody who did not believe in it. Quite the opposite: he was willing to enter into peace treaties with non-believers, which would end warfare and leave Muslims able to practise Islam and non-believers to practise their own religious beliefs. It is clear that Muslims were instructed to lay down arms as soon as enemy fighters desisted from fighting.

Chapter 22: Verses 39–40

> **v.39** *Permission to take up arms is given to those against whom war is made, because they have been wronged and God, indeed, has power to help them.*

> **v.40** *Those who have been driven out from their homes unjustly, only because they said, 'Our Lord is God.' And if God had not repelled some people by means of others, cloisters and churches and synagogues and mosques, wherein the name of God is oft remembered, would surely have been destroyed. And God will surely help him who helps Him. God is indeed, Powerful, Mighty.*

The first verse shows that permission was given to Muslims to take up arms (swords, spears, bows and arrows) in self-defence. But this was not enough, as Muslims were routinely murdered, tortured or held captive. Muslims, despite dwindling numbers as a result of enforced exodus and immigration, were driven out of their homes by the disbelievers who wanted to eradicate Islam. This first occurred for several years in Mecca and then in Medina, where the Prophet was constantly harassed by Arabian tribes and the Quraysh (pagans) who wanted to exterminate Islam. The Prophet and his companions had little choice in the taking-up of arms in self-defence to protect Islam. The Prophet thought of others during this time and paid attention to protecting churches and synagogues from destruction during the war because he valued these holy places where the word of God was spoken.

Chapter 8: Verses 58–62

> **v.58** *And if thou fearest treachery from a people, throw back to them their covenant with equity. Surely, God loves not the treacherous.*

v.59 *And let not those who disbelieve think that they can outstrip us. Surely, they cannot frustrate our purpose.*

v.60 *And make ready for them who fight you of armed force and of mounted pickets at the frontier, whereby you may frighten the enemy and others besides them whom you know not, but God knows them. And whatever you spend in the way of God, it shall be paid back to you in full and you shall not be wronged.*

v.61 *And if they incline towards peace, incline thou also towards it, and put thy trust in God. Surely, it is he who is All Hearing, All-Knowing.*

v.62 *And if they intend to deceive thee, then surely God is sufficient for thee. He it is who has strengthened thee with His help and with the believers.*

These verses relate to the breaking of covenants by enemies. God gave his permission for Muslims to attack back with all their might should a covenant be broken, resulting in war being waged against Muslims. The Prophet wanted to talk to opponents, but if they were not prepared to talk, he would cancel the agreement if they persisted in breaking the treaty. However, the Prophet advised his armies that there were to be no surprise attacks. He also advised against battle at night-time.

Verse 61 in particular carries an important principle about making peace treaties, an overriding feature in Islamic wars – denoting that Muslims sought not to force Islam upon anybody, but rather that they be left in peace to practise their own religion.

A question asked by many Muslim scholars is: did these verses contain a warning and a prophecy about future Islamic wars – and not just the wars against Arab pagans, which were prevalent during the time of the Prophet? It has been argued that they might even have referred to the wars against the Byzantine and Persian Empires, which Muslims had to fight in the centuries following the Prophet's death.

Chapter 8: Verse 65

> **v.65** *O Prophet, urge the believers to fight. If there be of you twenty who are steadfast, they shall overcome two hundred; and if there be a hundred of you, you shall overcome a thousand of those who disbelieve, because they are a people who do not understand.*

The forces that fought against Islam at the time did not believe in God. They were coerced into going to war against Muslims by the leaders of idolater tribes. Most of the men who fought Islam felt no personal interest in the war against the new religion. They did not understand it. It meant nothing to them, so that they considered they were fighting for the sake of fighting. The opposite was true for Muslims, who fought the war to safeguard their religion, and for the love and belief in God and the trust they had placed in the Prophet. The verse promises victory to Muslims over an enemy ten times their number. In war, 20 soldiers were required as a minimum to comprise of a fighting unit, and were obliged to fight if they met an enemy as many as ten times their strength. They were strictly forbidden to flee.

Chapter 8: Verse 67

> **v.67** *It does not behove a Prophet that he should have captives until he engages in a regular fighting in the land. You desire the goods of the world, while God desires for you the Hereafter. And God is Mighty, Wise.*

It was a practice at the time for Muslims to be taken captive and held as slaves irrespective of whether or not there was a war in progress at the time. This verse condemns this practice and forbids Muslims to engage in it, stating that it is wrong and an unworthy misuse of power. Such a practice was only allowed in times of war or regular fighting, when it was considered permissible for enemy soldiers to be taken prisoner. Slaves should never be taken for pleasure, nor should they be beheaded, unlike the practice of ISIS.

It was deemed permissible to accept a ransom for the release of a prisoner.

Chapter 9: Verses 4–5

> **v.4** *And when the forbidden months have passed, kill the idolaters wherever you find them and take them prisoners, and beleaguer them, and lie in wait for them at every place of ambush. But if they repent and observe prayer and pay the Zakat, then leave their way free. Surely, God is Most Forgiving, Merciful.*

> **v.5** *And if anyone of the idolaters ask protection of thee, grant him protection so that he may hear the word of God; then convey him to his place of security. That is because they are a people who have no knowledge.*

The first verse relates to those who did not enter into any treaty with the Muslims and who continued fighting – pagans entered into treaties but often failed to keep to them. They were often thought of as being two-faced, in the sense that they were pleasant to Muslims but plotted against them when their backs were turned. Notwithstanding this, the second verse states that any enemy who repented and accepted Islam should be forgiven and their life saved.

Many men at the time, particularly amongst the idolaters, favoured Islam but felt the need to keep quiet, fearing reprisals from their own tribes. Muslims even allowed some of these men to come to their homes, where they would receive instruction about Islam without any risk being placed upon them, even if they did not accept the religion during these meetings. There is no evidence in these verses that Muslims forced anybody to accept their faith by using violence or the threat of violence to advance its propagation.

There were many tribes spread throughout the Arabian peninsula. They were filled with hatred towards Islam. The Prophet approached these tribes and entered into peace treaties with them. During his time in Medina there were five tribes – two of which were pagan and three Jewish. The Prophet gathered forces with these five tribes and together they entered into a solemn agreement known as the Charter of Medina to support each other should outsiders come into Medina and attack any of them. The most likely aggressors at the time were pagan tribes who came from Mecca to seek out the Prophet and kill him to restore polytheism.

Although Zakat was primarily a Muslim tax, non-Muslims were covered by these peace treaties and were expected to pay it.

Chapter 4: Verses 71–76

v.71 *O ye who believe! Take your precautions; then either go forth in separate parties or go forth all together.*

v.72 *And among you there is he who will tarry behind, and if a misfortune befall you, he says, 'Surely, God has been gracious to me, since I was not present with them.'*

v.73 *But if there comes to you some good fortune from God, he says, as if there were no love between you and him, 'Would that I had been with them, then should I have indeed achieved a great success!'*

v.74 *Let those then fight in the cause of God who would sell the present life for the Hereafter. And whoso fights in the cause of God, be he slain or be he victorious, we shall soon give him a great reward.*

v.75 *And what is the matter with you that you fight not in the cause of God and of the weak – men, women and children – who say, 'Our Lord, take us out of this town, whose people are oppressors, and make for us some friend from Thyself, and make for us from Thyself some helper?'*

v.76 *Those who believe fight in the cause of God, and those who disbelieve fight in the cause of the Evil One. Fight ye therefore against the friends of Satan; surely, Satan's strategy is weak!*

These verses discuss cautions and precautions about matters that Muslims must be prepared for when they enter jihad. People had to remain vigilant and notice if tensions were gathering to the point of hostility. There were followers of the Prophet who acted to keep watch for threats from their enemies. Other precautions refer to body armour, consisting of steel vests, and also the need to divide soldiers up into various groups – both small and large, depending on the circumstances.

Going to war was never easy for anyone. People had to make sacrifices. They left their wives and children behind. They had to show bravery, and have the motivation to fight for their religious freedom. But not all Muslims went to war. The Prophet was fine with that. There was never any pressure placed on anybody to enter battle. Those who fought in self-defence did so in order to protect their religion and to save their weaker co-religionists.

PREVENTING AND STOPPING TERRORISM

Politicians, as well as some commentators in the media, often say that Islamic terrorism has nothing to do with Islam. Perhaps they do so to seek approval, fearing that if they said otherwise they would get accused of being Islamophobic or expressing anti-Muslim sentiments that portray ordinary Muslims in a poor light. But saying that extremism and Islamic terrorism has nothing to do with Islam is wrong, foolish and untrue. The truth is it has everything to do with Islam. Extremists and those radicalised misinterpret the religion, which justifies their jihad. To them they are the only true Muslims who are correctly interpreting Islam.

Although jihadists only make up a small fraction of Muslims they have nevertheless created a poisonous ideology – a poisonous version of Islam that has spread in the last two decades at an alarming rate. This is definitely a problem that arises within Muslim communities, and it is only there that it can be resolved. Every Muslim extremist is a Muslim.

Every Muslim extremist has been brainwashed into believing that they have been chosen by God to carry out a deadly mission – a necessary task – of entering into jihad to spread Islam, for everybody to become Muslim, to live in lands where full Sharia law can be practised, where Muslims are Sunni only and are governed by a caliphate. They understand that the only way for this to occur is through killing and war. Those who disagree with them, whether they are Muslim or not, are branded as disbelievers who should be killed.

Experts predict that the current crisis of Islamic terrorism could remain with us for at least another 25 to 30 years. So what solutions are there for resolving this huge problem and preventing other Muslims from moving away from the true teachings of Islam, which preaches peace and tolerance? The following pages offer thoughts from Islamic scholars and ordinary Muslims, who feel anger, passion and a commitment to restoring the damage that has been done to the image of Islam by the wicked deeds of a small number who commit atrocities in the name of their faith.

There is a denial of the extent of the problem. Muslims are not taught to be introspective or self-critical. This is seen as a betrayal, a treachery, with some believing that our 'enemies' will benefit from this if we exposed any vulnerability. There are others full of conspiracy theories, believing that the terrorist attacks committed in the UK are the work of MI5 agents out to discredit the reputation of Islam. Then there are the sympathisers who debate whether the people responsible for the attacks were terrorists or freedom fighters, comparing them to Nelson Mandela, Gandhi or Martin McGuinness.

There are over 2000 mosques in the UK and the majority of these are Sunni, which are funded by the Saudi government. They have the mosques, mullahs and masses on their side. They have Mecca, Medina and money on their side. There is a saying, 'He who pays the piper, calls the tune,' and that's why imams dare not speak out. They have allowed themselves to become 'Arabised'. They are copycat Arabs. Do they not realise that Arabs are the worst type of Muslims? They are the biggest hypocrites who say one thing and do another. They think themselves superior because the 'Book' (i.e. the Qur'an) was given to its people.

What is needed are mass public demonstrations in cities like London and Manchester where thousands upon thousands of Muslims should march in huge rallies and cry out, 'Down, down, down with extremism!' This would clearly show to the world that we are no longer in a state of denial. We need to challenge their ideology and misinterpretations of the Qur'an and misuse of the Hadith, by using the same tools of defence (that they use) to contradict what they are saying in order to weaken their resolve. Instead, silence or lukewarm whispers is all we offer. **Kamar**

Education is key but then so too is leadership. Without a proper form of leadership, and indeed accountability, you are bound to have sweeping injustices and a spectrum of people incorporating the just as well as the unjust. True leadership and true education are two of the most crucial things needed in Islam today. A balanced and comprehensive teaching of Islam encourages members of the Muslim community to steer clear of extremism.

Many books have been written denouncing extremism and terrorism. These should be better promoted. These are the type of books that need to be in the libraries in mosques. Muslim scholars must become more vocal to explain repeatedly that jihadists are not martyrs, but instead are sinners and criminals. Politics should not be part of Islam. The bombing of the Middle East since 2001 (post 9/11) has led to the hate-filled views of these extremists. The root cause of the problem is the extremist imams teaching their warped ideologies in their mosques to those who are easily impressionable. Therefore, there should be a focus on monitoring the sermons and speeches given at these mosques, if not all mosques. This could easily be done in the UK. The government easily has the capability, in terms of technology, to do this. Clerics should not be allowed to be imported from Pakistan and Saudi Arabia, because they are the ones who bring extremism in with them. **Siyana**

When somebody who is at risk of being radicalised comes to me, I firstly listen to them. I like to gauge their argument so that their narrative is aired and exposed. I try to ascertain how much they know about Islam. More often than not, they fall short in knowing some of the basics or they display knowledge that is misinterpreted. It's simply a matter of deconstructing wrong ideas by establishing what the person's view or perception is on certain matters, before exchanging your views on the same point in question, in the hope that the truth will prevail and that they realise that their point of view contains falsehoods.

I remember talking to a young man in his mid-twenties who justified the actions of suicide bombers, as well as justifying the killing of civilians in the process. He saw the latter as mere collateral damage, implicated by extension, because he saw those who would get killed as somewhat complicit in being against Islam.

He had been told a story from the Hadith about a companion of the Prophet who during battle had been catapulted over enemy walls straight into enemy hands. The man knew that his job was to go and open the gate to allow his fellow troops inside, but in doing so, he would get killed. But he still went to open the gates. This was his destiny. His reward would be a glorious afterlife.

Another young man came to me and said, 'This country is at war with Islam. It is okay to steal – to rob banks. This country is an enemy station.' My response to him was, 'Really – but you are a British citizen, you are a British Muslim; what you are saying is a betrayal, an act of treachery; your views are totally impermissible within Islam – any book on Islamic jurisprudence would sanction against what you have just said.' I finished by telling him that he needed to be loyal to this country by virtue of his passport, or else renounce his citizenship. **Bassam**

To say that Muslims are commanded by God to carry out acts of terrorism is propagating an untruth. We must speak out against it. We must use our hands to stop it. We must hate it with our hearts. This is not for us. It will never be for us. This type of jihad is completely misguided and full of ignorance and contradiction.

I don't understand why those who are involved in jihad say things and do things that are completely different to the rest of us. The Prophet Muhammad never did this in any circumstance and similarly we must not do the same. God would hate the oppression it brings. I hate it when these idiots kill innocent people. They even kill young children, depriving them of ever growing up and becoming parents. Every time a terrorist attack occurs there is a backlash against Muslims who are appalled by the news of this senseless violence and latest atrocity like everybody else. **Leila**

When we see 10 or 20 innocent people killed on our streets due to terrorism we rightly mourn and complain about the perpetrators. But when we invade other countries for oil and trade and kill thousands, if not hundreds of thousands, why don't we share that same anger for those innocent lives?

Quite honestly, our foreign policies are the real cause of extremism and radicalisation. We cannot go into 'selected' foreign countries and kill innocent people and not expect a pushback. The pushback is clearly what we saw in the streets of London, Paris and Barcelona. The 9/11 bombers were all Arabs. All of the European bomb attacks were done by North African Arabs, so why did we attack Iraq and kill hundreds of thousand innocent people? Why did we invade Afghanistan? Name me one Afghan terrorist or an Iraqi one, other than those fighting against an invading army in their country. **Zyan**

Young people need to integrate in the countries in which they live; integrate but not assimilate. I feel there is sometimes pressure for non-English to assimilate and be like the indigenous population. This is dangerous because we want to hold on to our faith and culture.

As a Muslim, I am well integrated and have many non-Muslim friends. My children have a modern outlook and do things with their friends at school and work. They socialise and eat out and go to sports events, without having to compromise their faith and culture, which they are very proud of, but if it is expected for young people to give that up, then we end up heading towards rebellion and radicalisation.

The Brexit immigration issue is all about Brits wanting foreigners to 'assimilate' and become English. Most migrants integrate but Brexiteer attitudes want them to assimilate and become like the English and change our faith and culture. I'm not saying that everything is perfect in Muslim communities – that is certainly not the case. In the UK there are Pakistani communities that are ghettoised in places like Burnley and Rotherham, which desperately needs to change. **Hania**

Radicalisation is an ideal that is 'taught'! Hitler sold his radicalisation to people who were slaves to the banking system, and this system reduced them to fertile ground for Hitler's ideals. How did we actually solve that? We bombed them. Seriously, we let the ideal be taught. We waited and watched it foster and grow. We watched it invade country after country and only intervened once it became apparent that our own country was at risk.

So what should we have done? Recognise that a dangerous ideal is getting airtime, or gaining ground in the hearts of people, or threatening the peace? The time for action had elapsed by the time we got round to stopping them.

Is it the same this time? We have created vast vacuums of power in the Muslim world. Then we fund any opposition against the sovereign governments, and when the resultant 'terrorists' emerge from the rubble, we look to find a solution to this problem that we created. Then we ask, how do we stop radicalisation? In reality, the question really is: what should Muslims do to eradicate radicalisation? The answer is: we have unhappy young men with no jobs or future. Therefore we need to ensure that such easily influenced people are identified and measures put into place to make them valuable members of our society. Identify hate preachers and have them removed from society permanently;

not deported so that they can continue to preach their hate via the internet. An example needs to be made of such people.

The process of radicalisation can only be stopped if it can be identified as early as possible. After that, it is merely the act of locking the stable door. How do we identify radical teachings and teachers? That's where the authorities need to be more active. Tighter social media laws need to be implemented to deny free propaganda to those at risk of extremism, which includes terrorist training videos and anti-Western rants posted on YouTube. Authorities need to take Muslim communities into mutual confidence and trust; they need to learn the true concept of Islam. Then they will be in a position to challenge and change the misguided concepts accepted by victims of radicalisation. Taking Muslim communities into confidence will open more doors into a close-knit society and help to more easily identify trouble before it becomes unmanageable. **Pamir**

* * *

The Counter-Terrorism and Security Act 2015 is an Act of the UK Parliament commonly referred to as Prevent or the Prevent strategy. It came into force in July 2015. The aim of the Prevent strategy is to stop people becoming terrorists or supporting terrorism, as well as providing support to de-radicalise those vulnerable to being drawn into terrorism with an appropriate support plan for the individuals concerned.

The Government has defined extremism in the Prevent strategy as 'vocal or active opposition to fundamental British values, including democracy, the rule of law, individual liberty and mutual respect and tolerance of different faiths and beliefs. We also include in our definition of extremism calls for the death of members of our armed forces, whether in this country or overseas.'

However, despite the intention behind Prevent, many Muslims I spoke to were critical about its implementation and were angry that the strategy makes them feel that all Muslims are viewed as possible terrorism suspects.

> The government needs to engage with all Muslim communities, not just individuals or groups that are on the same wavelength. In the last few years, countering extremism and terrorism has turned into a big money spinner. The Home Office's Prevent programme is currently funded to the tune of £40m a year and I have seen think tanks emerge who are unqualified in providing information to the government about communities they do not understand. This is further exacerbating the problem of extremism. **Aniza**

Prevent gives out huge amounts of money to Islamic clerics and police forces to combat radicalisation in their communities. The police, generally speaking, won't have sufficient training or knowledge to properly challenge young people steeped in radical thoughts and desires. They won't have the skills to challenge misinterpretations of the Qur'an. The Islamic clerics obviously have greater knowledge, but their ability to challenge varies from person to person.

I know that both the police and Islamic clerics have been warned to steer clear of discussing foreign policy with those susceptible to radicalisation. They are not supposed to discuss the Palestine situation or any of the wars in Afghanistan or Syria. Neither can they address human rights abuses or discuss how the UK is an ally to Saudi Arabia and America.

I don't see how anybody gets rescued from extremism by this approach because it is too weak. One meeting with somebody whose mind is filled with extremism will not 'cure' them of this affliction. It took time to take root. It will take time to deconstruct. Remember, young people who get into extremism are usually angry with the world. My approach would be to deconstruct their religious justifications by going through the Qur'an and Hadith with them in fine detail to bring balance to the argument. I would discuss foreign policy with them, and dare I say it, I would probably agree with them on some points. But the difference would be that I would instruct them on the golden rule of not allowing emotion to guide you, rather letting intellect guide your emotions.

I would talk to them about work, family and the importance of family life. They need to be brought back to basics about respecting their parents. Leaving your family for ISIS is the highest level of disrespect and dishonour. They need to become more aware of God, the Prophet and the beauty and power of prayer.

Obviously, I can't tell any one person all of this in one sitting, but would endeavour to sow seeds with the intention of arranging to meet them again for further discussion. By meeting them again and again, I would draw them back to the true teachings of Islam, the Islam I know, which is about love, peace and honour. **Gabriel**

It's certainly not perfect, but I wouldn't dismiss it. It has done good work in spotting and apprehending would-be terrorists as well as placing hundreds of others under surveillance. Its current strategy needs improving rather than seeking an alternative programme. The government should take advice and criticism in order to improve it.

Prevent does not focus on ideology to counter extremism and terrorism and does not explain the difference between normative Islam and extremist ideology. The terminology of Prevent includes 'moderate' Muslims, and 'radical' Muslims and 'fundamentalists', the latter two often being used interchangeably. The strength of any strategy will lie in the research put into its development.

Strategists should have spoken to Muslims throughout the UK and should have taken into account their wide range of opinions and ideas on extremism and its causes. Prevent lacks a proper definition of what extremism is and should have a narrower and tauter meaning. Inadequate training to service providers who lack religious literacy seems to be another overarching deficiency. Doctors, teachers, social workers and the police need better training to understand what normative Islam is, and not to confuse everyday practices with extremism. A big pitfall of the strategy is its cautious 'better to be safe than sorry' approach, which has resulted in Muslims being wrongfully arrested and excused of extremism when it was later discovered that they were innocent. Every Muslim is seen as a potential threat. Individuals and their families have been deeply affected by this. Once a person is arrested their reputation is marred, resulting in a lasting detrimental effect. **Laham**

In preventing extremism it must be about striking a balance and looking at the various perpetrators, as opposed to looking at just one group. Admittedly, Islamic extremism is currently an unprecedented and global phenomenon, but along with this, white supremacy – another extremist ideology – is taking root across the world. Here in Britain, several far-right extremist groups are bringing religion into the equation by misquoting the Bible to justify their racist, xenophobic and anti-Muslim prejudices, and in doing so incite hatred and violence to achieve their aims. **Baari**

A FATHER'S STORY

'Please, doctor, save my son,' I pleaded with the consultant, and cried tears of joy when he survived. He was born a healthy weight but had some kind of severe protein deficiency, and the first few days were touch and go. A nun at the hospital nursed him during those tense days when we doubted his survival, and I remember thanking her so much and commenting she was a blessing from Allah. It was her gentleness and tender care that helped my son to recover.

Jamal was always an intelligent child. Even as a young boy he could read maps far better than I ever could. I used to joke that he was better than a satnav. Once when driving to Manchester he was able to memorise roads and streets with such ease that it would have been impossible to get lost with him by my side.

I endeavoured to raise my children as decent human beings, and tried to instil in them a firm belief and fear of the good Lord. I used to regularly take Jamal and his brother to a local cemetery where I explained death to them. They were taught not to believe in materialism because we're all going to die one day, and they were told to pray for people who had passed away as well as for themselves. Afterwards we would either go to the seaside or for a picnic if the weather was good. I also taught the boys to respect differences in others, and how the colour of someone's skin didn't matter because we are all creations of the good Lord.

Jamal was a very friendly child and would speak to anybody. He loved learning about everything from snakes and birds, to the moon and stars. I encouraged his inquisitiveness because I am a curious person myself. One day, Jamal and I took a bus journey and on returning home, I tested his knowledge about the buildings and landmarks we had passed, but he wasn't able to remember certain things. However, the next time I tested him he excelled and was able to describe everything he had seen – including the different buildings, roads, people, cars and trees. This was a good lesson because it had taught him the ability to observe. It paid off too because I remember a teacher at his grammar school once remarking to me that Jamal was the most intelligent young man in the entire school. There were times, though, when he got bored and lazy if he didn't find the curriculum challenging enough, but his high grades never wavered. There was incredible joy and pride amongst our family when he got his A-level results and was accepted into medical school.

My wife and I went to visit Jamal in London one day, and filled the car with shopping and some of my wife's home-cooked food for him. His landlady was a Muslim and widow. She remarked to us that she felt the good Lord had blessed her with Jamal, as he was so kind and respectful. In return she treated him like a son.

Jamal loved medical school. He would return home some weekends and during the holidays, and was always happy and full of life. He had friends, he played sports. He used to come to the mosque with me and always did his daily prayers. Life was good. Life was normal. We laughed together. We spoke about anything and discussed everything. That was the type of relationship everybody had in the family with each other. There was harmony in our home. Nobody bickered. Nobody disagreed or squabbled over trivial things. That wasn't the way we lived.

More good news arrived when Jamal announced he had been accepted by a top London hospital to train to be a surgeon. I was overjoyed that the good Lord had blessed my son with such a wondrous gift to save lives. We even spoke about what he planned to do once he qualified. He agreed to my request to go and work amongst the poor in Palestine. I planned to buy him the plane ticket and promised I would put money into his bank account every month to cover his rent and living expenses.

I told him not to charge for any operations he undertook, and he agreed – whether the patients were Muslim or not. He was going to Palestine to help those in need because Islam teaches us not to harm humanity but to strive to be good human beings. Little did I know that these plans to go to Palestine would never come to fruition. In fact, they couldn't have gone more awry.

We didn't detect anything wrong until he came home one weekend. We attended an event at our mosque to celebrate the Prophet's birthday. I remember when we arrived at the event that he refused to sit with his mother, which was most strange. I asked him what was wrong but he wouldn't say. I knew something was deeply troubling him. On the way home in the car, he remained silent. My wife and other son engaged in some light conversation, but Jamal remained silent. When we arrived home he got out of the car and banged the door. Once inside, I asked him again what was the matter and it was then that he blurted out, 'I don't want to be a surgeon anymore.' I asked him why and he replied, 'I am not allowed to look at women or treat them. Islam does not allow this.'

I tried explaining that there were no such rules in Islam but he shook his head before saying, 'I don't like this brand of Islam that you follow.' I repeated his words to him, 'This brand of Islam?'

He went on to criticise everything about Barelvi Muslims – our sermons, how we celebrate the birthday of the Prophet, our belief in saints, how we send blessings to the dead by reciting the entire Qur'an in honour of somebody after their death. He continued insulting me at every opportunity during the discussion before looking me in the eye and telling me that he had joined another branch of Islam because the Islam he was made to follow by me was neither true nor pure in its original sense.

In the days, weeks and months that followed, conversations always led to the topic of jihad. We had argument after argument. He wouldn't agree with me when I told him jihad belonged to the past when it was necessary in the time of the Prophet. He used to shout at me and say, 'No, it is for now!' He thought I spoke nonsense when I told him we needed to do jihad with our heart to win people with love and forgiveness, and not to kill them. He merely replied it was a good thing that kafirs were being killed and that their bodies should be left to rot and be eaten by dogs. I pleaded with him to question why the good Lord would have created so many different races and religions if he didn't want difference to exist in the world. He retorted that it was haram to be surrounded by white people and Christians. There was simply no reasoning with him because he had reached the point of no return. He even told me I was a kafir and that he would not hesitate in killing me. Can you imagine a son saying this to his father?

My son had been brainwashed by these radicals who go to universities and choose certain minds before extracting and reprogramming them. Jamal had become embroiled with Islamists who belonged to an organisation called Al-Muhajiroun. Their ideology was devised from the international terror group Hizb ut-Tahrir. These evil people take the war verses from the Qur'an out of context by concentrating on the 'killing' aspects. Jamal wouldn't accept the context in which they were written; instead he would say Muslims were suffering around the world and white people were to blame, and that jihad was necessary until Islam was universal and every single human being on the planet was a Muslim. At that moment, I realised they had created a new version of Islam that the world had never seen before. I also realised that a different version of Jamal had come into existence. He had been transformed from a loving, compassionate and kind person into someone who was angry, hate-filled and vile.

Some days I sit in silence and repeatedly ask myself how this could have happened to my son. I used to tell him and his brother stories about when I was younger and how I'd saved two Hindu boys from drowning in a Kenyan river, and the time I had once found a black boy scavenging bins for food and gave him food and drink along with some money. I told them these stories not to make me look good but with the hope of instilling into them the need for people to show humanity to others. Thankfully, my other son, who went on to study dentistry, took notice of my parental guidance and never caused me any trouble, but Jamal went on to discount every word I had ever said.

I sometimes feel I am to blame, that I should have gone deeper and taught him more about Islam and the Prophet before his mind was taken. Perhaps further guidance from me could have prevented his belief in such bloodshed, murder and massacre. My wife, too, blamed herself. She always said that a child's education begins in a mother's lap; this is where children first learn about Islam and the importance of a mother's influence on her children. Instead we raised a son who does not value human life.

It beggars belief how any Muslim can think that blowing human beings to smithereens is good. We are commanded not to kill, not even an ant. Islam teaches us to be merciful to the entire creation, to Muslims and non-Muslims, to friends and enemies, and even animals. There is a Hadith which states that the Prophet said 'Those who are merciful will be shown mercy by the Most Merciful. Be merciful to those on the earth and the one in the heavens will have mercy upon you' (Hadith – Tirmidhi). But the Satan's army that Jamal joined does not care because they have taken Islam and revised it into a version that is a million miles away from the true, honest and unadulterated Islam that the Prophet bestowed on his people.

Jamal's life now lies in ruins. He no longer speaks to either my wife or myself and says he wants nothing to do with us. He lives by himself and has let the house we gave him go to wreck and ruin. He has never married and has grown a long beard. My other son speaks to him occasionally. I believe Jamal does occasional delivery work but has been sacked from many jobs because of being disrespectful to his employers. So can you imagine how I feel? He has gone from a place of immense high standing to being a practical outcast in society. My life, too, has been left in ruins. My heart bleeds red. My eyes sob oceans. My brain is a mess and unable to fathom how this could have happened. My voice has become a lone cry in the wilderness. Will there ever be an end to all this misery? When, oh, when will there be an end to all this misery? **Hassan**

JIHADISTS RETURNING TO THE UK

It is surmised that teenage jihadists who left the UK to go to and join ISIS and who are still lucky enough to be alive will wish to return to home to their families. Bearing in mind that these British citizens elected to go and fight of their own free will, the issue is should they be spared prosecution? Some are already believed to have returned undetected. The question most raised is, have they become sleepers? Are they waiting for an opportunity to commit terrorist attacks here in the UK? It is unlikely they have become reformed characters, and although they might regret going abroad to commit jihad because of the hardships endured, their minds will still be poisoned with the Islamist ideology that prompted them to go in the first place.

It would be plain wrong to just let them back in the UK without any punishment or restrictions. What example would this be setting to the next generation of young Muslims? How would this be a deterrent to prevent them following a similar terrorist ideology if this erupts in some other part of the world? If these young terrorists do come back, they must be detained and interrogated. It must be established what crimes have been committed and they must be imprisoned for them. Even those who are released must be electronically tagged and monitored for the sake of national security. We need to develop de-radicalising programmes for such people, and the only way to free their poisoned minds is to reinforce the three Ts – theology, theology, theology. Challenging them and teaching them is the only cure for their damaged minds. **Kadeen**

If they are British, they should be allowed to return home to the UK. But for anybody to return and try to make excuses that they joined ISIS because they were young and deluded is not good enough. There can never be any justification for what they did. These people have brought shame on Islam, Britain and their families. Upon return they must be arrested, detained and de-programmed from the cult of ISIS – before being given lengthy prison sentences, especially if they are still deemed a risk to the public. If they have committed war crimes in Syria, they should be held fully accountable for these and be given life sentences. If they have raped, tortured and murdered Yazidi women in Syria, then they need to face the full consequences of these actions too and be sentenced accordingly. **Dilbar**

CHAPTER 9

Anti-Muslim Prejudice

The British Runnymede Trust, an independent research and social policy agency, defines Islamophobia as the 'dread or hatred of Islam and, therefore, the fear and dislike of all Muslims'. It goes on to say that Islamophobia entails the practice of discriminating against Muslims by excluding them from the economic, social and public life of the nation. Meanwhile Emisco (European Muslim Initiative for Social Cohesion) defines Islamophobia as 'a form of intolerance and discrimination motivated with fear, mistrust and hatred of Islam and its adherents'. Each year the 21st of September is designated as the European Action Day against Islamophobia and religious intolerance.

Islamophobia often entails combined elements of anti-Muslim feeling and racism, and is frequently manifested in combination with, xenophobia, anti-immigrant sentiments and religious bigotry.

Research carried out in 2014 found that Muslims often face the worst job discrimination of any minority group in Britain, with Muslim men up to 76 per cent less likely to have a job of any kind compared to white, male British non-Muslims of the same age and qualifications. And Muslim women are up to 65 per cent less likely to be employed than white non-Muslim counterparts (Dobson 2014).

Islamophobes hold a perception that Islam has no values in common with other cultures. They consider it inferior to the West, and that it is a violent political ideology rather than a religion.

The 1990s saw much suffering and conflict in Eastern Europe that was emotionally damaging and draining to Muslims across the world. The Bosnian War was an international armed conflict that took place in Bosnia and Herzegovina between 1992 and 1995. Deemed as an act of genocide, 8000 Bosniak Muslim men and boys were rounded up in Srebrenica and killed by Bosnian Serb forces, the worst massacre in Europe since the Second World War. This war crime came to symbolise the brutality of the ethnic disputes that erupted in the Balkans in the 1990s. The inhumanity of what happened during this war had deep and far-reaching effects on Muslims, with some feeling their identity and religion were devalued. Episodes of inhumanity still exist in the world against Muslims; for example, hundreds of thousands of Rohingya Muslim refugees have had to flee Myanmar in recent years to neighbouring Bangladesh and India – in what the United Nations denounced as ethnic cleansing on a grand scale.

Islamophobia can be divided into four key areas:

Exclusion: There are currently only a handful of British Muslims in positions of power and influence in politics, police and judiciary, commerce and business.

Discrimination: British Muslims have the highest rates of UK unemployment. The UK also has high child poverty and in-work poverty amongst Bangladeshi and Pakistani communities who earn below the minimum wage.

Violence: This consists of verbal abuse, physical assaults, as well as criminal damage to mosques. Far-right extremists have made every Muslim 'fair game' to attack, but female Muslims are mainly targeted because of their visible traditional dress code.

Prejudice: There are some tabloid newspapers in the UK – aimed at a middle-class, white readership – that barely disguise their prejudices towards Muslims and Islam, and readily publish biased views to influence their readers.

It's a strange phenomenon to hate or dislike someone so greatly that you wish to do them harm, feeling compelled to insult, belittle or attempt to dehumanise them in some aspect or other. Black people, gay people and Jewish people, among other groups, have been on the receiving end of bigotry and discrimination for a long time. In the last 30 years the spotlight has switched to Muslims and Islam. Suddenly, it seems to be their time to experience intolerance from others about their religion, although a level of political motivation is suspected to be behind this as a diversion from when the Cold War ended.

British Muslims are men and women, young and old, heterosexual or gay, disabled or able-bodied. They may be white, black, Asian or come from other ethnic backgrounds. Like racism, homophobia and anti-Semitism – the core ingredients of Islamophobia are fear and ignorance, which spill over into physical violence and hate crime.

Islamophobia occurs far less in major cities where there is a large community of Muslims than in smaller towns and cities where Muslims may be a minority. But is the issue in essence a case of Islamophobia or Muslimphobia? It could be argued that it's the latter, because non-Muslims generally know little about the teachings of Islam, so have little to base any fear or dislike upon, whereas their dislike of Muslims is based on seeing Muslims in person and perceiving them as different, dangerous or both – as people who are a violent threat to the British way of life and a threat to customs and culture.

England adored Muslims in early 1970s. Muslims were still new to the country. We were different within the Christian setting. People loved to say hello. It was a beautiful country back then. People didn't care about us being Muslim. The opposite is true now. People are scared of us. For many years there was no hatred.

Now, they want us to leave because they think we are terrorists. **Shajaat**

But not every Muslim feels so strongly about feeling unwelcome in the UK. Some say they are blessed to live in the UK, which they see as being far less Islamophobic than some other European countries.

I truly believe Britain is a tolerant society that respects other people's faith and culture. It is from my experience and that of my family and friends living in Britain that makes me make this statement. When I read and learn about the wider disparity of Muslims and non-Muslims in other parts of Europe, I feel that many are still at the overt racism stage, whereas in the UK we have legislation and hate crime that is recorded and reported, and recently the Government have included Islamophobia as a hate crime. **Aasif**

However, despite Aasif's belief that Britain is a tolerant society, when Islamophobia shows its ugly face, it brings misery, rejection and violence in its wake. Frequently, the media carry reports about attacks on Muslims and mosques. There is a small but enduring stream of despicable acts, such as a pig's trotter being thrown into the entrance of a mosque, or a Muslim finding a slice of bacon on their car door handle. These hate crimes are sometimes carried out by lone individuals, or by groups associated with far-right movements or by sympathisers to their cause, who see Muslims as alien, non-integrating immigrants.

EVENTS THAT LED TO AN ESCALATION IN ISLAMOPHOBIA IN THE UK

When the fatwa was imposed on Salman Rushdie in 1989 after the publication of his novel *The Satanic Verses*, some Muslim communities welcomed it and reacted violently. There was a demonstration in Bradford that resulted in a public burning of the book, an act widely seen as barbaric. Muslims seen on TV were often unfavourably viewed as men with long beards who spoke poor English, resulting in a prejudiced view of Islam. Here the religion was suddenly being put under the spotlight and seen in a wider context of 'migrants causing trouble'. This was the first crystallisation of the identity of British Muslims in a negative way.

Muslim communities experienced internal disputes. There was a division of views amongst Muslims, leaving some feeling very ostracised. This period also saw the beginning of calls for better integration of Muslims into British culture. At the same time there was huge resentment from Muslims, who found Britain's fundamental stance on the rights to speak and publish freely hard to comprehend because they came from dictatorial societies.

The Gulf War in 1990 also saw Islam come under unfavourable scrutiny. The war began when Saddam Hussein, the president of Iraq, accused neighbouring Kuwait of stealing Iraqi petroleum by slant drilling. He declared Kuwait the nineteenth province of Iraq, and invaded and occupied the country. The seven-month-long occupation only ended after a short but brutal American-led conflict in which 47 British soldiers died. The war was seen as selfish and needless, and the fact that so many innocent people died destroyed any positive views about Muslims living in the UK. This was unjustified to them and, indeed, other Muslims elsewhere around the world, who had nothing to do with what happened between Iraq and Kuwait. But their religion and identity was blamed for the deaths of British soldiers. Sometimes it was overt and other times covert, but always consisting of prejudice and discrimination.

The 1990s saw rapid developments and changing cycles of political power across the Middle East and Eastern Europe, and in places Muslims began to feel their identity was threatened. Some were unable to speak out, while others felt less inclined to be quiet and sought action. There was a definite rise of religiosity amongst some younger Muslims in the UK, partly as a result of the Islamic revolution in Iran and as a result of what occurred in Bosnia, but it was a development of an 'evangelical' version of Islam. This resulted in young Islamic militants distributing leaflets outside mosques in Finsbury Park and East London, telling other Muslims that their brothers and sisters were dying and that they must fight. These leaflets were reported in the media to widespread disapproval, and while the leaflets were not indicative of the views of mainstream Muslims, they nevertheless were all grouped together with regard to the matter. Foul propaganda espoused by far-right extremists (including the British National Party (BNP) and English Defence League (EDL)) added fuel to the fire, and thus began the transformation of Muslims as a whole being viewed as violent and dangerous people.

ISLAMOPHOBIA IN THE UK

Reports from by Tell MAMA (Measuring Anti-Muslim Attacks), a UK Muslim charity that monitors incidents of Islamophobia, have noted Islamophobia occurring in relation to the following:

1. Schools and colleges: A general low level of Islamophobia occurs amongst children and young people. This may be sparked by a news item in relation to a terrorist incident – for example a non-Muslim child may make cruel remarks about these killings to a Muslim child.
2. Visible Muslim women: Muslim women become prime targets when they are out in the community by themselves. Attacks range from being verbally harassed to being spat at and having their hijab pulled off. These attacks often happen when the attackers, mainly men between the ages of 15 to 40, have seen something on the news that reinforces their dislike towards Muslims.
3. Assets and resources: There has been a steady rise in the number of attacks from neo-Nazi and far-right sympathisers on mosques, houses and other property owned by Muslims. These attacks may take the form of graffiti, bringing pork into

a mosque, breaking windows and bomb threats. The attackers are males, usually aged 25 to 45.

4. Workers in late-night take-away restaurants: This situation usually involves people who have being drinking and going to kebab outlets at the end of the night. Unfortunately, these visits sometimes turn into drunken racist rants but also extend to those perceived to be Muslim, who receive abuse as a result. Police involvement in such incidents is not uncommon.

5. The plethora of grooming scandals in the UK: Public outrage at these abuse cases has spilled over towards taxi drivers and others who are Muslim, or perceived to be Muslim. They have been at the receiving end of passengers and customers who think it is acceptable to be both verbally and physically aggressive.

6. Bus stops and train stations: These attacks often take place when cars drive past and drivers or passengers shout abuse at Muslims, or those perceived to be Muslim, who are waiting for a bus. It is also known for people to shout abuse from trains and on the concourse of train stations (particularly at mainline stations).

7. Employability and interviews: Institutions can have Islamophobia and racism ingrained in their management structure, ensuring that Muslims, or those perceived to be Muslim, are not offered interviews or jobs, regardless of excellent qualifications and work experience pertaining to the role.

8. Goods and services: Some people tend to think it is acceptable to be rude to a sales assistant or a waiter who they perceive to be Muslim. This can also extend to making a complaint in a spiteful and unjustifiable manner against a Muslim worker.

9. The online world: This is particularly widespread, especially with US-based Facebook groups with pro-Trump or extreme far-right views. They distribute internet memes demonising Muslims in general. There are also several online Islamophobic Facebook pages and websites in the UK with far-right propaganda, which have thousands of followers without any degree of censorship to veto their content.

LIVES AFFECTED BY ANTI-MUSLIM PREJUDICE

When they see my hijab, I sometimes receive disgusting looks from men parked in vans or at traffic lights when I'm crossing the road. I see anger and aggression in the way they look at me. That's why I have adopted a friendly smiling face as I walk to college because I want to be seen as approachable, that Muslims are not horrible people. **Naima**

I have experienced random incidents where I have been abused. I remember travelling home on the underground one night after attending the mosque. I was dressed in a tobe and topi (cap) when a man shouted at me, 'This is a British country, and we don't welcome Muslims here.' I answered him back, telling them that I was born here and that this was very much my country. I felt sadness that he could be so ignorant, but also angry. How dare he accuse me of not being from this country? Did he not have any understanding of history, of how my forefathers from Bangladesh came to Europe and helped fight for this country in both the First and Second World Wars? People have short memories. But honestly, how can people say things like that and think they can get away with it?

I love this country because it is my country. If there was an enemy attacking this country, I would fight to protect it like my forebears did. I'm English in every possible way. I love fish and chips and even support Tottenham!

On another occasion, another man, young with an Eastern European accent, shouted at me on a train, saying 'Hey you, get out of this country.' I could tell he had drunk alcohol by his demeanour. I just laughed at the absurdity of it. Here he was, probably having only been here a few years himself, telling me, somebody who was born here, to leave.

Overall, these were both minor incidents, but I've had male friends who've had sandwich wrappers and drink cans thrown at them. So yes, Islamophobia is a problem in Britain, and it appears to be on the increase. Many Muslims encounter it but do not speak out. They fear that doing so may do more damage than good. So they insulate and protect themselves; however, more people are informing advocacy groups of their experiences and are encouraged to report more serious incidents to the police. **Musawwer**

This is caused mainly by the media in the West who are against Muslims and Islam. They want to paint a bad picture of Islam and to give it a bad image. They always strive to highlight the wrongs of Islam. They know well that only a tiny number of Muslims are terrorists and that those who turn to violence like this are petty criminals and not really Muslims.

Just because somebody says they've converted to Islam and have a Muslim name does not make them a Muslim. There is no better example of this than Khalid Masood, the man who caused the carnage in Westminster. The media come with their own agenda. Look at the proprietors who own these news agencies. They have right-wing views. They have Zionist views. They believe that the events of 9/11 paint a bad picture of every Muslim, but it doesn't. You simply can't put everyone in the same basket.

Personally, I have never experienced direct discrimination, but I know several of the women who come to the mosque have had swear words shouted at them. There were also a few nasty threatening letters addressed to the mosque I attend, which the imam passed to the police. **Qasid**

Occasionally, somebody might shout from a car that I shouldn't live in this country. Some people's minds are poisoned by what far-right extremist groups say about Muslims (i.e. that we are trying to take over England). Then some aspects of the media try to scapegoat Islam by referring to the religion when somebody commits a crime, whereby they don't state a non-Muslim's religion in similar circumstances. **Abbas**

AIZA'S STORY

During the past 25 years I have witnessed several incidents. I remember after the first Iraq war in 1990 when some women, who I had been friendly with at the nursery where I dropped off my son, suddenly stopped speaking to me. I wondered what was going on that caused this, so after a few days of being ignored I asked them what was going on. Mutterings of 'war and all that' was their reply to which I responded, 'Okay, but what have I done to cause that?' They were unable to answer me so we discussed the subject and we all agreed that the war was indeed concerning. After that they resumed their greetings to me every time we met.

Another ten or so years passed by and we had the Crawley fertiliser bombers after 9/11. This was a big news item in the media at the time. One day I answered the phone, to be subjected to a woman shouting down the line, 'You people are the root of these problems, why don't you go back to your country?' I started asking her questions, 'Did I do this? Was I arrested?' I was glad I didn't simply put the receiver down because after turning the tables on her, we were able to have a much calmer conversation, ending in me advising her to do some research into the true teachings of Islam, which would show her that no rational Muslim would ever become a bomber.

Over the years I have noticed people refraining from sitting next to me on the train if they can avoid it. It has become so noticeable. Once upon a time, it offended me because I couldn't understand what they could imagine I had done for them not to trust me. But over time I have become indifferent to it.

Let me tell you something amusing: one day I was getting off a train after having encountered the usual suspicious glances. I was wearing a head scarf that had beads on its end. It was a cold day and as I swung the scarf around to cover up, the end bit with the beads accidently hit a man in the head. I automatically apologised. He smiled and said not to worry about it before I added, 'Sorry again for attacking you with my weapon of mass destruction.' People in the carriage understood the joke and laughed.

I remember the time when they introduced restrictions on liquids at airports. There was a knock on the door one day. I went to answer it and found a woman outside. She started screaming abuse about Muslims causing problems for everyone with these new security measures at airports. She was literally screaming in my face, 'How dare you do this to Britain!' My eldest son, who was 17 at the time, came to my assistance. I wanted to close the door on the woman but my son said, 'Mum, let me talk to her.' He asked her to stop shouting and calmed her down before entering into a discussion about Islam and told her what was happening had nothing to do with the proper teachings of Islam. I was so proud of him. The woman left without saying another word.

On another occasion, I was in my local supermarket walking down an aisle with a shopping trolley when I overheard a middle-aged woman who was smartly dressed remark out loud, 'those ignorant Muslims'. I ignored her and carried on with my shopping. She repeated the remark again, so I decided to turn and ask her if there was a problem. She reiterated her comments about Muslims being ignorant, before turning to her husband who was standing next to her, adding that Muslims don't know how to be civilised. I told her I found her remarks offensive, but she continued with her tirade before I suggested I call the police to settle the matter. Her attitude then changed. She said she was only voicing an opinion and that she wasn't out to cause trouble. I told her I meant what I said about calling the police, before adding that Muslim women aren't all meek and shy and that lots of them are like me, who do not take abuse lying down. She apologised. I told her not to do it again to me or anybody else, or she might be held accountable, before continuing with my shopping.

ANTI-MUSLIM PREJUDICE AS A RESULT
OF ISLAMIC TERRORISM

Wherever the terrorist act occurs, whether it's Europe, here in Britain or somewhere else in the world, Muslim communities have to face up to their mosques being targeted and their women being attacked on the street. Males are given a hard time too. I've lost count of the number of times I get stared at on the tube.

Once I was running late for a tube and just managed to board it before the train doors closed. There were a group of people laughing and joking amongst themselves as I boarded, but the looks I got when they saw me dressed in my tobe robes and topi cap carrying a bag –they stopped smiling, but I smiled at them. You can imagine what they were thinking when they saw a young Muslim male dressed in Islamic clothing carrying a rucksack enter their carriage with the train moving forward. There was silence. I managed to get a seat, and after a few stops a middle-aged woman boarded the train. I got up and offered her my seat. She thanked me. She was from Jamaica like me, so we got chatting and the ice began to thaw amongst my fellow travellers. **Babr**

The actions of a minority of people have damaged the good reputation of Muslims in the UK. I remember during Friday prayers after one of the sexual abuse cases when three men from a far-right political group broke a window in our mosque, scattering some holy textbooks onto the floor in the process. They then came into the mosque where there were 300 people present. I told my congregation to let the men have their say but not to answer them. Afterwards, they left peacefully.

Our neighbours were very supportive. I received several text messages. One woman even brought us a box of biscuits to say how sorry she was for us. She complimented the congregation on having been so patient when confronted with such unpleasant behaviour during the service, which was very sweet of her. **Yazan**

Islamophobia is continued racism from the 1960s. The far-right movements will always target immigrant families, and they love to pick and choose verses from the Qur'an and misinterpret them. They will take a line about slavery and turn it into something it isn't. They would never show you a verse that talks above love and tolerance.

There is also what is called 'the white flight', referring to white people who move out of the neighbourhood when Asians move into it. It still happens to this day, with people not wanting to live next door to a Muslim. What they expect will happen, I don't know, but they move at the first opportunity.

These days xenophobia is prevalent in the UK. Some black people have short memories. Recently, a friend of mine told me a story about how a black driver pulled out in front of him and when he beeped his horn, the man turned around and shouted at him, 'Go back to your country, you Muslim terrorist.'

The fact that people need to realise is that working-class Muslim neighbourhoods are far safer than other working-class areas. You don't hear of Muslims attacking people. But do you think it would be safe for a Muslim to enter a predominantly white working-class area and escape verbal abuse of some kind. They may even get physically assaulted. But Muslims are resilient people. They are strong in their faith. They carry on minding their own business. Respecting differences in others, though, is always a two-way process. Muslims have made mistakes in the past. Integration should have been a higher priority in past decades, with people making more of an effort to learn English when they came to live in Britain. **Radwan**

GROOMING SCANDALS AND THE FEAR OF BEING LABELLED ISLAMOPHOBIC

In recent years the UK has seen several high-profile court cases involving sex offenders from the Muslim communities in Newcastle,

Rotherham, Rochdale, Telford and Oxford. The perpetrators were identified as predominantly Asian with seven in ten believed to be of Pakistani and Bangladeshi Muslim heritage (Adil and Rafiq, 2017). These men sexually exploited white women and girls (some as young as 12) by drugging, gang raping and trafficking them. Some fell pregnant and underwent abortions. Several of the perpetrators were known in their families and communities as practising Muslims before they were arrested. These racist sex crimes were motivated by greed and contained aspects of machismo and contempt for people who were not of their own ethnicity. Several questions remain unanswered. Was it because of cultural prejudices that led to these Muslims to prey on white females, rather than women within their own communities? Were these white women seen as unworthy disbelievers who were 'fair game' for the cruelty and abuse unleashed upon them?

These are valid questions to ask in this chapter because the perpetrators of these crimes brought self-inflicted shame on their communities and besmirched the good reputation of Islam at a time when it is already under attack because of extremists and terrorism. One thing that emanates from these abuse scandals is the backlash against ordinary Muslims and their religion. This backlash came from ordinary members of the public, who questioned what Islamic community leaders would do to stamp out the malaise in their communities to prevent further abuse happening. When the Newcastle grooming scandal ended in lengthy prison sentences for the men responsible, this led to questions being raised in the media by people who cast mistrust on the religion, coupling this with derogatory remarks about the way the religion supposedly treats women. Alleged poor treatment of women was believed to be a factor responsible for the mindset of the perpetrators with the way they viewed women.

Aspects of political correctness entered the debate, with some media outlets questioning if pointing out the race of the men involved was a distraction to constructive discussion about the grooming scandals. Others in the media were bold enough to say that they thought Britain has a problem with British Pakistani men raping and exploiting white girls, and that Muslim communities needed to address this issue. All of these differing views led to tension and unrest and a fear of saying the wrong thing in case it caused offence. In that sense, political correctness became a hindrance and prevented honest and frank discussion with those seeking solutions by being fearful of being called Islamophobic or racist. Indeed, some commentators questioned if being called Islamophobic has now eclipsed being called racist, a fear leading to some suppressing and self-censoring their opinions, and the counter idea that ideas should be allowed to be expressed without labelling or blaming. In other words, being able to identify the true extent and cause of the problem without fear of being accused of bigotry for doing so.

So what are the answers to these grooming sex scandals? I asked six imams for their views on what local communities need to do to convince the public that abuse scandals like these are not being brushed under the carpet, that Muslim communities are not in denial or oblivious about what is occurring, or that attention is being deflected away from the issue.

I remember after the Oxford grooming scandal when one of the perpetrator's mothers blamed the victims for wearing short skirts to tempt her sons. This is part of the 'them' and 'us' mentality that unfortunately some Muslims have developed in the UK. Their mindset towards the victims is: they drink; they smoke – so let's have sex with them because they are going to hell anyway.

These men have been brainwashed into believing that as long as the declaration of faith is uttered on their lips before they take their last breath, they will be pardoned for their wrongdoing and will go straight to paradise, such is their perceived privilege for being Muslim.

There is a social apartheid here in the UK between Muslims and non-Muslims. Some Muslims think that they are integrated just because they speak English and watch *EastEnders*, but there are ghettos existing in cities like Leeds, Leicester and Luton where

Muslims never associate with non-Muslims. Again, this is the 'them' and 'us' scenario where non-Muslims are seen as the kafir (disbelievers) who go to hell, while 'We Muslims go to paradise.' They fail to notice that Mrs Jones living next door to them is a lovely, moral and upright woman, so why should she deserve to go to hell?

What needs to change is a shift in the theology movement – to stop this exclusivity that creates these divides between Muslims and non-Muslims. We need Islam in Britain to be rooted and relevant to this society. Every time something like this happens, it must feel like mana from heaven to far-right organisations, adding fuel to their existing antagonism against Islam and Muslims. It isn't helped by a lack of outcry from Muslim communities at these scandals affecting their communities.

I am doing my bit to change this. After the Oxford grooming scandal I read out the names of each of the people jailed for these horrific crimes in my Friday sermon because I wanted to name and shame them. I wonder how many of the other 2000 mosques in this country did something similar to this? I did this because each of these Muslims brought shame on Islam and on Britain. They are criminals who deserve the prison sentences they received for their wickedness and deceit. **Dr Hargey**

Unfortunately there are cultural attitudes amongst Asian people in the UK, particularly Pakistani, who for unknown reasons take a particularly dim view of white girls who are troubled or in the care system. They view these girls as not being as good as everybody else. These men would have been brought up listening to their parents denouncing the poor attitudes towards girls of this kind, who felt stricter parenting would have prevented their poor behaviour.

Then there will be imams from the Pakistani community who will share these views – so there won't be any discussion about these scandals in the mosques. Personally, I don't know why these men committed these crimes but suspect it's to fulfil their own personal needs and that it involves money. It has nothing to do with the religion.

We need to reflect on these scandals. We need young Muslims to undergo a personal development course that deals with living in the Western world and how best to respect others. The problem is that most young Muslims these days stop attending madrassah at the age of 13, which is a most important development stage in a young adolescent's life when moral teachings most need to take root.

I believe some of the men jailed for these crimes will be remorseful, but others will blame the females. I don't believe that the Western ways of rehabilitation will work on these men because they will not accept Western intervention. What they need is a programme for Muslims in prison that looks at the principles of Islam – differences between right and wrong that will enable them to take responsibility for their actions.

Islamophobia and hate crimes always increase after Muslims are involved in criminality. These men will not have considered the long-term consequences of their actions. I believe human beings who have come to that level of what these men did are those who are only capable of thinking of their own personal needs. **Imam Choudhury**

They will definitely have been influenced by upbringing, which I would guess wasn't right because they lacked moral reasoning. Some might even have had bad experiences with white people and decided to seek their revenge. I have heard of people who have had a bad experience with a Muslim and then go on cause to harm to other Muslims. Their actions are evil and there can't be any excuses. The Prophet once said, 'No man will ever enter paradise because of his actions, but it is only out of God's mercy.'

There is a lack of moral guidance being given to young Muslims in our communities. A lot of the imams are elderly and speak little English and therefore Friday sermons will not be conducted in English. Only 20 per cent of our mosques, if that, have an English-speaking imam.

These clerics usually preach about disbelievers and how they need to improve themselves. But Muslims need to improve themselves. Talking about any type of sexual behaviour in mosques is considered taboo. A few months ago I discussed pornography in my Friday sermon. A few men came up to me afterwards and told me that I needed to be careful of the wording when discussing such matters. Another told me that he didn't think my sermon was necessary and another questioned why I discussed this subject before insisting their kids were good.

We need to focus on the next generation growing up. We need to talk about practical issues – about stress, anger, desires. Muslims are lacking in contribution in debates about the world, how to raise children, the pressures of young people growing up – stuff like that. If we don't do it now, when should it be done? The world is not getting better or easier. There are some mosques in the UK already doing this good work but they are only a minority. Poor management and poor pay and conditions do not yield scholars to work in mosques. Even when the elderly imams have passed away there is not a younger generation of imams ready to take over who can create unity in diverse communities. **Imam Rafiq**

There are two scenarios to be considered here. There's the home-life culture and life outside of the home. At home, these men will have been taught to have respect for their mothers, grandmothers and sisters. They will have heard how well the Prophet treated his wives and daughters, and the importance of modesty and women covering themselves. They will be used to women in their families not going out that much. They will have grown up in a culture where men hardly ever talk to women outside of their families, and they certainly will never have socialised externally with women from their own culture.

At home, sons are well behaved in front of their parents. Parents interpret this as a sign that if they are respectful at home then they are the same outside. But outside the home, sadly some men are not the same. Those involved in these grooming scandals are criminals who will have sought to get their hands on easy money. They may start selling drugs and one thing leads to another. They learn that Western women are easy to talk to and they seek to socialise with them, but deep down while they have respect for women from their own culture, they see Western women as different and less worthy of respect. They are also viewed as easy prey to corrupt for their own means.

I know from being an imam that Asian families, those from Bangladesh, Pakistan and India, will seek to hide any family problem they have. To them, it's about protecting the family status. It's about protecting themselves from a sense of shame they might feel, fearing that others will think that it's their fault if shame is brought to their doorstep. That's a big problem we have in Muslim communities. The cultural norms help to hide the problem. Asking for help only draws attention to it. The first instinct is to cover it up and pretend it doesn't exist, to protect reputation. There is no thought put into having a prevention strategy. Only when somebody is caught up in a crime and is forced to accept what has happened do people seek to 'fix' it. **Imam Osman**

People shouldn't be afraid to speak out. Wrong is wrong. Muslims should not be defended, especially those who call themselves Muslims but carry out actions that are not Islamic, that have no decency. I am appalled that people who consider themselves Muslim would do such a thing to females. Could they not imagine how they'd feel if it was their mother, sister or cousin who was treated like this? Did the Prophet never once cross their minds? 'Wish for others what you wish for yourself?' (Hadith – Tirmidhi).

It angers me that Muslims have to take the blame for what a handful of criminals do to others, especially when these people are operating outside of their religion. The problem isn't Islam. The problem is culture. Men from Pakistan, India, Bangladesh and Afghanistan think white women are easy to have sex with. They seek pleasure from them because they believe white women want to sleep with as many different men as possible. It's a disgusting attitude to have towards women, to see them as being so worthless like this. Unfortunately, there is corruption in Hindu texts that has made its way into cultural norms, which affects Muslims from India, Pakistan and Bangladesh. Then there is the Taliban, who oppress women in Afghanistan at every opportunity. These are not new attitudes coming to the surface. They have been there for centuries, seeping their way through the ancestral lineage of these countries that I mentioned.

Men who carry out these disgusting acts do not fear Allah. As I said, they have no shame. The immediate solution is tough punishments for those who carry out these acts. They must be held accountable, and for others doing these things they need to be mindful of what will happen if they are caught. They need to repent and make amends for the harm they have done, because Allah will definitely punish them on earth, and I'm not talking just about prison sentences when I say that. **Imam Akram**

Desires are fine but it's how you fulfil them that can be a problem. A lot of Asian people have puritanical Victorian attitudes towards sex because they have never been able to talk openly about the subject.

Sex within the rules of Islam is quite liberal. The only things not permissible between married heterosexuals are anal sex and having sex when the woman is menstruating. But a lack of discussion about sex leads to poor knowledge, and it is with this that these weak Muslims (who are also weak human beings) will not have been satisfied with their wives and therefore will have looked outside their marriages for adventure.

Of course, greed, money and power are also alluring factors towards sin. Men involved in these grooming scandals used vulnerable females to satisfy their unfulfilled desires because of ill-suited arranged marriages. It beggars belief that Muslims could do such a thing – how any man can do such wicked things –

right under our noses. And to think that this is probably going on unnoticed in other parts of the country boils my blood with anger and disgust.

Men who do this type of thing are criminals from stop to start. It's not just a problem of white girls getting abused; there are young Asian Muslims also being abused. The numbers are still low, but I would estimate that they will increase after more young people have the confidence to speak out, and are believed.

Professor Alexis Jay's report in 2014 on the abuse scandal in Rotherham highlighted that out of the 1400 female victims, between 150 to 200 of these were young Asian Muslims who had been groomed for sex. From my own understanding into this terrible problem, it is believed that Asian men target these young Asian girls coming out of school by paying them compliments and telling them how beautiful they look. They know that they won't meet them in pubs or nightclubs and therefore won't be able to ply them with alcohol or drugs. They use other tactics – offering lifts and buying them gifts. They also use psychological tactics, eventually telling them that they are in love with them. These young impressionable girls are flattered and feel obliged to do 'anything' for the man who loves them.

The true scale of this epidemic is yet to reveal itself, I feel – remember, the cover-ups in Rotherham and Telford went on for years because the victims weren't believed by their parents and also by social services. It will be the same in Muslim households. These girls will fear telling their parents or siblings in fear of not being believed or of retribution. There is also the possibility of a cover-up within families to protect honour and prevent shame. Therefore, there will be Muslim parents who are in denial. But this type of grooming is definitely happening and it is the responsibility of Muslim communities to report inappropriate behaviour.

Ask yourself: is it normal to see an older man giving gifts to a female unrelated to them? The media just focus on one aspect of the problem and will imply that it is a matter of race and religion, but the fact that it's occurring within communities has yet to be discussed widely. Media reports of these grooming scandals inevitably fuel the various far-right extremist groups operating in the UK, who will organise marches in large towns and cities intent on stirring up hatred against Muslims and spreading as much Islamophobic poison as possible. But the behaviour of the men involved in these grooming scandals is not indicative of the thousands of other law-abiding Muslim males living in Britain, and the actions behind grooming certainly have nothing to do with the teachings of Islam. But these points are not what you will hear being announced in these demonstrations. **Imam Mahmood**

RECOMMENDATIONS TO COMBAT ISLAMOPHOBIA

Muslims I spoke to in my research feel the following six suggestions would make a difference in combating Islamophobia in the UK.

1. Workshops in schools/colleges and universities: Greater emphasis needs to be placed on human rights and female emancipation, as well as on how to respect and value difference in others, so as to improve society for the next generation. Schools need to incorporate this into PSHE (Personal, Social and Health Education) studies, and student unions can challenge Islamophobia through debates.
2. Mosques: They have already begun having open days, but need to do this more frequently and advertise these events, inviting more people from the community to come in and ask questions. This way non-Muslims would get to know Muslims and develop some understanding of Islam, and will realise that Muslims are ordinary people with shared similarities and needs. Mosques also need to use their pulpits against paedophilia and promiscuity.
3. Role models: Some Muslims feel there are too few positive Muslim role models for non-Muslims to look up to and respect,

although there are some well-known sports people, mainly cricketers, boxers, and a handful of politicians. But role models do not have to be rich or widely famous. Local communities need to be seen to value the contributions of Muslims as integral parts of their communities.

4. Policing: A greater understanding is needed on the part of the police regarding online abuse and Islamophobic language. Both the upper echelons of police management and police recruits need to be given a better education and cultural sensitivity about Islamophobia and its effects on Muslim communities. In this way it can be dealt with delicately, with an increased likelihood of prosecutions against perpetrators.

5. The legal and criminal justice system: Sometimes courts and the Crown Prosecution Service have a poor understanding of the issues. They need to know what far-right extremism looks and feels like for its victims, and the impact it has on lives. There must be consideration as to whether the right to 'free speech' is sometimes used to protect Islamophobic harassment, especially that which might incorrectly be viewed as being at a 'low level', and therefore 'acceptable'.

6. Media: It is felt that there should be more newspaper articles and more documentaries that educate people about the lives of Muslims and Islam; that too much emphasis is placed on extremism and radicalisation and not nearly enough on the teachings of Islam and how most Muslims, who are average law-abiding citizens, live their lives.

CHAPTER 10

Other Thoughts and Opinions

AN IDEAL WORLD

I could introduce you to many young Muslims who would greet you warmly because they feel obliged to be friendly. Their affability is because they are cautious of being misunderstood or giving the wrong impression. So they make a point of displaying good character – to appear as normal, regular people and to smile in the hope of removing any perceived ideas non-Muslims may have about them.

Many of these young people will tell you they feel more comfortable dressed in Islamic clothing than Western, but that's not to say they don't wear jeans and T-shirts when they go to the cinema, for example, with friends. Some love football and cricket, and eat many types of halal food, including burgers and kebabs. Some read novels, and many of them will be happy to tell you that *The Kite Runner* by Khaled Hosseini is one of their favourites. Most expect to get married by the time they reach their mid-twenties. These young Muslims generally dislike the British media who, they feel, misinterpret them by failing to report how good Muslims are, in general, at practising their religion and how seemingly well they contribute to British society day in and day out.

These young people will tell you stories about discrimination as well – like the young student who told me that one day he and his friend, who were both dressed in Islamic clothing, were walking down a corridor and came into contact with a group of males advertising a paintballing challenge. One of the men said to the two Muslim friends, 'You two lads look like you could handle a gun.' It may have been intended as a joke, but it caused offence.

My intention for writing this is to go further than simply introducing young Muslims to you. I want to take you inside their ideal world. Before I started writing this book, I was on a bus in London one day when a young male Muslim boarded, dressed in his Islamic tunic, and sat opposite me. He, like so many other Muslims, wasn't the happiest looking of young men, but there was something about him that caught my imagination. I wondered what sort of person he was, what he was thinking about, how he perceived the world, and what would have made him happier than his outward expression suggested.

Having a culture and religion that is so different to my own, my mind wandered further and I began to consider what his ideal world would look like and what could be done to make it happen. What would please him most about life and the universe? As a result of my musings, I decided to include this in the book, and the conclusion outlines a selection of answers young Muslims gave me after I posed the question to them.

> I would love to see a world where everyone was able to enjoy peaceful lives alongside those of different faiths and cultures and not just to put up with one another: a world that was filled with mutual respect and an ability to live in harmony. I would love to see this happen – where everybody could feel free and at ease enough to have good public debates with each other about religion and other worldly affairs without the need to resort to violence. **Bazil**

I would like to see greater proper organised interfaith dialogue across the world amongst Muslims and non-Muslims. I am friends with many people of different faiths and I never understand why others can't follow suit. Religion should not divide people. I believe all religious leaders should come together in order to develop understanding and respect, and for this to disseminate down to their communities and congregations. This would include various groups of Muslims too who are alienated from each other through petty grievances. **Raani**

I would remove the current Muslims who are MPs because they are merely token gestures to ensure the government and politics are seen as diverse and inclusive. But these Muslims are dead weight and do not represent the three-million-plus Muslims. They should not be silenced when speaking out about foreign policy. We need people who can represent us because currently we have non-Muslim MPs who respect Muslims more than the current Muslims in politics. **Ibrahim**

I would like cities to be compatible with nature. There is far too much pollution in the world. We need to be more eco-friendly. People need to listen about the dangers to the planet as a result of CO_2 emissions. I would make growing trees mandatory practice in every country. I would get every human being on the planet to grow a tree. Can you imagine how much better our world would be without pollution? Can you imagine how this would improve people's health and well-being? **Tabana**

I would eradicate poverty. Do we really need to live in the modern world where people are still short of food, clothing and shelter? The answer is 'no' because it's not unrealistic that all of these basic needs could be provided to those without. Muslims are expected to give 2.5 per cent of their income to the poor. Can you imagine if everybody in the world made this contribution, and honest governments used it appropriately? How soon would poverty become a thing of the past? But for this to happen, all world leaders would need to believe in justice and fairness for all its citizens. **Chaker**

I would like to see the reintroduction of the caliphate for Muslims. I would start with just six countries – Saudi Arabia, Iran, Pakistan, Turkey, Indonesia and Morocco. I would like to see these countries form a coalition that would stabilise the Middle East. They could easily form an economical alliance, and this would entail a distribution of wealth amongst each other, as well as drawing up a plan to protect their borders. **Pania**

I would like everybody to be really happy living on earth – for everybody to have a nice family, good job, nice house and enough money to live on comfortably for their entire life without ever having to struggle. I would like for all children to be happy – to feel included and not be isolated. For every child to have a home and never have to live on the streets or be in the care system. For every child to have loving parents, food, toys, friends and to receive a good education. **Fazan**

I would de-militarise the world and get rid of guns. The world doesn't need guns – or if it does they should only be used in exceptional circumstances. I would also ensure that there was no more nuclear energy. I would like war to be an unknown concept, something only remembered in history books. Without it, the world would be such a fairer place, where all individuals have the opportunity to flourish, not just privileged groups. A place where I have peace of mind and don't become anxious every time I hear about an attack in some part of the world – because it's going to be blamed on my religion. We can start taking steps to create this ideal world by the media taking responsibility, by consciously avoiding labelling, misrepresenting and fuelling tensions through sensationalised reporting. And we should take individual responsibility, by being kind to one another, being more compassionate and open-minded. We should judge others less, be kind to ourselves, and as the adage goes – live and let live. **Khyber**

I would like everybody in the world to be treated as equal. There would be no poor, no rich, just everyone on the same level of quality of life and wealth. There would be no discrimination or hate, and people would be able to live their lives freely. To make the world a better place, in my opinion, would need us to move away from the social ills prevalent today such as drugs, gambling and deceit. We would also need to learn to live together in a more cohesive way, with less discrimination and hatred. I truly believe a lot of these ills arise due to money. People are rarely satisfied with what they have, especially in the first world, where we are more fortunate than others. People feel money will be the answer to all their problems, but in my opinion, it's only the worship of the one true God which can give your heart true content. I'm not sure of the statistics, but I read somewhere that a larger proportion of the poor are religious as compared to those well off. Another statistic shows that those who are living in poorer countries tend to be happier than those who are living in first-world countries. I think there must be a correlation between happiness and God! **Talah**

I would like to live in a world where every person could practise their religion in total peace without hatred or jealousy – where they would be able to support each other irrespective of whether they are Muslim, Hindu, Buddhist or Christian. People need to start living as a community where they automatically support people of different religions and cultures without giving it a second thought. I believe if this mentality becomes engrained in our way of life, we would slowly begin to eradicate social ills in society (e.g. homelessness, which would cease to exist under this framework). **Ghurah**

I would like to live in a world that is crime free and peaceful. I would like to see a system in place that ensures equal rights and justice to everyone irrespective of their colour. A world where there is no corruption and where peace will ensure that there's solidarity amongst everyone, allowing tolerance, love and harmony to flow freely. Ultimately, my ideal world would have no suffering in it. **Yalina**

PLANS FOR THIS LIFE: PLANS FOR THE HEREAFTER

It is said that life is all about making plans. Muslims pay attention to two sets of plans: those for this life and those for the afterlife. Most young Muslims desire the same outcomes as most other young non-Muslims – a good education followed by a job/career, being able to provide well for their families, enjoyment of good health and being able to contribute towards their community/society. But why should somebody who is young think about dying and the state of their soul? And yet there are Muslims who constantly keep check on their virtues and good deeds, which might bring them favour in the next life, and they urge others to do the same. Husni, a young Muslim I spoke to, who was in his early twenties, told me that it is best to start preparing for the afterlife as soon as possible. There was nothing dark or sinister in his thinking, but it was like listening to a financial advisor saying how it is best to start contributing to a pension fund as soon as somebody starts earning. The young Muslim told me that nobody is guaranteed a long, healthy life so that's why he makes special effort to pray five times a day and be a good Muslim in all other areas. This, he said, was his preparation for the hereafter because he wanted to ensure that he was doing all he could to ensure salvation in the next life.

Husni told me that he didn't believe in an ideal world because we will never live in a world that is perfect. He considered there will always be challenges and difficulties so therefore people need to deal with problems and learn to adapt to circumstances beyond their control. Instead of daydreaming, Husni said we should make the best of what we are able to do right now. This means delivering a better education of Islam to Muslims who only have a grasp of the basics, contributing towards good community relations between Muslims and non-Muslims, becoming more confident at presenting Islam to non-Muslims, and being warmer and friendlier to those outside the faith. Despite his pragmatic stance towards life, I ventured again and asked what Husni would change if he had a magic wand. He replied, 'irresponsible media representation of Islam' before adding, 'How can we live happy lives surrounded by propaganda and misconceptions – how can we live normal lives when the media won't stop insinuating that we want to take over the world?'

BRITISH ISLAM: THE NEXT GENERATION
– WHAT ZEBI THINKS

My parents weren't born in Britain. They came from Pakistan and moved here when they were teenagers. I don't speak their language properly, and when I visit Pakistan, I am instantly spotted as being different to the natives. Although people see me as a Muslim, they put me into a different category – like that of a tourist.

I don't have a problem with this because, after all, I am British. I was born here and this is where I have become rooted through school, friends and now university. I have adapted to being Muslim in a non-Muslim country. Islam asks for Muslims to obey the law of the land wherever they live, but surely this must include respecting the culture of this country too? I have lots of female friends and do not see the harm of giving any of them a lift in my car, provided they are able to put up with my singing! I love to have the stereo on in the car and sing. I go to pubs with friends where we watch football or rugby matches. They drink alcohol and I drink Pepsi, and there is never any pressure on me to do otherwise. My friends respect me for who I am. I also go to nightclubs with friends because I love music – not to chat up girls and have sex. Dining out with non-Muslim friends isn't a problem either. They can eat anything they like as far as I am concerned. They know what I can and can't eat. That doesn't stop friendly camaraderie occurring amongst the group – for example if I'm out in town with friends one of them might ask who wants a bacon roll and nod at everybody before reaching me and saying, 'Oh, sorry, Zebi. You're not allowed one.'

Restrictions according to one's religion don't have to be viewed negatively. You can adapt your lifestyle to that of your country without becoming assimilated and going against the values of your religion. You must trust yourself, and as a young person you must ask your parents to trust you, too, and never betray them. It is perfectly possible to be a fully integrated Muslim in Britain without shunning non-Muslims and fearing their lifestyle.

It is perfectly possible to respect others who, in turn, will respect that Muslims pray five times daily, do Ramadan every year and don't drink alcohol or eat pork. Life needs to be about welcoming people into your life, not trying to keep them out. I really feel there will be far more of this in the next few generations of Muslims in Britain. There will be less emphasis on the culture and traditions of our grandparents and ancestors and more on what is important in our lives in the here and now.

THE OXFORD INSTITUTE FOR BRITISH ISLAM

The Oxford Institute for British Islam (OIBI) was launched in 2017. This new enterprise will change the landscape of Islam in Britain, and elsewhere, through its radical and proactive approach. The Institute was set up as a prototype initiative for Muslims living in the UK, and its goal is for British Islam to represent a firm adherence to a progressive and pluralistic Muslim faith based exclusively on the Qur'an. This means that following the Hadith is not a requirement, partly because of its questionable authenticity, but mainly because the Qur'an is the direct word of God, which provides every answer required for mankind. OIBI advocates placing full trust in the Qur'an – rather than people becoming overly reliant on the Hadith and, in certain cases, believing that the Hadith is on par or superior to the Qur'an – something the Institute believes is both untrue and misleading.

> God wants people to question things. Why else would he have given them brains? Wouldn't it be bizarre if he allowed you to question everything else except him? The first words spoken to Muhammad were 'read'. He wanted the Prophet to think and to understand. And that is precisely what the Oxford Institute of Islam wants Muslims to do. That is why we are becoming a major think tank in Britain, and able to respond intellectually and accurately to what the Qur'an has to say about any issue presenting itself in the world. Islam in Britain is Islam in the West and not the East. Why should we be expected to follow our faith blindly? Britain is a secular society and that critical distinction allows and encourages people to think about their religion, instead of following something they don't understand. Here at the Institute we are reviving each concept of the Qur'an and intellectually and analytically dissecting the facts contained in our divine text. There is no other organisation in Britain operating from this progressive outlook. We want to re-establish the faith of Abraham. We want the Qur'an to stand out by itself away from manufactured secondary sources like the Hadith. We hold the utmost respect for the Prophet. Here was a man who battled polytheism for 23 years, against all odds, and succeeded in bringing about a belief in monotheism. What a phenomenal achievement. Muhammad was a multitalented and inspirational human being, who was also a great teacher. But we don't recognise the Hadith as a primary source of knowledge and therefore refuse to give it the credit other Muslims do who follow it blindly. **Chaman**

OIBI feels that owing to Islam's tarnished and bruised reputation in the UK, and indeed in other parts of the world, the time has come to teach Islam directly and exclusively from its primary, authentic source – the Qur'an. They feel this must entail turning away from medieval interpretations, political bias and bygone practices from distant ancestral homelands. This means welcoming public debate on difficult questions, topics and ideas relating to Islam in the UK and effectively challenging prejudices against the faith. They freely debate about the Qur'an holding answers to every one of mankind's problems. OIBI also wants to garner debate amongst Muslims on issues that they point out are not specifically mentioned in the Qur'an, for example: eating only halal meat, the need for men to grow beards and be circumcised, and for women to wear either the hijab and/or burqa, to name but a few.

OIBI feels that far too many cultural restrictions have taken root here in Britain over the past 50 years. This prevents integration, and hinders progress for those trying to become UK citizens and have a faith that is relevant to twenty-first century British life – and not because of misplaced loyalty to parents or grandparents, who may not have developed an ability to think independently and thus promote healthy debate. The Institute feels it is time to end Muslims being ghettoised in towns and cities across the UK. Some Muslim themselves are, in fact, adopting a self-imposed apartheid mentality that avoids association with non-Muslims.

Real Islam, I feel, is contained in the Qur'an. For me the Hadith is an unnecessary addition whether or not anything it says can be found in the Qur'an. Bluntly speaking, it will always be a secondary source. The Qur'an is the direct word of God. The Hadith is not and therefore can never be on par with God. The Hadith only came into existence in Persia by Sahih al-Bukhari, who was the first to start compiling them. This was through political aims against the Arabs, who were hated at the time. It was determined that something should be created which would be equal to the Qur'an and make people less dependent on it. Nobody questioned then, and even in today's world, why anybody could be drawn towards the Hadith and not the Qur'an in the first instance. Ultimately, Muslims have strayed so far away from what Islam is that it has become unrecognisable. But Islam in the Qur'an is a very different matter, and this is what people should be practising today. More and more people are reading the Qur'an these days, which is a great thing because it is a book of guidance that holds all the answers. Its authenticity is beyond doubt. The Hadith needs to be viewed as a historical document and nothing else. It should never be used for day-to-day living. It should never be used as a supplement to the Qur'an because the Qur'an does not need supplements. **Ghafur**

OIBI was established to create an indigenous Islam, which is at home in Britain and appreciates the essence of British life by accepting its personality and culture without compromising any of the fundamentals of the faith. This does not mean diluting Islam or not adhering to any of its practices, rather the Institute seeks religious independence and theological autonomy to individual believers, which harmonises with the core values of the Qur'an.

The Institute wants an Islam that is rooted and relevant in Britain: an Islam that is respected and not feared, with Muslims who are free to live their lives without mimicking Islam in Pakistan, Saudi Arabia or Bangladesh. It wants an Islam that belongs here in Britain, not something that has been imposed or implanted – an Islam that is accepting of all aspects of life where Muslims can live freely as long as it does not conflict with the core values set out in the Qur'an.

I want my children to grow up with love and respect first for themselves and then for others. If they cannot love and respect themselves then they cannot love and respect others, and that to me is an essential teaching of Islam. I also want them to pray and meditate so they are conscious of the ever-present. The ever-present is one of the Qur'anic attributes of God. I want them to be mindful that each and every one of us is precious; the world and the environment we live in is precious and they have a responsibility to look after it. Islam advocates this principle. I want them to give time and thought to helping those less fortunate than ourselves because that is a charitable tenant of Islam. I also want them to be educated so that they develop their minds and are able to think for themselves and be open and thoughtful. Seeking knowledge is a duty for every Muslim. The Qur'an teaches us that God has made us into nations and tribes so we can get to know each other. This benefits the society we live in and acknowledges the fact that people may come from different backgrounds but they have a similar purpose, which is for the benefit of each other. I want my children to understand that there are other religions and none is superior to the other. The fact that the Qur'an refers to Prophets who are associated with other religions, and who have entered different nations to spread the message of God, is testament to the fact that Islam aligns its origin to God no matter what religion one follows. **Pamir**

MUSTAFA'S STORY

The Dawoodi Bohras (mainly referred to as Bohras) is a close-knit sect within Shi'a Islam with a global population of around one million. Bohras are mainly found in India, Pakistan, Yemen and East Africa, but there are also a significant number living in Britain, where they have a large mosque in London. The majority are wealthy, educated and professional. Men dress distinctly in white two-piece tunics (known as kurtas) along with a white and golden embroidered cap. Members of Bohras are all issued with an identification card, are only allowed to pray in their own mosques, are forbidden to marry outside of their community and have an obligatory means-tested Zakat. They use their own interpretation of the Qur'an and forbid members to read other interpretations. They do not follow the Hadith. Although integration with other Muslims and non-Muslims is not forbidden, neither is it encouraged.

Mustafa comes from this sect. His journey as a Muslim has been anything but smooth. He is a tall, good-looking and well-educated man with a professional career. Mustafa grew up in India but has lived in Britain for the past decade. He has gone through periods of practising Islam but has also become disillusioned with his faith and, at times, feels complete ambivalence towards it, fellow Muslims and himself. Mustafa is now in his mid-thirties and desperately wants to get married – despite never having had an enduring relationship. He admits to periods of confusion and anger but has a desire for spiritual enlightenment in order to live his life as a good-hearted person. Let me roll back Mustafa's story to the beginning for you.

Mustafa's father was a doctor, and his mother an organic chemist. Mustafa was their only child. His parents were liberal thinkers, but he had a much better relationship with his mother than his father. His father wasn't a strong family figure. Mustafa viewed him as weak because he didn't challenge his authoritarian parents when they forced him into his first marriage – from which he got divorced and married Mustafa's mother. Both Mustafa and his mother, in turn, were rejected by his father's parents because they favoured their son's first wife.

Mustafa went to a private secular school. He said his parents appreciated education and wanted him to have the best chance in life. Only a tiny number of Muslims attended this school, and Mustafa was the only Muslim in his class. He didn't mind, though, because he made friends easily, mainly with Hindus. But as a child, Mustafa felt different to other children. His father was away a lot of the time and although his mother used to take him to the mosque, he got picked on by his peers because he was overweight, which resulted in low self-confidence and self-worth.

Mustafa disliked the imam at the mosque who taught him the Qur'an. He also felt detached from the people there because he felt he did not belong among them. Mustafa's mother taught him to read and write Arabic, which enabled him to study the Qur'an at home. He stopped going to the mosque and thereafter, during his teenage years, lived a carefree life, although his parents trusted him and knew he would never eat pork or experiment with alcohol, cigarettes, drugs and sex. In his late teens, Mustafa's father suddenly died of a heart attack. He said he didn't cry when his father died because he had never got to know his father as a person. They had rarely shared father-and-son moments. His mother, on the other hand, was very upset and went into purdah after the funeral for four months and ten days, resulting in her never leaving the house, or coming into close contact with men, except close male relatives during this period.

Mustafa went to university and shortly afterwards saw his personality change as his life expanded in surprising ways. He met new people from all over India at university and this included different types of Muslims, although religion at this point was no longer a big part of his life. But this was soon to change. The 9/11 tragedy shocked Mustafa as he watched the events on television. He began to realise it felt as if the world was holding Muslims responsible for what happened, and decided to take a closer look at Islam and what it taught. He started reading various interpretations of the Qur'an but couldn't find anything which advocated violence or radicalisation. His reading gradually drew him back within the folds of Islam, but instead of returning to his own mosque, he started attending a Sunni mosque after purposefully befriending some of his Sunni university friends. Here, he grew a beard and shaved his moustache and began praying five times a day.

Life ticked along quite nicely for a while until one of Mustafa's Hindu friends invited him to a seminar one night at a temple where a speaker criticised Muslims and accused the Qur'an of perpetrating violence by quoting the line 'kill the idolaters' contained in Chapter 9:5. Mustafa felt affronted by this and re-read various interpretations of this chapter, which all contained slightly different words and meaning. Although he realised that the Hindu scholar was mistaken to just randomly select a line from the Qur'an and not put it into context with the rest of the passage's meaning, it made him realise how different translations of the Qur'an can easily mess up Islam. He admits that at this point he too felt messed up, despondent, lonely and in need of some spiritual nourishment. A visit to his cousin loomed and with it brought new openings. In London, Mustafa met Muslims from all over the world who were open to discussing and debating topics in Islam, unlike the restraints he felt placed on him in India. He was still frustrated, though, that Islam was associated with terrorism, and sad that his identity as a Muslim was not viewed in a positive way.

When Mustafa returned to India, he shaved off his beard because he didn't want his outward appearance to distract from his religion. He stopped attending the mosque and talking openly about Islam but behind closed doors he continued to practise. He formed his own kind of Islam that was private to him. After completing his degree, he moved to Britain, with his mother later joining him. Through her, he became acquainted with Bohras in the UK, which saw another turning point in his life. Mustafa admits to having always been socially nervous around females, and attributed this to childhood bullying, but to his surprise he fell in love with a beautiful girl from his community. They got engaged and were in the process of planning their wedding when a disagreement led to their estrangement. Mustafa remembered going home one night and in a fit of rage against God he picked up a copy of the Qur'an and screamed at it. Mustafa wanted so desperately to be given a chance to love his future wife. He thought he had found somebody who could share his compassion, truthfulness, intelligence and integrity but instead he felt self-loathing and rejection. He said having a partner would have been everything to him. So great was his despair at losing out on what he thought was his entitlement, he took a few weeks off work. He spent most of this time crying in bed and wondering what was so wrong with him to have been rejected by the woman he loved.

A further detachment from Islam followed but this time it was more severe because Mustafa began to turn against Muslims. He began to notice lies and hypocrisy before deciding to remove himself from everything and everybody associated with Islam. From that moment onwards, he decided he would only pray on his terms, praying from within rather than having to recite certain prayers. A visit back to India reinforced his disquiet about Muslims when, during dinner with his cousins, they enticed him to drink alcohol, something he said had never happened in Britain when he dined out with friends who drank alcohol.

Mustafa's mother, who was suffering health problems, wanted to go on the pilgrimage to Mecca, and Mustafa agreed to accompany her. He wanted to ensure that his mother had the ultimate experience, so he booked an expensive package and they stayed in a hotel overlooking the Kaba. But what should have been the trip of a lifetime became a nightmare. When they arrived in Mecca, Mustafa felt immediate discomfort. He felt like the air was burning him, so great was his unease. He quickly realised that he disliked being in a place that was 100 per cent Muslim. He found fellow pilgrims rude as they pushed their way through the multitude of crowds, and felt that people were on a mission to reach Mecca just for the accomplishment of completing the pilgrimage. All his life Mustafa had prayed towards the Kaba, and now as he stood in front of it, he realised that he felt nothing. The same emptiness was felt when he touched its holy stone and did not feel any divine presence. He concluded to himself that Mecca was the worst place he had ever been to in his life. But when he travelled a few hundred miles away to Medina, he felt the complete opposite. He reflected how the Prophet had fled Mecca for Medina. Mustafa felt his sudden sense of ease, and imagined this mirrored how safe the Prophet must have felt after arriving there, with its calm and positive energy.

After Mustafa returned to London, he decided to leave Islam for good. He felt the religion was making him more and more unhappy, and not bringing him closer to God. Although sad, his mother accepted his decision. These days Mustafa is reading the *Bhagavad Gita* from the Hindu faith and says that he is beginning to work out what elightenment is about. However, he says he has no wish to convert to Hinduism or any other religion. He feels religion traps people and pushes them away from enlightenment because of overuse of discipline and scare tactics. There is still a small part of Mustafa that holds affection for the Qur'an, but he no longer wishes to read it. He has found spiritual contentment elsewhere. Mustafa said everybody's destination is to reach enlightenment and it's a journey we are all experiencing. He compares religions to cars that come in different makes, sizes, colours, models and engines. You either drive the car or get driven in it. As good as any car is, there will be side-effects attached to it – pollution, congestion, traffic jams and accidents. But you don't have to use a car to get to your destination. There are other modes of transport. These days, in addition to continuing his quest for spiritual enlightenment and freedom, Mustafa is looking for a non-Muslim partner, a soulmate to share his life. In the meantime, he is enjoying his life in the UK, where he has a professional job and earns good money. He travels all over the world on different types of adventures and believes he has found true peace, away from the trappings of religion, and does not feel shame or guilt for changing his mode of transport, which continues to steer him towards happiness.

OPINION PIECE ON MUSTAFA'S STORY BY SHAYKH ASRAR RASHID

I would like to know the root cause of his distress. Is Mustafa depressed? Does he regret the past or is he worried about the future? He comes from a fringe Shi'a sect, which seems to play a part in his emotional angst. To a non-Muslim, the best way to differentiate Bohras from other Muslims is like explaining the difference between a Catholic and an Amish. They are poles apart. I do not wish to overly speculate, but Mustafa's void of any true sense of spirituality may have been caused by the rigidity and strictness placed on him while growing up as a Bohra. I know he attended a Sunni mosque for a while, but this appears not to have helped – his basic knowledge of Islam seems weak. Growing up he may have been told to do things without questioning any of the logic. Maybe this blind conformity led to his crisis of faith? At the moment it is clear to see that he is an upset individual. Muslims need to be free to question their beliefs. They need to develop their own understanding of Islam rather than have it blindly foisted upon them by a cleric who may not be so well educated in the faith.

There is no quick fix to Mustafa's pain because first of all he needs counselling. He has a lot of anger to release. I wish I could help him in that respect, but there are only a handful of imams in the UK who are trained counsellors. We definitely need more and this is something I have considered pursuing myself with help from my mosque. I can see Mustafa is sexually frustrated and needs to find a suitable wife to ease this distress. I empathise with him about his experience in Mecca, but pilgrims get very annoyed in 40-degree heat. You also must consider that many different nationalities travel to Mecca from around the world, some of whom come from underdeveloped countries, and they can present as being a bit rough and rude. But that is a separate issue to his religious experiences and the void in his life.

From a religious-support perspective, I would love to guide Mustafa. I would listen to him without lecturing. He needs to understand why he is disillusioned with Islam, and the only way to achieve this is to have him reinvestigate his entire faith and its meaning. But I feel he's not ready for that yet. He needs to first have counselling to deal with his anger, followed by marriage, and after that he could embark on a fresh exploration of his faith. If he was under my tuition I would help him rationalise Islam step by step, think of every possible question he wanted answering about Islam, and bring his list to me. Then I would consider them and answer slowly, reflectively and rationally. We would also read the Qur'an together and I would provide him with close guidance. Mustafa needs rational proof, which somebody like me would give him. He doesn't seem to have ever sat down and talked over his fears and reservations about Islam with an Islamic scholar.

Mustafa says he has now left Islam. That's his personal choice and nobody should force him to do otherwise. They might try to persuade him, maybe, but to use coercion would be very wrong. He has already had some bad experiences of Islam and doesn't need more to add to his list of grievances. He must find his own way forward. Mustafa's story is really not that original. There will be other Muslims who are confused and angry because of their lack of understanding. For me, a lack of understanding always leads to problems, and this is clear in what has happened to Mustafa. When somebody truly understands that rational basis of Islam, thcy become good Muslims. They are happy peoplc. They do not live their lives by a blind conformity, but through knowledge and understanding, which leads to a relaxed approach and confidence in their faith and in their life, something Mustafa sadly is missing out on at present. But I pray that he receives the help he needs and finds the correct answers to the questions he has yet to ask about Islam. And may Allah guide him and keep him safe always.

References and Further Reading

Abbot, L. *et al.* (2013) *The Religions Book*. London: Dorling Kindersley.

Abdal-Ati, H. (2011) *Islam in Focus*. Oak Brook, IL: American Trust Publications.

Acheson, I. (2016) 'Tackling Islamist Extremism in Prisons: The Acheson Review.' *Law & Religion UK*, 23 August, 2016.

Adil, M. and Rafiq, H. (2017) *Group-Based Child Sexual Exploitation: Dissecting Grooming Gangs*. London: Quilliam Foundation.

Ahmed, M. *et al.* (2016) *Milestones to Militancy*. London: The Tony Blair Foundation.

Ahmed, M.M. (2011) *Would You Like to Know Something about Islam?* New York: Crescent Books.

Al-Yaqoubi, S.M. (2016) *Refuting ISIS*. 2nd Edition. Reading: Sacred Knowledge.

Ali, A.Y. (2013) *The Qur'an*. New York: Tahrika Tarsile Qur'an Publishers.

Ali, K. (2016) *Sexual Ethics and Islam: Feminist Reflections on Quran, Hadith and Jurisprudence*. London: Oneworld Publications.

Armour, R., Sr. (2002) *Islam, Christianity and the West: A Troubled History*. Maryknoll, New York: Orbis Books.

Azzam, M. (2016) *The Burdah*. Jeddah: Al-Madina Institute.

Brown, J.A.C. (2014) *Misquoting Muhammad: The Challenge and Choices of Interpreting the Prophet's Legacy*. London: Oneworld Publications.

Channel 4 (2016) 'C4 survey and documentary reveals what British Muslims really think.' Accessed on 17/01/2018 at http://bit.ly/c4_survey

Charfi, M. (2005) *Islam and Liberty: The Historical Misunderstanding*. London: Zed Books.

Clarke, A. (2013) *Shariah: Islamic Law*. London: Ta-Ha Publishers.

Cranston, R. (1949) *World Faith*. New York: Ayer Company Publishers.

Dahlan, S.A.Z. (2015) *The Essential Islamic Creed*. London: Heritage Press.

Dobson, R. (2014) 'British Muslims face worst job discrimination of any minority group, according to research.' *The Independent*. Accessed on 17/01/2018 at http://bit.ly/Independent_Job_Discrimination

Eger, A.A. (2016) *The Islamic-Byzantine Frontier*. London: I.B. Tauris Publishers.

Encyclopedia Britannica (2009) *The Britannica Guide to the Islamic World – Religion, History and the Future*. London: Constable & Robinson.

Farid, M.G. (1967) *The Holy Quran*. Surrey: Islam International Publications Ltd.

Frampton, M. *et al.* (2016) *Unsettled Belonging: A Survey of Britain's Muslim Communities*. London: Policy Exchange.

The Gallup Coexist Index (2009) *A Global Study of Interfaith Relations*. Accessed on 17/01/2018 at http://bit.ly/gallup2009

Haddad, G.F. (2007) *The Four Imams and Their Schools*. Cambridge: Muslim Academic Trust.

Hadeeth, A.I.K. (2013) *The Signs before the Day of Judgement*. CreateSpace Independent Publishing.

Hadith Collection (2012) *Sahih Al Bukhari, Sunan Ibn Majah, Sunan Abu Dawud, Jami At Tirmidhi, Sahih Muslim, Sunan An Nasai, Riyad As Saliheen, Al Lulu Wal Marjan*. Riyadh: Darussalam Publishing.

Haleem, M.A.S.A. (2008) *The Qur'an (Oxford World's Classics)*. Oxford: Oxford University Press.

Hamid, A.W. (1989) *Islam the Natural Way*. London: MELS Publishing and Distributing.

Hamid, S. (2016) *Sufis, Salafis and Islamists: The Contested Ground of British Islamic Activism*. London: I.B. Tauris Publishers.

Hathout, H. (1995) *Reading the Muslim Mind*. Oak Brook, IL: American Trust Publications.

House of Commons/Home Affairs Committee (2012) *Roots of Violent Radicalisation*. London: HMSO.

H.R.H. Prince Ghazi Bin Muhammad (2017) *A Thinking Person's Guide to Islam: The Essence of Islam in Twelve Verses from the Qur'an*. London: Turath Publishing.

Imam an-Nawawi (1998) *The Complete Forty Hadith*. London: Ta-Ha Publishers.

Islam, Y. (1999) *A is for Allah*. London: Mountain of Light Publications.

Itani, T. (2015) *Quran in English*. Berlin: CreateSpace Independent Publishing.

Jalandhari, M.A.A. (2012) *Death on the Cross*. 8th Edition. London: London Mosque.

Jay, A. (2013) *Independent Inquiry into Child Sexual Exploitation in Rotherham (1997–2013)*. Commissioned by Rotherham Metropolitan Borough Council.

Kamali, M.H. (2017) *Sharia Law: Questions and Answers*. London: Oneworld Publications.

Kathir, I. and Waley, M. I. (1994) *The Signs Before the Day of Judgement*. London: Dar Al Taqwa.

Kattab, H. (1994) *The Muslim Woman's Handbook*. London: Ta-Ha Publishers.

Kugle, S.A. (2010) *Homosexuality in Islam: Critical Reflection on Gay, Lesbian and Transgender Muslims*. London: Oneworld Publications.

Latif, S.A. (2002) *Principles of Islamic Culture*. Chennai: Goodword Books.

Lawson, T. (2017) *The Qur'an: Epic and Apocalypse*. London: Oneworld Publications.

Lemu, B. and Heeren, F. (1992) *Women in Islam*. Markfield, Leicestershire: The Islamic Foundation.

Lewis, B. (2003) *Holy War and Unholy Terror*. London: Weidenfeld & Nicolson.

Ling, M. (1991) *Muhammad: His Life Based on the Earliest Sources*. Cambridge: The Islamic Texts Society.

Mabon, S. and Royle, S. (2016) *The Origins of ISIS*. London: I.B. Tauris Publishers.

Malik, N. (2016) *The Children of Islamic State: The Cubs of the Caliphate*. London: Quilliam Foundation.

Manning, R.R. (Ed) (2015) *30-Second Religion*. Lewes: Ivy Press.

Mawdudi, S. (1989) *Towards Understanding Islam*. Markfield, Leicestershire: The Islamic Foundation.

McDermott, M.Y. and Ahsan, M.M. (1996) *The Muslim Guide*. Markfield, Leicestershire: The Islamic Foundation.

Michon, J.-L. and Gaetani, R. (Eds) (2016) *Sufism, Love and Wisdom*. Bloomington, Indiana: World Wisdom.

Molana Sayad Muhammad Iqbal Shah Hazrat Imam Jalal-ul-Din (2006) *Tafseer Dur-e-Mansoor*. Lahore: Zia-Ul-Quran.

Momen, M. (2016) *Shi'i Islam: A Beginner's Guide*. London: Oneworld Publications.

Mondal, A.A. (2014) *Islam and Controversy: The Politics of Free Speech after Rushdie*. London: Palgrave Macmillan.

Mustafa, P. (2017) *The Quran: God's Message to Mankind*. London: Xeitre-Signat.

No-Mani, M.M.M. (2002) *Ma'Ariful Hadith – Volumes I to IV*. Keighley, West Yorkshire: Darul-Ishaat.

Nanji, A. (2008) *Dictionary of Islam*. London: Penguin Books.

Newby, G.D. (2002) *A Concise Encyclopedia of Islam*. London: Oneworld Publications.

O'Donnell, K. (2006) *Inside World Religions*. Oxford: Lion Hudson Publishers.

Picktall, M.M. (1996) *The Meaning of the Glorious Quran*. Beltsville, Maryland: Amana Publications.

Qutb, S. (2006) *Basic Principles of the Islamic Worldview*. Morden: Islamic Publications International.

Ramadan, T. (2017) *Islam – The Essentials*. London: Pelican.

Rapoport, Y. (2010) *Ibn Taymiyya and His Times*. Karachi: Oxford University Press Pakistan.

Raudvere, C. (2014) *Islam: An Introduction*. I.B. Tauris Publishers.

Revesz, R. (2017) 'Bangladeshi village burned down after "Prophet Mohammed insulted" in resident's Facebook post.' *The Independent*. Accessed on 17/01/2018 at http://bit.ly/FB_post_Asia

Ridgeon, L. (Ed) (2015) *The Cambridge Companion to Sufism*. Cambridge: Cambridge University Press.

Roy, O. (2017) *Jihad and Death: The Global Appeal of Islamic State*. London: C Hurst & Co Publishers.

Runnymede Trust (1997) *Islamophobia: A Challenge for Us All*. London: The Runnymede Trust.

Rushd, I. (1996) *The Distinguished Jurist's Primer*. Reading: Garnet Publishing.

Sarder, Z. (2012) *Muhammad: All that Matters*. London: Hodder & Stoughton.

Stuart, H. (2017) *Islamist Terrorism: Analysis of Offences and Attacks in the UK (1998–2015)*. London: The Henry Jackson Society.

Swidler, A. (Ed) (1993) *Homosexuality and World Religions*. London: Trinity Press.

Talib, A.I.A. (1985) *Nahjul Balagha: Peak Eloquence*. New York: Tahrike Tarsile Qur'an.

UKIM (2015) *Who Is Muhammad?* Birmingham: Learn Islam 4 Free.

Waines, D. (1995) *An Introduction to Islam*. Cambridge: Cambridge University Press.

Warsi, S. (2017) *The Enemy Within: A Tale of Muslim Britain*. London: Allen Lane.

Yusaf, M. (2017) *Inside the Soul of Islam*. London: Hay House.

Zebiri, K. (2008) *British Muslim Converts: Choosing Alternative Lives*. London: Oneworld Publications.

Index